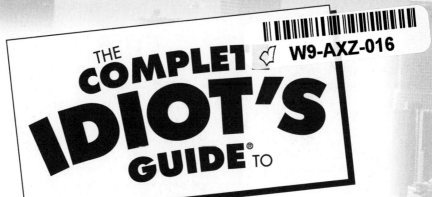

THE
COMPLETE
IDIOT'S
GUIDE® TO

W9-AXZ-016

NEW YORK CITY

by Anita Gates

ALPHA

A member of Penguin Group (USA) Inc.

ALPHA BOOKS

Published by the Penguin Group

Penguin Group (USA) Inc., 375 Hudson Street, New York, New York 10014, USA

Penguin Group (Canada), 90 Eglinton Avenue East, Suite 700, Toronto, Ontario M4P 2Y3, Canada (a division of Pearson Penguin Canada Inc.)

Penguin Books Ltd., 80 Strand, London WC2R 0RL, England

Penguin Ireland, 25 St. Stephen's Green, Dublin 2, Ireland (a division of Penguin Books Ltd.)

Penguin Group (Australia), 250 Camberwell Road, Camberwell, Victoria 3124, Australia (a division of Pearson Australia Group Pty. Ltd.)

Penguin Books India Pvt. Ltd., 11 Community Centre, Panchsheel Park, New Delhi—110 017, India

Penguin Group (NZ), 67 Apollo Drive, Rosedale, North Shore, Auckland 1311, New Zealand (a division of Pearson New Zealand Ltd.)

Penguin Books (South Africa) (Pty.) Ltd., 24 Sturdee Avenue, Rosebank, Johannesburg 2196, South Africa

Penguin Books Ltd., Registered Offices: 80 Strand, London WC2R 0RL, England

Copyright © 2008 by Anita Gates

THE COMPLETE IDIOT'S GUIDE TO and Design are registered trademarks of Penguin Group (USA) Inc.

International Standard Book Number: 978-1-59257-812-2
Library of Congress Catalog Card Number: 2008927329

10   09   08   8   7   6   5   4   3   2   1

Interpretation of the printing code: The rightmost number of the first series of numbers is the year of the book's printing; the rightmost number of the second series of numbers is the number of the book's printing. For example, a printing code of 08-1 shows that the first printing occurred in 2008.

Printed in the United States of America

Note: This publication contains the opinions and ideas of its author. It is intended to provide helpful and informative material on the subject matter covered. It is sold with the understanding that the author and publisher are not engaged in rendering professional services in the book. If the reader requires personal assistance or advice, a competent professional should be consulted.

The author and publisher specifically disclaim any responsibility for any liability, loss, or risk, personal or otherwise, which is incurred as a consequence, directly or indirectly, of the use and application of any of the contents of this book.

Most Alpha books are available at special quantity discounts for bulk purchases for sales promotions, premiums, fund-raising, or educational use. Special books, or book excerpts, can also be created to fit specific needs.

For details, write: Special Markets, Alpha Books, 375 Hudson Street, New York, NY 10014.

Publisher: *Marie Butler-Knight*
Editorial Director: *Mike Sanders*
Senior Managing Editor: *Billy Fields*
Executive Editor: *Randy Ladenheim-Gil*
Development Editor: *Michael Thomas*
Senior Production Editor: *Janette Lynn*

Copy Editor: *Lisanne V. Jensen*
Cover/Book Designer: *Kurt Owens*
Indexer: *Angie Bess*
Layout: *Ayanna Lacey*
Proofreaders: *Laura Caddell, Mary Hunt*

Contents at a Glance

Contents

Part 4:   Downtown 181

Part 5:   Plan My Trip—All Around Town. . . . 247

Introduction

So … you're going to New York? If you've visited before, you already know the city can be quite a challenge. If it's your first time, you may be worrying about the fast pace, the crowds, the prices, the seemingly endless list of sights to see, and just how you're going to get around in a city where most people don't drive cars in their everyday lives.

What you need is a book that will make your visit effortlessly fun, infinitely satisfying, actually affordable, and amazingly easy to plan. You've come to the right place.

This is the full-service New York City guide, including a batch of ready-made itineraries for different interests, different time frames, different parts of town, and even different energy levels. I've lived in New York for close to four decades—on the Upper East Side and Upper West Side of Manhattan and in the heart of the Village (Greenwich Village, that is). But I haven't drawn only from my years of experiences in the city; I've also consulted with in-the-know colleagues and friends. So what you have here is the benefit of insiders' tips from an entire circle of longtime New Yorkers.

This book is called a *Complete Idiot's Guide*, but that's not a reflection on its readers. We all feel like complete idiots at times, especially when we're tackling something big and new. It takes a very smart (and confident) person to recognize what he or she doesn't know and where to go to find answers.

To make that process as simple as possible, we've divided the city into manageable neighborhoods, drawn easy-to-read maps, and gone into endless (but necessary) detail about little things such as taking the bus.

When people do studies to determine the most popular American travel destinations, New York City almost always turns up at the top of the list (or very near it). Those of us who choose to live there understand why, and most will tell you the same thing. It's not just because of the theaters, restaurants, shopping, or museums. New York City has a special energy—something vibrant in the air.

Come breathe it in!

What's in This Book

The Complete Idiot's Guide to New York City was designed to make your life simpler. Part 1 is all about planning and anticipation, dealing with topics ranging from unique characteristics of New Yorkers and New York City life to the nitty-gritty details of planning and booking your trip. Parts 2 through 4 divide the city into three parts: the East Side (plus Queens), the West Side (plus the Bronx), and Downtown (plus Brooklyn and Staten Island).

Two very different chapters are devoted to each part of town.

The "Getting Comfortable" chapters introduce you to the area and its specific neighborhoods as well as provide a list and description of a number of hotels there in various price ranges. Then, I suggest pleasant but sight-packed walks that will help you start to feel at home. Obviously, you'll need some of this material during your trip planning. Ideally, you'll take a look at the rest before your arrival (or, at the very least, on the plane or train).

The "Enjoying" chapters are for guidance while you're in New York. They list and describe restaurants and stores in the area, famous and lesser-known sights to see, nightlife opportunities, and interesting places to go for a drink. (Here's one exception to the rule about reading these chapters after you've arrived, however: if you're hoping to have dinner at one of the city's super-popular, super-expensive restaurants, you may want to make reservations weeks or even longer in advance.) Each chapter ends with a one-day itinerary in that area, arranged for maximum logistical ease—because the toughest thing about New York City is getting from Point A to Point B.

Those special itineraries are a unique feature of *The Complete Idiot's Guide* series. You'll find more of them in Part 5, "Plan Your Trip—All Around Town."

Bonus Features and Tips

This guidebook also contains a number of bonus features that will provide interesting background on a topic or to alert you to something special about a place.

The book includes numerous unique boxed features throughout like this one here.

Useful tips occur throughout the book, marked by icons. These include:

⊘ —No matter what you've heard, it's really not worth the time or effort.

▨ —Tips and tricks to help you make the most of your trip.

▨ —Places and experiences beyond the global-mall mentality.

¢ —Ways and means for cutting costs in one of America's most expensive cities.

You'll also find that phone numbers and names of important destinations throughout the book are placed in **bold.** Look for bold when you want to locate information about the Big Apple at a glance.

What Things Cost

Throughout this book, you'll see dollar signs next to hotel and restaurant listings. The more of them you see, the more of your budget that expenditure is going to eat up. Here's how the symbols translate into real dollars.

For Hotels:

Prices are for a standard double room.

$\boxed{\$}$ = under $100

$\boxed{\$}$ $\boxed{\$}$ = $101–$250

$\boxed{\$}$ $\boxed{\$}$ $\boxed{\$}$ = $251–$350

$\boxed{\$}$ $\boxed{\$}$ $\boxed{\$}$ $\boxed{\$}$ = $351–$500

$\boxed{\$}$ $\boxed{\$}$ $\boxed{\$}$ $\boxed{\$}$ $\boxed{\$}$ = over $500

For Restaurants:

Price ranges are per person for dinner, including an appetizer, entrée, dessert, one drink, and tax. Deduct roughly 30 percent for lunch prices. And keep in mind that ordering the most or least expensive item on any restaurant's menu can make a big difference in your bill at the end of your meal.

$\boxed{\$}$ = under \$40

$\boxed{\$}$ $\boxed{\$}$ = \$41–\$80

$\boxed{\$}$ $\boxed{\$}$ $\boxed{\$}$ = over \$80

Bon Voyage!

So … get started on your research. For inspiration, watch a movie set in New York (preferably not *Mean Streets* or *American Psycho*; if you're planning to spend much time on the Upper West Side, go for *You've Got Mail*). Next thing you know, you'll be gazing out an airplane, train, bus, or car window at the country's most spectacular skyline. You're going to have an unforgettable time.

Acknowledgments

First, many thanks to Janet Piorko and Harvey Chipkin, the dashing husband-and-wife team who first talked to me about this project.

Like them, many friends and colleagues shared their expertise on New York City with me. Some even gave me a place to work (and live) while I waited for my apartment to become available again. (I had sublet my place … it's a long story.) A thousand thanks to Emma Brantley, Trey Brantley, Bob Burrichter, Cornelia Dean, Lizbeth Dison, Rik Fairlie, Sylviane Gold, Lisa Higgins, Peter Keepnews, Donna Kermeen, Ann Kolson, Susan Millar Perry, Dan Perry, David Perry, Jennifer Quale, David Santos, Dr. Rand Stoneburner, Abigail Sturges, Jennifer Whitaker, Craig Whitaker, and Hope Wurmfeld.

Many thanks to Marilyn Allen, a gracious and understanding agent, and to Randy Ladenheim-Gil, my editor, for her expert guidance.

Trademarks

All terms mentioned in this book that are known to be or are suspected of being trademarks or service marks have been appropriately capitalized. Alpha Books and Penguin Group (USA) Inc. cannot attest to the accuracy of this information. Use of a term in this book should not be regarded as affecting the validity of any trademark or service mark.

Part 1

Anticipation Is Half the Fun

Getting ready for your trip to New York isn't only about making airline and hotel reservations, ordering theater tickets, and calling ahead for hard-to-get restaurant reservations. It's also a matter of learning about the city, its people, and all the things it has to offer—then looking forward to just how much fun this big-city adventure will be.

The Big Apple: The Big Picture

In This Chapter

- 🍎 What you need to know about geography, weather, and time zones
- 🍎 What to pack for your stay in the Big City
- 🍎 The best times to visit
- 🍎 How the natives walk, talk, drive, and live

Nobody knows for sure why New York City is called the Big Apple.

One theory is that the term was coined by jazz musicians in the 1930s because there was a jazz club by that name. Another theory is that a newspaper columnist, John J. Fitzgerald of *The New York Morning Telegraph*, introduced the term in the 1920s when writing about horse racing. (He said he'd picked it up from New Orleans stable workers, who had always referred to a race's prize as an apple and saw New York races as the biggest of all.)

There's even a reference in a book published in 1909, Edward Martin's *Wayfarer in New York*. Referring to the city, he wrote, "The big apple gets a disproportionate share of the national sap."

But because he didn't capitalize the term or put it in quotation marks, Martin was probably just being metaphorical.

Whatever its origin, the term has stuck. It reminds us all that in terms of population, ambition, and energy, the city is very big. And you're going to tackle it.

Discovering New York City

No matter how long you plan to stay in New York, you're going to enjoy it more if you know a little about the place beforehand. And that can mean anything from what weather to expect to how the natives live their day-to-day lives.

Geography: Not Technically the Center of the Universe

Ask New Yorkers where their city is located, and they'll tell you in a minute: it's the center of the universe. More specifically, New York City is in the Northeastern United States, in the southeastern corner of New York State, and nestled between Connecticut (a half-hour drive away) and New Jersey (visible across the Hudson River).

Manhattan is an island—a relatively small one (approximately 12 miles long and $2^1/_2$ miles wide at its widest point)—surrounded by the East River on one side and the Hudson River on the other.

Brooklyn lies to the southeast, across the famous bridge of the same name, and has great beaches. Staten Island lies to the south. Queens is to the northeast, and the Bronx is to the north.

GETTING ON AND OFF THE ISLAND

To get to Manhattan and all its many sights, you have to traverse a river—and most people do that by driving across one of the city's bridges (including the George Washington, the Brooklyn, the Manhattan, the Queensborough, and the Triborough) or driving under the river through a tunnel (including the Midtown, the Holland, and the Lincoln). If you hear a reference to "the bridge and tunnel crowd," it means people who live in the suburbs or outer boroughs. Strangely enough, people who live in Staten Island have never been referred to as "the ferry crowd."

Rain or Shine

North of Philadelphia, south of Boston, and on roughly the same latitude as Madrid, Spain, New York City has a true four-season climate. Books describe it as temperate and humid. Average rainfall is about 45 inches.

Fall is crisp and slightly cool (the average high in October is 65°). Winter is cold but not generally bitter (January's average low is 25°), and it snows a good bit—anywhere from December to March. (The first year I lived in New York, it snowed on Easter Sunday.)

Spring is pleasant and warms up to an average high of 72° in May, although the evenings are still cool (an average low of 44° in April).

Summer is hot. Highs in the 80s and heat waves in the 90s aren't unusual. But average lows in the 60s mean heavenly summer nights.

Clock Watching

The city that never sleeps is in the Eastern time zone of the United States, one hour ahead of the Central time zone (Chicago), two hours ahead of Mountain (Denver), and three hours ahead of Pacific (Los Angeles). Most of the year, it's five hours behind London and six hours behind Paris and other Western European cities.

Eastern Standard Time (EST) is usually in effect from October or November to March or April. In the spring, *Eastern Daylight Time* (EDT) goes into effect and clocks are set forward one hour so that in the summer, it's still light at 8 P.M. or so.

When to Go: Anytime

There's a reason Vernon Duke wrote a song called "Autumn in New York." In many ways, fall is the most beautiful time of year here. The weather is crisp and just turning cool. All the rich people are back from their summer houses in the Hamptons. There's a grown-up equivalent of back-to-school energy in the air as the new theater, dance, concert, and opera seasons get under way. And while the place is busy, the true mobs of tourists are gone—replaced by actual New Yorkers.

Holidays in New York City are absolutely magical. The Rockefeller Center Christmas tree, the store windows, and of course the joys of holiday shopping make this the most beautiful time of year to come to town. But beginning around Thanksgiving, the traffic becomes hellish and the crowds around the major sights are daunting. It's a tradeoff.

Deep winter has the disadvantage of cold, sometimes dreary weather, but there are lots of off-season bargains and it's easier to get into hit Broadway shows and fashionable restaurants than at other times of the year. Plus, most of New York's great sights aren't weather-dependent.

Spring can be lovely, but winter weather sometimes hangs on longer than expected. If you're lucky and get warm, sunny days, this is a fine time for theater (a second round of Broadway openings in anticipation of the Tony Awards), the parks, and outdoor cafés.

And finally, there's summer—the traditional vacation season. The city is crowded with out-of-towners, and the best of the cultural season is over until fall—but there are tons of special events and a sense of warm-weather festivity that's contagious.

MORE REASONS TO COME IN THE SUMMER

1. Sidewalk cafés. (New Yorkers, unlike Parisians, don't bundle up and sit outdoors having coffee or drinks in November unless there's a sudden heat wave.)
2. Outdoor concerts in the parks
3. Outdoor movies in the parks (the next best thing to a drive-in theater)
4. Holiday fireworks spectaculars

What to Pack: The Best-Dressed Visitors' List

If you want to stand out like a sore thumb, by all means wear shorts and sneakers in Midtown on a weekday. But if you've chosen New York City for your vacation because you love being part of the most exciting big city in the world, it might be fun to dress for it.

Not that things are formal in New York. Unless you're invited to a black-tie gala of some kind, you won't need tuxedos and evening dresses. Most New Yorkers go to a Broadway theater straight from work (well, with a short detour for pre-theater drinks or dinner) and don't change clothes for the occasion. You'll see people at the theater in jeans, too, but mostly the audience comes in office wear.

If you want to dress up just a little more, the basic black dress for women and the basic black suit for men is the way to go. The same is true for dinner in Midtown restaurants on weekdays and weeknights. Restaurants in residential neighborhoods tend to be more casual, and you can play around with fashion in the chic downtown areas.

For daytime shopping and sightseeing, bring casual but polished clothes and comfortable shoes. Jeans are fine in most places, but they look best with nice tops—not wrinkled T-shirts making sociopolitical statements or advertising brand-name products.

King Kong's old hangout: The Empire State Building, once again the city's tallest skyscraper.

Summer can be hot and steamy, so sleeveless fashions are fine. Fall is generally mild but can turn suddenly cool, so packing sweaters and a raincoat is a good idea. If you're visiting in winter, you'll need a good, heavy coat as well as gloves, a wool scarf, a warm hat, and boots (snow boots, if the weather forecast warrants). Spring can come late, so a coat is often in order well into May.

It's always smart to pack an umbrella (at least a small, portable one). But if you find yourself without one when a shower starts, no problem: umbrella vendors pop up immediately on street corners. And if you don't see one, just run into the nearest drugstore and pick up a cheap one. You're probably going to leave it in the taxi anyway.

Most hotels offer hair dryers these days, and lots offer bathrobes and toiletries (but it's a good idea to check with them first). When packing, throw in Band-Aids for your feet if you're planning to walk more than you usually do. And you probably will, since walking is the preferred method of transport.

New Yorkers and How They Got That Way

It started with the Lenape Indians, who lived in Manhattan starting around the end of the last Ice Age. Then, one day in 1609, the English explorer Henry Hudson came sailing down the river that today bears his name. Soon came the Dutch settlers (Hudson was working for the Dutch), who named the place New Amsterdam and got heavily into fur trading.

The English took over in the 1660s, promptly renaming the place for the Duke of York, and they hung on to it until the Revolutionary War. Then, New York entered the nineteenth century as a truly American city.

NOT A BAD PRICE FOR 14,000 ACRES

The old story about Dutch colonists buying the island of Manhattan from the local Native Americans for $24 isn't quite true. Historians say such a transaction did take place in 1626 but that the 60 guilders the colonists paid was closer to $670. Today, you can rent a Manhattan parking space for a month for a little less than that.

New York was a fairly calm, compact city, and pretty much everything above Houston Street was farms and fields. The population in 1825 was about 170,000, and most of those New Yorkers were white Anglo-Saxon Protestants. But everything was about to change.

By 1865, the city's population was almost one million, and it was rapidly becoming more diverse. Immigrants were arriving (the Germans and the Irish came first), and they have never stopped. The term "melting pot" came from the title of a 1908 play that got awful reviews. But the title became a metaphor for the city's close-quarters diversity and its inevitable effect.

In the early twenty-first century, New York is still melting. Some 170 languages are spoken here. The population is roughly 44 percent white, 25 percent black, and 30 percent other. More Jews live in New York City than in Jerusalem, and we have more Puerto Ricans than in any other place outside Puerto Rico. The largest immigrant groups include Italians, Irish, West Indian, and Chinese, with growing numbers from Pakistan, Guyana, the Dominican Republic, Albania, Colombia, and Russia.

DEALING WITH LANGUAGE BARRIERS

Even if you're a native English speaker, you may have occasional language problems in New York. Many people who will be part of your experience in the city (taxi drivers, waiters, and store employees) may speak either very limited or very heavily accented English. The best way to handle this, after polite requests to repeat whatever you or the other person said, is to deal with one- or two-word sentences with just the key words needed to convey the information (for example, "Closed? Sunday?" "Supermarket? Left?"). Growling, "Hey, buddy, this is America! Speak English!" is generally not an effective communication method.

And it's not as if immigrants come to New York City and find wide, open spaces in which to live out their American dreams. The city has one of the densest populations in the world. If 26,403 people per square mile sounds like an astonishing number, take note: that's just for New York City as a whole. In Manhattan, the number is 66,940 people per square mile.

No wonder city folks can be a little short-tempered at times. And no wonder a spacious apartment is the greatest luxury many New Yorkers can imagine.

Talking Like a New Yorker

The first day I set foot in New York, at the tender age of 21, I gave myself away as an out-of-towner with a simple mispronunciation. In a taxi on the way back from my lunchtime job interview, I noticed a street sign and said aloud, "Houston Street"—pronouncing the name like the city in Texas. No, no, no. I was quickly informed by my future bosses that it's HOW-ston.

Luckily, the New York experience isn't scarred with pronunciation potholes like that. Certainly, you don't want to refer to "Green-Witch" Village (Greenwich is pronounced GRIN-itch, just like the places of the same name in Connecticut and England)—but you shouldn't really be referring to Greenwich Village anyway. It's just "the Village."

Another dead giveaway, if you're trying to avoid being taken for an out-of-towner, is to refer to the Avenue of the Americas by its real name. No self-respecting New Yorker has ever acknowledged Sixth Avenue's new name (officially changed in 1945).

If you have reason to visit Lexington Avenue, a quick way to sound like a local is to abbreviate it: "We're going to 78th and Lex, please." New Yorkers don't abbreviate the word avenue, however. If you hear someone mention going over to "Madison Ave." (rhymes with "have"), he or she is probably a visitor from Boston.

Then, there's the matter of direction. In many American cities, "downtown" just means the center of the business and shopping district—the heart of the city. In New York, downtown literally means down. If you're heading downtown, you're going south—at least to the Village and possibly all the way down to the Financial District at the tip of the island.

Uptown is, logically enough, north. The Upper East Side and Upper West Side are uptown neighborhoods, but Harlem is *really* uptown (as in the 1970s movie title *Uptown Saturday Night*). And if you're going crosstown, that means you're traveling east or west.

Otherwise, New Yorkers speak pretty much like other Americans. Despite rumors to the contrary, we do say "Excuse me" before making a request and "Thank you" when we've been helped. (Well, at least a lot of us do.)

THE PAUSE THAT CONFUSES

If you're asking someone on the street for directions or guidance, here's a tip. Don't stop after "Excuse me" and wait for acknowledgment. The New Yorker you're addressing may think you're going to ask for money (no matter how nicely you're dressed). Run your request all together in one sentence: "Excuse me, but could you tell me which way Park Avenue is?"

New York City accents differ from borough to borough, and of course New Yorkers come from everywhere (from Rhode Island to Korea, from Alabama to Albania). But you may occasionally still hear someone pronounce 33rd Street as "Toity-Toid." And you'll definitely hear someone say, "Fugged-aboudit" ("Forget about it"), although it may well be said in fun.

Oh, and when New Yorkers refer to "the city," they usually mean Manhattan.

Walking Like a New Yorker

New Yorkers walk fast. They stride. They move purposefully. And the main reason is that they're almost always on their way somewhere—to work, to a lunch date, to an appointment with the tax accountant or divorce lawyer, to the movies, the dry cleaner, the liquor store, the shoe repair shop, and so on. You, if you're a visitor to the city, may be on a particular block just for the sake of sightseeing. These differences of purpose can create conflict.

This phenomenon can be seen most painfully in the Times Square area on weekdays, when busy office workers find themselves stuck behind pokey tourists—and out-of-towners on leisurely strolls find themselves almost knocked down by rude, impatient locals.

If you want to enjoy New York at a slow pace, the best place to do that is in residential neighborhoods (particularly on weekends). Leisurely strolling is also encouraged in the city's parks. But in general, what you want to do in the city is get there fast and then take it slow.

After all, you've come to New York City at least partly because of its unparalleled energy, so you might as well be part of it. To get into the mood, make an appointment for a certain time and then leave your hotel room five minutes later than you should in order to arrive comfortably on time. Soon, you'll find yourself picking up your pace (see, doesn't that feel good?), bobbing and weaving among the crowds, and crossing against the light.

Yes, New Yorkers regularly cross the street when the sign says, "Don't Walk." And they always cross when the red "Don't Walk" sign is blinking. This is the Manhattan pedestrian equivalent of a yellow light, which—as many have observed—appears to mean, "Speed up." You should also know that after the "Don't Walk" light has stopped blinking, you still have seven seconds or so before the traffic light turns green and vehicles start moving again. (I don't recommend emulating New Yorkers in this respect. You could be killed. I'm just telling you what you may observe.)

Think of walking in New York City the same way you think of driving on a multilane highway. Walk on the right (although international visitors will sometimes get into the mix and confuse things). Pass on the left. If you find yourself facing a lot of oncoming foot traffic, pick a person walking in front of you in the same direction and follow him or her, letting that person do the hard work of clearing a path for you. I do this all the time.

If you're traveling with more than one other person, please don't walk three or four abreast on busy sidewalks. You're blocking traffic. If at all possible, without losing sight of your children, break into groups of two and give others room to pass.

In general, New York couples do not hold hands while walking, although unorthodox behavior has been known to break out in parks or on holidays. It's advisable, however, to hold onto small children while walking in crowded parts of town.

Back in the early 1980s during a transit strike, New Yorkers—faced with the prospect of walking long distances to work—came up with the bright idea of wearing sneakers and running shoes with office attire. You don't see this so much anymore, but you will want comfortable, low-heeled shoes for walking.

THINKING IN BLOCKS

In Manhattan, a mile is about 20 blocks—which means *street* blocks (as in going from 34th to 35th Street). Avenue blocks (as in going from Second Avenue to Third Avenue) are longer. They vary a lot, but in general you can think of them as two and a half times as long as street blocks. So if you're planning to take a walk from Times Square (42nd Street) to the heart of Chelsea (23rd Street), you're talking a two-mile trek.

Driving Like a New Yorker

If you really wanted to drive like a New Yorker, you'd leave your car at home. The majority of Manhattanites don't own cars. They get around by a mix of subway, bus, and taxi travel and good old-fashioned walking. And those who do own cars and pay the exorbitant rates for monthly garage parking (or go through the agonies of finding parking spaces on the street every day) tend to use their cars only for getting out of town. Their automobiles sit quietly in their garages all week—then, on Friday afternoons, they're brought out to make the weekly drive to weekend homes in Connecticut, New Jersey, Long Island, or upstate New York. (Not every car owner has a country house, but a lot do.)

But if you absolutely must bring your automobile to New York City or rent a car while you're here, you should at least know what you're in for. That can be summed up in two words: slow going.

The good news is that because Manhattan traffic tends to move slowly (count on at least 20 minutes for a two-mile trip from the Upper East Side or Upper West Side to Midtown), there aren't a lot of speed-related accidents. The bad news is that you'll spend a lot of valuable time sitting in traffic.

Traffic: New York's 13,000 taxis can probably navigate Times Square better than most of us.

Most of the avenues are one-way. Fifth, Seventh, Ninth, Lexington, and Second Avenues go downtown only. Madison, First, Third, Sixth, Eighth, and Tenth (Amsterdam) Avenues go uptown only. Park Avenue, Broadway, West End Avenue, and parts of Riverside Drive, which have two-way traffic, are the exceptions to the rule.

In general, avenues—which run north and south—are big and broad while most streets, which run east and west, are narrow. Streets are almost all one-way, too. The general rule is "even east, odd west." That is, streets with even numbers (68th, 44th, and so on) go east only, and those with odd numbers (77th and 25th) go west only. Again, there are exceptions. The broad streets, such as 42nd, 57th, 72nd, 79th, 34th, 23rd, and 14th, have two-way traffic—but you may run into unexpected rules about turning onto and off them.

All bets are off when you drive below 14th Street. This part of town, from Greenwich Village down to the Financial District, is Old New York—built before the nice, neat grids of the rest of Manhattan became the norm. You'll find curving, narrow streets with a mix of names and numbers—and, at times, a seeming lack of rhyme and reason. One of the most famous intersections in the Village, for instance, is the corner of Fourth Street and Tenth Street. But this is the age of *global positioning systems* (GPS), so maybe you'll be fine.

If you're going a fairly long distance, you may want to head over to the periphery highways (FDR Drive on the East Side and Henry Hudson Parkway, or the West Side Highway, on the West Side) to make better time. Even if you end up getting stuck in traffic on those highways, too, at least you'll get to enjoy the nice river views.

Just keep in mind that many of your fellow motorists are taxi drivers. Their skills, knowledge, and personalities vary widely. It's considered perfectly proper to roll down your window periodically and ask a taxi driver for directions.

ELEVATOR ETIQUETTE

In some parts of the world, it would be considered appallingly rude to enter an elevator without acknowledging other occupants with a "Good morning" or "Good day." In New York City, no problem. You can enter silently, ignore anyone else who's already there, and stare into the distance for the length of your ride. But if someone does say "Good morning" or something equally innocuous, you're not risking your life by replying. The same goes for asking someone the time or telling them their dog or baby is cute. And of course, if the elevator breaks down, the rules change and you can feel free to tell total strangers your entire life story while waiting to be rescued.

How the People Live

Thank goodness for movies and television (especially television—from *I Love Lucy* to *Seinfeld* and *Sex and the City* to *Gossip Girl*). Otherwise, life in New York would seem extremely peculiar to some Americans.

Most sizable American cities have downtown neighborhoods where people live in high-rise apartment buildings and walk to the market, rather than driving to the nearest shopping center whenever they need a gallon of milk—but in New York City (or Manhattan, at least, and many parts of the other boroughs), that's pretty much the only way of life.

A few Manhattanites live in private homes. Some are fabulously rich (when Michael Bloomberg was elected mayor in 2001, he chose to stay in his five-story East 79th Street limestone townhouse rather than move into Gracie Mansion, the official mayoral residence). Some got lucky on the real estate market. And some rent out a floor or two to make ends meet.

But the fabulously rich live in apartments, too, (Jacqueline Onassis always did—a 14-room place on the 14th floor at 1040 Fifth Avenue, near 85th Street). The most prized apartments are the ones in prewar (World War II) buildings because of their larger rooms, higher ceilings, gracious layouts, and solid construction. But there has been a recent trend toward ultra-contemporary buildings with floor-to-ceiling windows.

New Yorkers rely on their doormen and their supers (short for building superintendents). If you live in a doorman building, you can head off for work or even vacation while knowing that your FedEx and UPS packages and overflowing mailbox will be taken care of and that strangers won't be popping up to your apartment in your absence (unless you've left the key for them—with the doorman, of course). If you live in a non-doorman building, you rely on a buzzer/intercom system for security and on your super for repairs and emergencies.

Most New Yorkers go to work by subway, bus, taxi, or even commuter train (mostly suburbanites). A few of the more fortunate live close enough to their workplaces to walk. And a few of the even more fortunate are picked up by car services (those handsome black town cars you see everywhere) or by limousines.

They work all kinds of hours and run errands at lunch. The so-called three-martini lunch (for which the expense account was invented) may still go on here and there. And the ladies who lunch, at their leisure in painfully expensive restaurants, still exist. But more and more, New Yorkers tend to eat lunch at their desks or go grab a quick bite—alone or with colleagues.

At the end of the day, New Yorkers often go straight from the office to their dinner, movie, concert, or theater dates. Lots of dog walkers and nannies make this possible. The overall difficulty of getting from Point A to Point B in New York City makes this desirable.

In fact, New Yorkers are notoriously lazy about traveling outside their neighborhoods unnecessarily. If you have friends or family in New York, don't be offended if they don't volunteer to pick you up at the airport. That's not done so often here.

EVERYBODY DELIVERS

Shopping can be a challenge in the city. New Yorkers have a tendency to create their own little core neighborhoods within a three- or four-block radius where they have their favorite supermarket, produce market, dry cleaner, drugstore, deli, hardware store, and the like. There are a few huge supermarkets, but you won't find big parking lots behind them. (And that's just as well, because most Manhattanites don't own cars.) Luckily, just about every business delivers—usually for a small fee. That includes restaurants and not just the pizzerias and casual Chinese places. New Yorkers do eat out—a lot—but they also cherish evenings at home cuddled up with takeout or delivery food.

New Yorkers thrive on the energy and physical intimacy of their city. (At least, the ones who are happy to be here do.) Truly, they don't even hear the sirens and garbage trucks and other street noises that keep many visitors awake.

But when they feel the need to get away from it all, they don't have far to go to enjoy the country. Lots of them have weekend houses in Connecticut, on Long Island, in New Jersey, or in New York State (just north of the suburban counties). And those who don't often have friends who do.

And now you know how New Yorkers remain sane.

Chapter

2

The Good Life:
Food and Culture

In This Chapter

- 🍎 Great restaurants, plus food and drink of all kinds
- 🍎 The best shopping neighborhoods and streets
- 🍎 The joys of theater, all over town
- 🍎 Places to see great art and architecture
- 🍎 Where to find all kinds of music and dance
- 🍎 Football, baseball, basketball, and other spectator sports

Before New York City adopted the Big Apple nickname, it was known as Fun City (and with good reason). Just about everybody's favorite form of recreation can be enjoyed here, from fine dining to night baseball and wine tastings to professional wrestling.

Food and Drink

If part of what you're hoping for from your New York visit is some interesting places to eat, you won't be disappointed. But if you're planning to go home having covered the New York City restaurant scene, good luck.

Restaurants, Restaurants Everywhere

No human being has ever eaten at every restaurant in New York City—and not just because there are 10,000 or so of them. You could, after all, have lunch and dinner at a different restaurant every day of the year—but just as you were nearing completion of the list (this would be close to 14 years after you started), someone would break the news to you that since you started, another couple thousand places had opened.

So, you may want to plan ahead which aspect of the restaurant scene you want to explore. Or, you may just want to wing it and decide when you arrive. If you want to have dinner at one of the super-elegant, super-expensive restaurants at the peak of their popularity, however, decide now and make reservations by phone or online before you leave home (maybe a month or more before you leave).

To say that New York offers the potential for an international dining experience is a major understatement. Try to look up Italian restaurants in New York City on a directory website, and you'll find more than 950 (actually, more like 1,700 if you count the 800 pizzerias). Right behind the Italian restaurants are the Chinese ones—600 or so. Then, there are hundreds of French, Mexican, Japanese, Thai, and Indian places, followed by more than a smattering of Greek, Mediterranean, Middle Eastern, Vietnamese, Korean, Caribbean, Spanish, South American, Irish, and German.

You can find American food in New York City, too, of course—literally thousands of American restaurants. Sometimes that means haute regional cuisine or what food critics have started calling "haute barnyard" (fancy food with a major emphasis on farm-fresh ingredients). And sometimes it just means a great hamburger.

NO CHAIN, NO PAIN

You can find chain restaurants—Red Lobster, Olive Garden, Applebee's—in New York City. But they are there strictly to cash in on the tourist dollar because out-of-towners are familiar with them. (You'll find one of each of them in Times Square.) If you want a New York experience, go to New York restaurants—not places that are so uncharacteristic of the city. (That is, unless you're feeling homesick—in which case, we understand.)

Restaurants are listed by price category in the East Side, West Side, and Downtown chapters (Chapters 6, 8, and 10)—complete with addresses, telephone numbers, and other details. Here are a few thoughts on places that critics and real New Yorkers like a lot.

Best Italian

Del Posto on Tenth Avenue in the southern end of Chelsea is one of the newest stars in this category. So is A Voce in the Madison Square Park area (east of Chelsea).

If the great Italian restaurants do seem to be downtown, maybe that's because that's where the original Italian immigrants first settled. You'll find Pó on Cornelia Street, Il Mulino between Sullivan and Thompson Streets, and Lupa on Thompson. Babbo, a relative newcomer to the Village, is on Waverly Place, and Il Giglio is in TriBeCa.

But you can find a fabulous Italian meal farther uptown, particularly on the East Side. Alto is in the East 50s, Erminia is in the East 80s, and Sfoglia is all the way up on 92nd Street. And if you really feel like traveling, there's Roberto's (popular with Zagat's real-people critics) in the Bronx.

Best Chinese

It's nice to report that some of the city's best Chinese food can actually be found in Chinatown. Oriental Garden, Ping's Seafood, Mandarin Court, Golden Unicorn, and Dim Sum Go Go are among the neighborhood stars.

Midtown on the East Side is also the home of a few of the best, including Phoenix Garden on East 40th Street; Mr. K's and Tse Yang, both on East 51st; Shun Lee Palace on East 55th; and a star newcomer, Philippe, on East 60th.

Upper West Siders have Shun Lee's sister property, Shun Lee West. The New York University area, east of the Village and north of SoHo, has Chinatown Brasserie—another newcomer winning a lot of praise. Or just go out to the Chinatown in Flushing, Queens.

Best French

Not surprisingly, you'll find some of the finest French food in the city on the Upper East Side, where the people who can afford it live. Daniel is on East 65th, Café Boulud on East 76th, Jojo on East 64th, and the Payard Bistro is located between 73rd and 74th Streets.

Two of the absolute top French restaurants, Jean Georges and Le Bernardin, have West Side addresses—but the first is on Columbus Circle, right next to Central Park, and the second is solidly in Midtown on 51st Street.

Other impressive Midtown choices include La Grenouille, which has been on East 52nd Street forever and a day; the Modern, inside the Museum of Modern Art on 53rd Street between Fifth and Sixth; and L'Atelier de Joël Robuchon, the elegant newcomer, on East 57th.

But there's also incredible French food downtown. Consider the superstar restaurants Bouley and Chanterelle, both in TriBeCa, and the lesser-known Le Gigot, specializing in Provençal dishes, in the Village. In between, there's Fleur de Sel, a touch of Bretagne in the Flatiron district.

Best American

Where to begin? How about in the West 60s with Telepan, one of the most highly praised New American spots in town? Just on the other side of Lincoln Center you'll find Per Se, in the Time Warner Center, which is sort of a blend of New American and French.

The Upper East Side's star American restaurant is lovely Aureole, going strong since 1988.

STREET EATS

Who needs restaurants? You can find dozens of dishes being sold from stands on just about every street corner in Midtown. The Sabrett's hot dog (with mustard and onions or sauerkraut—your choice) is the classic. Every visitor to New York City (except vegetarians!) should have at least one. The morning coffee, bagels, and doughnuts are serviceable. The giant salted pretzels are a matter of taste.

In Midtown you'll find fashionable Michael's, known for its California cuisine, on West 55th. In the Flatiron area, there's Gramercy Tavern, a longtime favorite, and Veritas, with its knockout wine list, across the street from each other on East 20th Street, and Craft nearby on East 19th.

Downtown, there's the venerable Gotham Bar & Grill, the splashy Perry Street (on the street of the same name), the heavenly Annisa, and the neighborhoody Little Owl, all in the Village. The Great Jones Café is nearby in NoHo.

Eat here: Restaurants inside Grand Central Terminal include Michael Jordan's Steakhouse, Métrazur, and the Oyster Bar.

Best Steak

Some people say you have to go to Brooklyn—to Peter Luger's—to find New York City's best steak. But there are plenty of big, masculine steakhouses in Manhattan.

Midtown has Sparks on East 46th Street; Del Frisco's on West 49th; and a relative newcomer, Quality Meats, on West 58th Street. The Time Warner Center has Porter House New York. Wolfgang's is at the southern edge of Midtown, on East 34th Street, with a newer branch down on Greenwich Street.

Strip House is in the Village. Craft Steak is in southern Chelsea. And vowel-resistant STK is, appropriately enough, in the Meat Packing District.

Best Seafood

Some of the most terrific seafood restaurants in town are downtown. Aquagrill is in SoHo, as is Balthazar (not a seafood restaurant, per se, but known for its raw bar). Pearl Oyster Bar and Mary's Fish Camp are in the Village, and Mermaid Inn is in the East Village (although there's a newer location on the Upper West Side).

In Midtown, you'll find Le Bernardin (French seafood) on West 51st, Milos Estiatorio (Greek seafood) on West 55th, and Oceana (New American seafood) on East 54th.

Best Vegetarian

So much for downtown's reputation as forward-thinking: most of the best vegetarian dining in the city is on, of all places, the Upper East Side. That includes Candle 79 and Candle Café, vegan places in the East 70s, and Gobo in the East 80s.

Gobo does have another location, however, and it's in the Village. Counter is in the East Village. Pure Food and Wine is on Irving Place near Gramercy Park.

The best-known vegetarian restaurant in New York City is Zen Palate, which has one location in the Theater District (West 46th Street) and one on Union Square.

TO RESERVE OR NOT TO RESERVE

Some restaurants (usually the new, hot, and very expensive ones) require calling a month or more in advance for reservations. And even then, they may not find a table for you. With most places, calling a day or two ahead is fine—and with lots of neighborhood restaurants you can just walk right in, especially on weeknights. Friday and Saturday nights are busiest in most neighborhoods. You should also call a few days ahead, even on weeknights, for 6 or 6:30 P.M. reservations in the Theater District. (But after 8 P.M., when the theatergoers have left, you can get in almost anywhere.)

Best Sushi

If money is no object, Masa—in the Time Warner Center—is the place to go. Nobu in TriBeCa (now with an uptown location on West 57th) is a relative bargain. Other great sushi places include Sushi Yasuda in the East 40s, Sugi-yama in the West 50s, and Sushi Seki in the East 60s.

Best Mexican

The restaurant Hell's Kitchen is in—surprise—the Hell's Kitchen neighborhood (West 46th). Pampano is in the East 40s. Maya is in the East 60s. Itzocan has an uptown location on the Upper East Side but not that far from Spanish Harlem.

Otherwise, you'll have to go downtown for the finest Mexican meals. The other Itzocan is in the East Village; Mexicana Mama has one location in the Village and one in the East Village. So does Mercadito.

Best Burger

Only in New York would you find one of the most delicious hamburgers in town at a fancy French hotel: Burger Joint at Le Parker Meridien on West 56th. Then, there's Corner Bistro, which has been in the Village forever. Shake Shack is just a food stand in Madison Square Park, but *New York Magazine* proclaimed their cheeseburgers the best in town.

And Perhaps a Refreshing Beverage

The three-martini lunch is a thing of the distant past, but New Yorkers do enjoy a drink now and then (after work, before dinner, at dinner, pre-theater, during theater intermission, after the theater ...). Surprisingly, for a place with so many fantastic restaurants of all kinds and price ranges, New York is not a fabulous city for drinks. That's because, although most restaurants have bars, many are tiny (just enough seats for a couple of parties to wait for their dinner tables to become available). Many others are packed at cocktail hour—sometimes with drinkers standing three or four deep, shoulder to shoulder. That's an arrangement that has all the charm of a rush-hour subway trip (except with more noise).

You'll find suggestions for a few fun places to visit at cocktail hour in Chapters 6, 8, and 10 on the East Side, the West Side, and Downtown.

In general, the earlier you go to a place, the more likely you are to find an empty stool at the bar—or, even better, an empty table in the bar area. The idea is to get there before the working Manhattanites start pouring out of their offices and into the bars, so consider 4 or 4:30 P.M. for drinks.

Early is good, too, because of lower happy-hour prices (sometimes for wine, sometimes for beer, and sometimes for all cocktails).

Most bars have bar menus. You can just drink, or you can have a bite as well (anything from French fries to chicken or beef satay). This spontaneously turns many drink dates into dinner dates without having to move an inch (except to get out their wallets).

SUNDAYS AND SUPERMARKETS

Unlike many states, New York does not allow the sale of wine or liquor in supermarkets. (But you can buy beer in supermarkets as well as in delis.) Until a few years ago, wine and liquor stores were all closed on Sundays—but a few now stay open on Sundays (as long as they close one other day during the week).

New Yorkers tend to be wine drinkers. If you are, too, but the rest of your party doesn't share your interest, that's generally no problem. Most restaurants have at least a few choices of decent wines by the glass.

And if you don't know a Zinfandel from a white Zinfandel (or don't know that a white Zinfandel isn't a white wine), feel free to ask your waiter or sommelier (wine steward, of which there aren't that many these days) for a recommendation. Even the best-informed oenophiles do.

Buying a bottle of wine as a gift or for your own consumption back in your hotel room is a snap. In most residential neighborhoods, you can't walk for more than a couple of blocks without running into a liquor store. But for a unique experience and an amazing selection, check out Sherry Lehmann. The store has been purveying wine (and spirits) since 1934 and in 2007 moved from its longtime (since 1948) Madison Avenue address over to Park (*505 Park Avenue, at 59th Street, New York, NY 10022, 212-838-7500, www.sherry-lehmann. com*). It still looks like a London gentlemen's club inside, and you can easily buy a $1,000 bottle of wine if you like—but you can also buy a $10 bottle and the staff will be just as nice to you.

If you're going out for a big formal dinner, wine and/or water are the logical choices. (And it's not considered déclassé to tell the waiter that tap water, not expensive bottled water, will be fine for your table.) But New Yorkers are beer drinkers, too, particularly with Chinese, Thai, and Mexican food.

At less-formal meals, you can get away with just about anything as your beverage. That means iced tea, lemonade, juice, milk, a Coke, or some other kind of soda (New Yorkers don't call it "pop").

One nice benefit of New York City life for drinkers is that it's unlikely you'll be driving home after dinner, so no one has to abstain as the designated driver. That will be the taxi driver's (or bus driver's, or subway motorman's) job.

Shopping

Some people come to New York City just to buy things, and few go home without at least a shopping bag or two in hand. Whether you're hoping to find a bargain handbag or a funky piece of jewelry from a street vendor or to score some glamorous piece of fashion or design from an elegant, slightly snobby store, the city has what you're looking for.

Fifth Avenue is still the premier shopping boulevard, even if it isn't as grand as it used to be. Old-timers shake their heads in dismay to see The Disney Store hawking cartoon-character merchandise in the middle of all the golden European designer storefronts. And the Apple store at 59th may be grand, but a cathedral of electronics doesn't fit the old Fifth Avenue mold.

Happily, some things haven't changed: Bergdorf Goodman still anchors the avenue at the border of Midtown, on 58th Street, followed by Henri Bendel, Tiffany, Cartier, and Saks and a number of smaller designer shops between. FAO Schwarz, the ultimate toy store, is also there.

Madison Avenue, just one block east, is an intimidatingly glamorous street—although its concentrated shopping area begins just above 59th Street, exactly where Fifth Avenue's ends. In the East 60s and 70s, Madison offers Barneys, Ralph Lauren, Calvin Klein, Donna Karan, Valentino, and Chanel. (We could go on, and it does.)

For a long time, Manhattanites took pride in the fact that the heart of New York City didn't have malls, but the Shops at Columbus Circle, at the Time Warner Center, come pretty close. The stores are fairly upscale, but many are friendly and familiar, too, such as Williams-Sonoma, J. Crew, Sephora, Coach, Cole Haan, and Borders.

That's a reminder that as the country (and, let's face it, the world) becomes more homogenous, you can find plenty of stores in New York that you can find in any good-sized city. In addition to Williams-Sonoma and J. Crew, there are branches of Pottery Barn, Crate & Barrel, Banana Republic, the Gap, Ann Taylor, Restoration Hardware, Bed Bath & Beyond, lots of Barnes & Nobles, and even a couple of Home Depots.

There aren't many true department stores left (Saks and Bergdorf don't qualify by most definitions because they don't have furniture departments), but Bloomingdale's still stands proudly at 59th and Lexington and Macy's still takes up an enormous amount of space on West 34th. The city's best-loved furniture store is now ABC Carpet & Home, on lower Broadway.

Times Square is one of the less-desirable neighborhoods in terms of shopping, although you'll find no shortage of souvenir stores. If you're looking for gifts for friends back home and would love to find something beyond T-shirts, coffee mugs, or Statue of Liberty tiaras, try the museum gift shops instead.

You may want to check out the Village, too. Bleecker Street, especially, has become a desirable, very upscale shopping area.

Most stores are open late at least a couple nights a week, and most are open on Sundays.

WHEN NEW YORKERS LEAVE TOWN TO SHOP

If you're visiting long enough to tear yourself away from the city and take a day trip, you could do as the Manhattanites do: head for Woodbury Common, about an hour north of the city, and shop in the more than 200 discount outlet shops there.

There are stores for every budget, starting with the Gap—but the real fun is in the upscale outlets such as Calvin Klein, Armani, Valentino, Dolce & Gabbana, Fendi, Judith Leiber, and Jimmy Choo. Gray Line buses (www.grayline.com) leave from the Port Authority bus terminal.

Woodbury Common Premium Outlets, 498 Red Apple Court, Central Valley, NY 10917, **845-928-4000,** *www.premiumoutlets.com.*

Theater

New Yorkers like to brag that their city is not a one-industry town like Los Angeles (entertainment) or Washington (government)—but if New York did have to claim one major product, it would be the arts. And if New York is known best for any one particular art form, it's theater.

Even in an age when New Yorkers are bemoaning the sorry state of things (too much Disney, too many shows based on movies, too much stunt casting, too little originality), you'll find three dozen or so Broadway theaters all lit up with musicals, dramas, and comedies, at least some of them original and exciting.

¢ An evening at the theater is an expensive proposition (well more than $100 per ticket for musicals and almost as much for plays). That's why so many people line up at the TKTS discount booths, run by the Theater Development Fund (www.tdf.org), every day. There are usually dozens of shows available (often including the biggest Broadway hits of the moment) at 25 to 50 percent off. The Times Square location (on a little island running from 46th to 47th Street between Broadway and Seventh Avenue, although during renovations it moved to the Marriott Marquis a block away) opens at 3 P.M. for evening performance tickets and at 10 A.M. for matinees. The South Street Seaport location (downtown, at the corner of Front and John Streets) opens at 11 A.M. and sells its matinee tickets the day before. No credit cards are accepted.

Don't count out off-Broadway productions, which tend to be less expensive and are sometimes done by prestigious playwrights with big-name stars.

FOR FILM FANS

Movies are serious business in New York City. You can catch one of the latest hits at one of the big multiplexes, just like the ones back home, but you can also see old and/or little-known films at Film Forum, IFC Center, or Anthology Film Archives (all downtown). There are also special screenings done by the Museum of the Moving Image (in Queens), the Museum of Modern Art, and the Film Society of Lincoln Center.

Art and Architecture

There are museums in every neighborhood, from the art giants such as the Metropolitan, the Guggenheim, the Whitney, and the Museum of Modern Art (MoMA) to the terribly specific and the esoteric. There's a museum devoted to firefighting in SoHo, one dedicated to television and radio in Midtown, and one in Brooklyn that's all about the history of the subway.

When you're not in the mood for an entire museum, there are galleries all over the city exhibiting paintings, drawings, sculpture, video, and photography. Check out the listings in *The New York Times, New York Magazine, The New Yorker,* or *Time Out.*

Fifth Avenue neighbors: The 1937 statue of Atlas faces the twin spires of St. Patrick's Cathedral.

Even if you or someone you're traveling with isn't a fan of museums or galleries, you'll be exposed to art during your everyday wanderings. You'll come across giant pieces of modern sculpture in front of office buildings and statues of literary and historical figures (from Eleanor Roosevelt to Alice in Wonderland) in and around the parks.

New York's architecture is a free art show in itself. True, there are stretches of Eisenhower-era high-rises that could put you to sleep. But the city is also filled with some lovely turn-of-the-century apartment buildings (especially on the Upper West Side), charming townhouses in the Village, and an array of modernist office buildings that range from the sublime (the Seagram's Building on Park Avenue) to the slightly odd (the Lipstick Building on Third and 53rd).

FOR GOOD LISTENERS

Plenty of cities have author signings and readings at local bookstores, but New York City has those and more. There are always readings, lectures, and panel discussions at libraries, museums, and the incomparable 92nd Street Y (on the Upper East Side) as well as at bookstores.

Music and Dance

You'll find free concerts, too, with musicians playing for donations in the subway stations and on the streets. And no matter what your favorite music genre (from country to klezmer), you can find someone performing it somewhere in the city.

Head for Lincoln Center or Carnegie Hall for classical works, including the grandest of opera productions at the Met. Check the listings in *New York Magazine* or *Time Out* to find out who's playing at the jazz clubs and at the smaller musical venues such as Mercury Lounge, Iridium, the Knitting Factory, and Joe's Pub. And you can still find glamorous, old-fashioned cabaret with big names at spots such as the Oak Room at the Algonquin.

Devotees of dance will find two major ballet companies—New York City Ballet and the American Ballet Theater—plus two important venues for other dance companies: City Center in Midtown and the Joyce Theater in Chelsea. But the most famous dancers in the city may be the Rockettes. The Radio City Christmas show is their annual moment of glory, but you may be lucky and find them in town at other times of the year.

Spectator Sports

The athletic life isn't the first thing that comes to mind when you think of New York City. But even Manhattanites manage to run, swim (mostly indoors at health clubs), and play tennis. There are basketball courts in various playgrounds, and amateur baseball and softball games are known to take place in the city's parks.

But the city has been home to major professional sports teams for as long as professional sports teams have existed. With a little planning, you can make a sports outing a memorable part of your visit.

Baseball

The New York Yankees play in Yankee Stadium in the Bronx, and if construction continues on schedule, they'll move to the new Yankee Stadium across the street at some point in 2009. The current address is 161st Street and River Avenue, and you can get there by subway—either via the No. 4 (which is the express train on the main East Side line), the B, or the D. (Both the B and the D stop at Washington Square, 34th Street, 42nd Street, and Rockefeller Center.)

Tickets and other information are available at www.yankees.mlb.com.

The New York Mets are slated to get a new stadium too, but right now they make their home at Shea Stadium in Queens. The No. 7 train, known as the Flushing line (that's the name of the town in Queens), goes straight there from Times Square and Grand Central Terminal. The website for tickets and other information is www.newyork.mets.mlb.com, and the telephone number is **718-507-TIXX.**

Football

It says something about big-city real estate or maybe about the closeness of the tri-state area (New York, New Jersey, and Connecticut) that both of New York's professional football teams play their home games in New Jersey.

Whether you're looking for the New York Jets or the Giants, you'll find them at the Meadowlands in East Rutherford, NJ. It's a short drive or a 15-minute bus ride from the Port Authority bus terminal (**212-564-8484**).

For Jets ticket information, write the New York Jets Ticket Office, 1000 Fulton Avenue, Hempstead, NY 11550-1099 or call **516-560-8200**. One way to buy single tickets is through ticket exchange, www.oss.ticketmaster.com, where season ticket holders can sell individual tickets online.

Ticket exchange works for Giants tickets, too. Or you can write the Giants Ticket Office, Giants Stadium, East Rutherford, NJ 07073 or call **201-935-8222**.

A new $1.4 billion Meadowlands NFL football stadium is in the teams' near future.

Basketball

The New York Knicks play their home games at Madison Square Garden, right in midtown Manhattan. The main entrance, on Seventh Avenue between 31st and 33rd Streets, leads to the box office. Seats can be purchased on the ticket exchange system at www.teamexchange.ticketmaster.com.

A GARDEN PARTY

Beyond basketball, Madison Square Garden has a lot of things going on, including NHL hockey games (the New York Rangers), wrestling, and even professional lacrosse (the New York Titans). There are also major pop music concerts. The arena's official website is www.thegarden.com.

Yes, it's a pretty amazing city. And now that you know a little about the aspects of New York that draw you to it most, it's time to start planning your visit.

Chapter 3

Researching and Booking Your Trip

In This Chapter

- Putting together a travel budget
- Websites to help you do online research
- Deciding the kind of hotel you want
- Planes, trains, and package deals
- All about travel insurance
- Your own personal budget worksheet

Here comes the fun part: turning your trip into reality by making a series of decisions. Will you do a three-day weekend or take two weeks of vacation time, or will you go for something in between? Which airline will you take, and what days do you want to fly? Where will you stay? What do you want to do when you get there? Unless you're a billionaire, money will be an important factor in much of that decision-making. That's why this chapter begins with a discussion of costs and ends with a budget worksheet.

How to Budget for Your Trip

Yes, New York is one of the most expensive cities in the country. But knowing what to expect in terms of price will make your trip less shocking financially. And your visit can be much more affordable if you give some thought to exactly where you want to be frugal and where you want to splurge.

What Things Cost in New York

There used to be an unwritten but often cited equation: the price of a subway token and the price of a slice of pizza always kept pace with each other. But in recent years, that's gotten slightly out of kilter.

Subway (or bus) ride	$2
Slice of plain pizza	$2.50
Taxi from Midtown to Upper West Side	$10
Bottle of water	$1 and up
Cup of coffee	$1.50
Newspaper (*The New York Times*, weekdays)	$1.25
Empire State Building admission* (adult)	$17.61
Broadway musical (orchestra, Friday night)	$110–$121.50
Metropolitan Museum admission (adult)	$20
Circle Line tour (adult, three-hour cruise)	$29.50
Cocktail at Gramercy Tavern	$12
Prix fixé dinner at Daniel	$98
Takeout chicken dish from Hunan Balcony	$10
Staten Island ferry	free

The observation deck, that is. You can just walk into the building and look at the lobby any time.

CASH AND DON'T CARRY

Early in 2008, a middle-aged music executive was robbed and beaten in broad daylight (about 2 P.M. on a Friday) in Midtown after coming out of a bank with $150,000 in cash. It was a horrible crime, but I don't know anyone who didn't think, "What was this man doing with all that cash?"

There are ATMs on almost every corner in New York, and the vast majority of businesses take credit cards—so there's no reason to walk around with more than $200 in your wallet at any given time.

Little Ways to Save Money

Money does have a way of vanishing in New York City—not by theft or loss, but all the little things you do during the course of a normal day have a way of adding up. So it's helpful to find little ways to cut back on expenses.

Transportation

Walk as much as you can. It's healthy, gives you a solid acquaintance with the city's street life, and is free.

¢ Buy a weekly Metrocard pass ($20) at the nearest subway station—but only if you're planning to use mass transit frequently. Do the math before you buy.

Feel free to take a taxi if there are three or four people in your party and you aren't going from one end of the island to the other. Four $2 subway fares is the same as an $8 taxi fare.

Food and Drink

When you want to try an expensive, elegant restaurant, go for lunch instead of dinner. Lunches cost less.

When you go to a nice restaurant for dinner, eat at the bar now and then. It may be a special bar menu, but even if it's the regular one, you're likely to have fewer courses and splurges in this casual setting.

Some nights, pick up food from the nearest deli or food shop, take it back to your hotel, and eat in front of the TV.

In the same vein, go back to your hotel at least one evening, pick up the phone, and order dinner to be delivered to your room. You have tons of choices, including pizza, a wide array of Chinese food, burgers, and barbecue.

¢ When you're running around during the day and it's time for lunch, pick up something from a street vendor (for example, hot dogs or Middle Eastern goodies such as falafel). You'll probably save about 75 percent, compared with eating at a typical neighborhood restaurant. And there's no tipping.

Drink at happy hour. The prices of beer, wine, and liquor are dramatically lower at certain hours of the day in many bars. And because you aren't working for a living while you're here, your schedule has flexibility.

Hotels

Look for hotel deals on websites such as www.hotels.com.

If you don't mind sleeping in the same room with your children, ask for a room with two double or queen beds and pile in together. All hotels won't allow this, but many will.

If you're traveling in a group of three, four, or more, reserve a one-bedroom suite. It's generally cheaper than two standard guest rooms, and most suite living rooms will have a sofa bed. (Be sure to ask, of course.)

Avoid the mini bar. It's fun, but the prices are outrageous. (The same goes for bottled water outside the mini bar.)

Don't use the telephone in your room. Many hotels still apply huge surcharges to calls from their guest rooms. Use your cell phone or an old-fashioned pay phone instead.

Doing Things

Many museums have one day or evening per week when admission is free. There may be larger crowds, but the price is right.

Buy your theater tickets at one of the city's two TKTS booths. Prices are up to 50 percent off, even for current hit shows. The one downtown at South

Street Seaport tends to be less busy than the one in Times Square, but don't take a $15 taxi there and cancel out part of your savings.

¢ Buy a Citypass. Pay $65, and you've purchased admission to the Metropolitan Museum of Art, the Museum of Modern Art, the Guggenheim Museum, the American Museum of Natural History, the Empire State Building observatory, and a three-hour Circle Line cruise around Manhattan. That's a well-chosen half dozen sights, and it's a value of more than $120 at regular prices. Plus, you get a 15 percent one-day savings certificate for shopping at Bloomingdales and a 15 percent discount at 10 restaurants, including the Sea Grill, the Brasserie, and Macy's Cellar Bar & Grill. The card is valid for nine days (much longer during the winter season). For young people ages 12 to 17, the price is $49. Visit www.citypass.com for more information.

Shopping

To save on sales tax, have your purchases shipped to your home address (assuming it's outside New York State). But keep in mind that clothing items under $110 are tax-free to begin with.

Check out Century 21 in the Financial District or Woodbury Common, an hour outside the city, for discount prices.

I'VE GOT A TIP FOR YOU

Tipping in New York is a fairly simple process, thanks to the sales tax (which is a little more than 8 percent). Just double the sales tax on your restaurant bill, and there you have a 16 to 17 percent tip—which is perfectly appropriate for all but the most elegant restaurants. (At those places, give 20 percent. And even if you're math-challenged, you can just drop the last numeral from the total and double that. So, a check of $144 would call for a 20 percent tip of $28 ($144 without the last digit is $14, and two times $14 is $28).

A 15 percent tip is appropriate for taxi drivers. A tip of $1 to $2 per piece of luggage is good for hotel bellhops (unless you have 20 pieces and there's a cart involved, in which case you can do less). If a hotel or apartment building doorman helps you with your luggage or gets a taxi for you, a tip isn't necessary but a couple of dollars would probably be appreciated.

Getting Started Online

How did we ever plan anything, much less a major trip, before the Internet? First, you can go online to explore and be inspired by the incredible city you're about to visit. Then, hit the travel sites to do the actual booking of flights, hotels, and anything else you want to nail down before leaving home.

New York Information Websites

www.manhattanusersguide.com: This is an insiders' site that lots of New Yorkers swear by. You may not need the tips on kitchen and bath renovations or moving vans, but the information on new restaurants, stores, events, gift sources, and sample sales could come in handy. Sign up for MUG's free e-mail newsletter, or just go to the home page and search the archives.

www.mta.info: This site belongs to the Metropolitan Transit Authority, the organization that runs the city's subways and buses. Its MTA Trip Planner is highly useful. (On the home page, look under Regional Travel and click "Trip Planner: Subway and Bus Directions.") Just plug in the address you're leaving from and where you want to go in Manhattan and the outer boroughs, and the planner will tell you how to get there by mass transit. It will also let you know how long the trip should take. This system may not always result in the most efficient route, but it will get you there.

www.newyorkology.com: This handy site reports on all kinds of events for that day and the weekend ahead. You might find news about film festivals, celebrity lectures, wine classes, house tours, or progress at the World Trade Center site.

www.nyc.gov: This is the official site of the city and the mayor's office. The information on the public advocate's office may leave you cold, but you'll definitely want to take a look at the section for visitors under Information and Services. It includes information on a variety of topics including historic tours, events, and N.Y.C. for Kids. When you get here, you should also take a look at "This Weekend in New York City" on the home page just to see what's up.

www.nycvisit.com: This is the site of New York & Company, the city's official tourism bureau. Its many features include a Plan Your Visit section, lists

of deals and promotions, and a daily bulletin on things going on in the city
during that particular day.

*You can't beat the
view: Ice skaters at
Wollman Rink in
Central Park.*

Travel Sites

www.expedia.com: Expedia offers bookings on flights, hotels, cars, and a
general category that it calls "activities." That means theater tickets, museum
admission, sightseeing tours, and package deals such as the $65 Citypass (see
page 39), which is good for admission at six major attractions. A test search
for Chicago to New York flights, a month ahead of travel time, turned up
fares well under $300 on several major airlines. Rooms at the Empire Hotel
were available for $289, at the Waldorf-Astoria for $369, and at the Carlyle for
$400.

www.orbitz.com: On Orbitz, you can book any combination of hotels, flights,
and rental cars. Roughly a month ahead of time, you might find two round-
trip airline tickets and four nights in a hotel ranging from less than $800 to
more than $1,700, depending on the hotel choice. The last-minute deals can
be real money savers. If you're prepared to book things the weekend before
you go to New York City, you'll find considerable discounts. The Marriott
Marquis, for instance, was offered at $419 per night roughly a month ahead of
time but was available for $299 on a last-minute basis.

www.travelocity.com: Travelocity lets you search for flights, hotels, car rentals, and packages. A test search for a trip from Phoenix for two people traveling together turned up packages with round-trip airfare on American Airlines plus two nights in a hotel for various prices per person, including $659 at the Waldorf-Astoria and $707 at the SoHo Grand.

www.hotels.com: Despite its name, Hotels.com does offer bookings on flights and vacation packages as well as accommodations. But hotels are its specialty, and the site's early booking specials might turn up rates as low as $168 at the Thirty Thirty, $189 at the Paramount, and $345 at the New York Palace.

www.tripadvisor.com: When you select New York and your dates, Trip Advisor brings up the hotels that are available (on your dates and/or within your price range) in order of popularity, as ranked by the site's readers. Then, of course, you can check out the various reviews of the hotel you're considering. You might book the Fitzpatrick Grand Central, for instance, for $259 a night. The site also reports on flights, vacation packages, and restaurants.

Booking Accommodations

Unless you're arriving by chartered jet or in first class from Australia with your entourage, your hotel stay is probably going to be the biggest expense of your New York trip. So, making the decision about where to stay is a big one.

Big Hotels

Big hotels have a bad name. And I can understand why when I walk into the lobby of a large chain hotel and see piles and piles of luggage taking up all the space, and I imagine all the people who belong to that luggage checking in and out at the same time.

Happily, every large hotel isn't like that. And big has its advantages. In a larger property, you're more likely to find all the amenities: 24-hour room service, a good-size fitness center, a choice of in-house restaurants, a big TV with lots of channels and movies, a wireless Internet connection, and a business center somewhere in the hotel.

Another plus for big hotels is that you're often more likely to be able to find a room there when you're making relatively last-minute plans. Granted, the desk clerk is unlikely to remember your name—but sometimes anonymity is an enjoyable part of the New York City experience.

Little Hotels

Small hotels have come a long way. Once, if you wanted to get a room with a four-poster bed and pretty antiques in an intimate little property with a friendly staff, you had to give up certain amenities. But today, you can find great small hotels that offer many of the perks of their bigger, busier counterparts.

Still, you're unlikely to find a real on-site gym or spa. And it's been my experience that in a number of smaller hotels, services are listed that aren't readily available. ("Oh, we get our room service from the restaurant down the block, and they're closed on Sundays. Didn't anybody tell you?")

It's important to keep in mind that just being small isn't a guarantee of charm. There are character-free 20-room properties out there. But if you can find just the right combination—of flawless personal service and little luxuries in an oasis of calm—there's nothing better.

Getting Yourself to New York City

Now, all you have to do is get here. It's time to think about airline fares, the best times to travel, and at which airport you'd like to land when you make your grand entrance.

Shopping for Airline Tickets

Just about every major airline and several minor ones fly to at least one of New York's three major airports: Kennedy, LaGuardia, and Newark. And you may find better fares to and from one of those airports than others, depending on the particular airline. All are relatively close to Manhattan and offer taxi, bus, and train service into the city. (See Chapter 4.)

There are at least three places to check out airfares. One is the websites of the airlines themselves. The others are the major travel sites (such as www.orbitz. com, www.expedia.com, and www.travelocity.com) and the airline consolidators.

The major airlines' websites let you see fares on as many possible dates and times as you have the patience to check on. While you're on the sites, you may want to sign up for each airline's e-mail bulletins, which notify you of super-discounted fares—usually for a three- or four-night trip starting the following weekend. (Airline telephone numbers and website addresses are in the Appendix.)

The major travel booking sites include: www.expedia.com, www.hotwire.com, www.orbitz.com, www.priceline.com, and www.travelocity.com.

Consolidators, the wholesalers also known as bucket shops, manage to offer low, low airfares because they negotiate with various airlines to buy seats that (for one reason or another) are expected to go unsold otherwise.

A test search for flights from Seattle to New York, booking four months ahead (the farther ahead the better when you're working with consolidators), turned up the following results:

Through www.flights.com, the lowest nonstop round-trip fare was $396.32 on Delta. The search on www.flycheap.com also came up with Delta as the lowest nonstop fare, but at $378. And www.airticketsdirect.com reported its lowest fare as $347, but that was with a stop in Milwaukee and it was on Air Tran, the low-cost airline that is a direct descendant of ValuJet.

Most consolidators are on the up-and-up, but it never hurts to check with your local Better Business Bureau.

Shopping for Package Tours

Don't be a snob about package tours. Taking one doesn't necessarily mean traipsing around the city with 20 other people, following a world-weary tour guide holding some odd object aloft to keep his or her flock together.

COMPARISON SHOPPING

Yes, it takes a little longer, but you can save a good deal of money by checking several possible sources for your airline reservations.

Smarter Travel (**www.smartertravel.com**) is one website that lets you check out several sources quickly. Just type in your travel destination (be sure to choose "all New York airports" for maximum flexibility) and dates. Then, click the various sites to check out each one's options.

A test search for round-trip flights between Cleveland and New York one month before the departure date turned up a $192.79 fare on USAir for a one-stop itinerary and $230 on Continental for a nonstop trip. The most inventive idea came from Hotwire, which showed a $260 fare on USAir but suggested leaving from Akron instead, which would result in a $149 round trip. Expedia, Travelocity, and Orbitz came up with exactly the same fares ($218 with one stop and $258 nonstop) on the same carriers. Kayak (**www. kayak.com**) and Farecast (**www.farecast.live.com**) came up with $265 and $260.

To get the savings that usually come with package tours, all you have to do is buy your airline tickets and hotel room together. Most packages will have a number of hotels to choose from, and you can check them out separately— doing your own research to help you choose the one you like best. If the package includes other features (sightseeing tours, for instance), you can either join or go off on your own.

Most major airlines sponsor package tours. Check with carriers that operate in your area and see what you can find. (Airline telephone numbers and website information are in the Appendix.)

Discount travel services often let you order packages. Not long ago, I found one via Orbitz with nonstop flights on American Airlines for two people and four nights at Le Parker Meridien for under $1,100 per person. For lesser hotels, the prices were in the $700 to $800 range.

Handy-dandy gadgets: Telescopes in Battery Park give visitors a close-up view of the Statue of Liberty without leaving the island.

As its name suggests, *New York City Vacation Packages* (NYCVP) specializes in this sort of thing. Some of their "extras" choices (such as lunch at Tavern on the Green or a horse-drawn carriage ride through Central Park) are straight out of Tourist Trap Central, but they certainly offer a lot of them. A trip for two people with a four-night stay in a suite at Doubletree Guest Suites and numerous extras, including Broadway theater tickets, priced out at $1,344 per person. *1-877-NYC-TRIP. www.nycvp.com.*

Also, look at ads in travel magazines and in the travel sections of newspapers. Just keep in mind that a travel agency is only as good as its most careless agent, and you could end up having him or her booking your trip.

Taking the Train

Amtrak trains come into Penn Station, right in the middle of Manhattan (Seventh to Eighth Avenues between 30th and 34th Street), so you can just grab a taxi or roll your luggage into the subway and head straight for your hotel.

There are lots of advantages to train travel. If you take the train, you don't have to arrive two hours early (as passengers have to do at airports) for security procedures. (Do have a photo ID with you, though, just in case you're asked for it.) And while train cars come in many degrees of comfort, they tend to be roomier and more pleasant than the economy-class cabin of a typical American airline. And the scenery is often a lot more interesting than three or four hours of cloud formations.

If you're on a long trip (perhaps an overnight train), you can even reserve what used to be called a sleeping compartment. (Today, it's known as a Superliner Roomette, Viewliner Roomette, or Bedroom.) That means reclining seats that turn into beds, turndown service, coffee, bottled water, a daily newspaper—and, in the case of the most expensive accommodations—a private bath with sink, toilet, and shower.

So ... why doesn't everybody just take the train to New York City?

Ⓞ Well, for long trips, it's slow and expensive. If you wanted to come from Dallas, for instance, it would probably be a two-day trip with a connection in Chicago or another city. The fare with a bedroom with private bath would very likely be more than $1,500. If you went with a Superliner Roomette, whose bathroom facilities are down the corridor, it would still probably be more than $1,200. And of course trains have delays, just like planes.

For shorter trips, it's another story. From Baltimore's Penn Station to New York's Penn Station, it's roughly a two-and-a-half-hour trip at $61 each way (a sample fare based on making reservations a month ahead). You could pay roughly twice as much for the Acela Express train, but it would reduce your travel time by only 15 or 20 minutes or so.

Amtrak's website includes sections on Hot Deals, weekly specials, and vacation packages (including a Broadway theater package). *1-800-USA-RAIL. www. amtrak.com.*

Rental Cars, If You Must

Ⓞ There's no good reason to rent a car in New York City. Parking on the street is virtually impossible, garage parking is expensive, and it's far easier to get anywhere you want to go by taxi, subway, bus, or on foot. Even if you're willing to brave the traffic and drive defensively in close quarters with a swarm of taxicabs and delivery trucks, it's just not practical.

However, some people insist on renting automobiles in Manhattan. And if you're planning a day trip to the suburbs or the country, driving there is definitely an option.

FAREWELL TO THE TWENTIETH CENTURY LIMITED

Grand Central Terminal, which opened in 1913, looks monumental enough to be an international facility—but it's strictly commuter country these days.

In a past era, Grand Central was the beginning and end of glamorous cross-country travel on trains such as the 20th Century Limited, which journeyed between New York and Chicago with such elegance that passengers boarded by way of a red carpet.

Now, you'll find subway passengers and train travelers going only as far as the New York and Connecticut suburbs. But thanks to the terminal's Beaux-Arts grandeur, the experience still has a touch of elegance. (New Jersey Transit and the Long Island Rail Road operate out of Penn Station, along with Amtrak's long-distance trains.)

To get off the island of Manhattan, you'll need to take FDR. Drive on the East Side; Henry Hudson Parkway (the West Side Highway); the Lincoln, Holland, or Midtown Tunnel; and/or one of the bridges, possibly the George Washington Bridge or the Triborough. Car rental offices will have maps, or you can use Mapquest (www.mapquest.com) to plot your course.

Manhattan alone has scores of car rental locations. You'll find them in most neighborhoods, including the Upper East Side, Upper West Side, Midtown, Times Square, Greenwich Village, the East Village, and the Financial District. Rental companies include Avis, Hertz, National, Budget, Alamo, Dollar, and Enterprise. (See the Appendix for telephone numbers and website information.)

Travel Insurance: What You Need

You can buy at least three kinds of travel insurance: protection from trip cancellation, lost luggage, and medical emergencies.

Most U.S. health insurance policies will cover medical expenses that may arise while you're traveling, but you should check to be sure that yours does. The airlines insure the contents of your luggage if it's lost, but if you're traveling with expensive clothing or other high-cost items, you may want to supplement that coverage. Some homeowners' policies also include some travel-related insurance.

The good news is that policies can cover a great deal more than they used to. You may be able to buy a policy that will cover trip cancellation not only because of weather or a terrorist threat but also cancellations because of last-minute work obligations or the death or serious illness of a close family member. Some policies will even reimburse you for lost tee time at a golf resort if your game is rained out. Of course, this kind of coverage will also cost you more.

To determine whether you want to buy travel insurance (and if so, what kind), the best way to start is at the website of the United States Travel Insurance Association (www.ustia.org). The site includes a "How to Shop for Travel Insurance" guide and a list of insurance companies that belong to the association, along with links to most of those member companies' websites.

Here are some of the best-known travel insurance companies:

- Access America (*www.accessamerica.com*)
- AIG Travel Guard (*www.travelguard.com*)
- Insure My Trip (*www.insuremytrip.com*)
- Squaremouth (*www.squaremouth.com*)
- Total Travel Insurance (*www.totaltravelinsurance.com*)
- Travelex (*www.travelex-insurance.com*)

Budget Worksheet

Thinking out your budget is one thing; actually putting it down on paper is another. This worksheet can help you nail down some expenses, estimate others, and reduce a lot of financial anxiety later.

PRE-TRIP COSTS

Childcare $_____

Pet care   _____

Transportation to the airport   _____

TRIP COSTS

Airfare to New York (for entire group)   _____

Hotel (rate per days
multiplied by number of days)   _____

Transportation to and from New York airport   _____

Taxis/subway fares/bus fares   _____

Restaurant meals (per day times
number of days)   _____

Entertainment (such as theater,
concert, or club tickets)   _____

Sightseeing (such as tours and museum admissions) _____

Drinks (cocktail-hour outings,
separate from meals)   _____

Souvenirs   _____

                                                   _____

ESTIMATED TOTAL $_____

Now don't you feel reassuringly organized? You may even have money left over for a little recreational shopping. And the next thing you know, you're going to be in the city, in the middle of it all.

Chapter 4

Getting Comfortable in New York City

In This Chapter

- ❦ The tricky trip from airport to hotel
- ❦ Getting acquainted with the city
- ❦ Getting around by subway, taxi, and other modes of transport
- ❦ An introduction to the city's neighborhoods

In an ideal world, you'd arrive in New York City by private plane and be met on the tarmac by the mayor, a chauffeur-driven limousine, and a personal tour guide at your beck and call. But then, you'd never have the sense of accomplishment that comes from navigating your way through the greatest city in the world (and maybe even coming to feel at home there).

Getting in from the Airport

The trouble with flying into New York is that you have to land at an airport. New York's three area airports—**John F. Kennedy International (JFK), LaGuardia Airport (LGA),** and **Newark Liberty International Airport (EWR)**—are crowded and seemingly disorganized.

Waiting for your luggage to arrive at the baggage carousel can seem to take forever, and then you'll probably have to stand in line for a taxi to get into the city.

Courage! Knowing what you're doing will help, and you do have choices.

JFK International

JFK is New York's largest airport, but farther from Manhattan than LaGuardia and about the same distance as Newark. It's really like a little city of many terminals, but luckily each terminal has its own ground transportation area and taxi line right outside the baggage claim area. Just follow the "ground transportation" signs.

Taxi fare: $45 flat fare, plus tolls and tip.

Tolls: $4.50 for the Triborough Bridge or the Midtown Tunnel.

Tipping: 15 percent is standard. But feel free to go up to 20 percent if your driver is particularly helpful or entertaining. (Just remember: the tip percentage is based on the fare alone, not including the toll or any other extras like nighttime or rush-hour surcharges.)

Bottom line: the simplest and one of the most comfortable ways to go.

Car service fare: varies, depending on your destination and the size car you need.

Tolls: $4.50 for the Triborough Bridge or the Midtown Tunnel.

Tipping: same as for taxis (15 percent or so; 20 percent if the driver is particularly helpful).

Car service information: Allstate, *1-800-453-4099* or *212-333-3333*. Carmel, *1-800-922-7635* or *212-666-6666*. Dial 7, *1-800-777-8888* or *212-777-7777*.

Bottom line: simple, and you can ask for whatever size car you want. But you have to call ahead to reserve a car, and there are horror stories about rudeness and bad service.

¢ **Bus fare:** adults $15 one way, $27 round trip, children under 12 free (but that only applies to one child per paying adult).

Bus schedule: every 20–30 minutes, depending on the time of day.

Bus stops: Follow signs to "bus" or "ground transportation." The bus will drop you at Grand Central Terminal (42nd Street and Park Avenue), Port Authority Bus Terminal (42nd Street and Eighth Avenue), Penn Station (Seventh Avenue between 33rd and 34th Streets), or Bryant Park (Sixth Avenue between 40th and 41st Streets).

Bus information: *New York Airport Service, 1-800-872-4577, 212-875-8200,* or *718-875-8200. www.nyairportservice.com.*

Bottom line: not a bad choice, but you still have to get to your hotel from the nearest bus stop. (There's a $2 additional hotel shuttle service you can pick up from the stops that run from 33rd to 57th Streets.)

¢ **Minivan fare:** $13 to and from hotels. $15 to residential addresses. ($22 from residential addresses back to the airport, but that's for the first passenger. Additional passengers in your party are $9 each.)

Minivan schedule: by arrangement.

Minivan stops: your hotel or residence, just like a taxi. But you'll probably be sharing with others, so your stop may not be first.

Minivan information: Super-Shuttle, *1-800-BLUE-VAN* or *212-BLUE-VAN, www.supershuttle.com.*

Bottom line: a good bet if you're not in a huge hurry.

AirTrain fare: $5, includes subway or bus fare to connect with it.

AirTrain schedule: departures every few minutes. Follow AirTrain signs at your terminal, parking lot, or car rental facility.

AirTrain stops: connects with the New York subway's A train (Howard Beach stop in Brooklyn) and its E, J, and Z trains (at the Jamaica stop in Queens.) It also connects with the Long Island Rail Road in Jamaica.

AirTrain information: AirTrain, *www.panynj.gov/airtrain*.

Bottom line: certainly a bargain but a little complicated at this point in its development—and not a great idea if you have luggage and/or don't know the city well.

BEWARE OF TAXI OFFERS

At New York airports, anyone coming up to you and saying, "Do you need a taxi?" is not to be trusted. You could end up seriously cheated. Get into the regular taxi line instead, and a dispatcher will put you into a nice, safe, licensed yellow cab.

LaGuardia

LaGuardia Airport, named for one of New York's most beloved mayors, Fiorello LaGuardia, is the closest airport to Manhattan.

Taxi fare: approximately $25–$35 (metered fare), plus tolls and tip.

Tolls: $4.50 for the Triborough Bridge or the Midtown Tunnel.

Tipping: 15 percent is standard. But if you fall in love with your driver, do 20 percent. (Remember, that percentage is based on the fare alone. Don't include the toll when you figure it.)

Bottom line: from any airport, this is the simplest way to go. From LaGuardia, compared with Kennedy, it's almost a bargain.

Car service fare: varies, depending on destination and car size.

Tolls: $4.50 for the Triborough Bridge or the Midtown Tunnel.

Tipping: same as for taxis (15 percent or so; 20 percent if the driver is particularly helpful).

Car service information: Allstate, *1-800-453-4099* or *212-333-3333*. Carmel, *1-800-922-7635* or *212-666-6666*. Dial 7, *1-800-777-8888* or *212-777-7777*.

Bottom line: simple and versatile (you can ask for a minivan if you have a large family or party). Just be sure to call ahead to make a reservation and to go online and check out customer reports on various services.

¢ **Bus fare:** adults $12 one way, $21 round trip, children under 12 free (but that only applies to one child per paying adult).

Bus schedule: every 20–30 minutes, depending on the time of day.

Bus stops: Follow airport signs to bus or ground transportation. The bus will drop you at Grand Central Terminal (42nd Street and Park Avenue), Port Authority Bus Terminal (42nd Street and Eighth Avenue), Penn Station (Seventh Avenue and 34th Street), and Bryant Park (Sixth Avenue between 40th and 41st Streets).

Bus information: New York Airport Service, *1-800-872-4577, 212-875-8200,* or *718-706-9658*. *www.nyairportservice.com.*

Bottom line: not a bad choice, but you still have to get to your hotel. (The $2 additional hotel shuttle service goes only from 31st to 60th Streets.)

¢ **Minivan fare:** $13 to and from hotels. $15 to residential addresses (same as for JFK). (Ditto: $22 from residential addresses back to the airport for the first passenger and $9 each for additional passengers.)

Minivan schedule: by arrangement.

Minivan stops: just like a taxi; your call. But if you're sharing with others (and that's likely), they may be dropped off before you.

Minivan information: Super-Shuttle, *1-800-BLUE-VAN* or *212-BLUE-VAN*, *www.supershuttle.com.*

Bottom line: a good bet if you have a little patience.

Public transportation (subway or bus) fare: $2

Public transportation schedule: departures every few minutes.

Public transportation stops: Follow airport signs to bus or ground transportation. The M60 bus connects with the New York subway's 2, 3, 4, 5, 6, A, B, C, D, N, or W trains. Going back to the airport, the M60 leaves from Broadway and 106th Street.

Public transportation information: *www.mta.org.*

Bottom line: cheap and fairly simple—but if you have luggage, it can be a major hassle.

ARRIVING BY TRAIN

If you decide to come to New York by Amtrak, your train will arrive at Pennsylvania Station (known as Penn Station) right in Midtown, between 31st and 33rd Streets and Seventh and Eighth Avenues. There are two subway stations within Penn Station—one that will take you anywhere on the West Side (No. 1, 2, and 3) and one that will get you to the East Side and Queens (the A, C, and E trains). Taking a taxi from Penn Station is easy, too. Upstairs on both Seventh and Eighth Avenues you'll find taxi lines, usually with a dispatcher at work keeping things in order.

Newark Liberty Airport

Newark may be in New Jersey, but it's actually closer to Manhattan than JFK is. It's an especially good choice if you're staying in downtown Manhattan as opposed to Midtown or Uptown. Sometimes Newark airfares are lower than those flying into the other two airports. And sometimes they're not.

Taxi fare: the dispatcher at the front of the taxi line determines the fare when you announce your exact destination. Expect $35 and up.

Tolls: $6 for the Lincoln or Holland Tunnel.

Tipping: 15 percent is standard, and 20 is kind. (Be sure to figure the tip on the fare alone, not including the toll.)

Bottom line: it couldn't be simpler.

Car service fare: varies, depending on your destination and the size car you need.

Tolls: $6 for the Holland Tunnel or the Lincoln Tunnel.

Tipping: same as for taxis (15 percent or so; 20 percent if the driver is a sweetheart).

Car service information: Allstate, *1-800-453-4099* or *212-333-3333*. Carmel, *1-800-922-7635* or *212-666-6666*. Dial 7, *1-800-777-8888* or *212-777-7777*.

Bottom line: simple as long as you remember to call ahead and make a reservation. And keep in mind that there have been service complaints about some companies.

¢ **Bus fare:** adults $14 one way, $25 round trip, children under 12 free.

Bus schedule: every 20 minutes.

Bus stops: Follow airport signs to bus or ground transportation. The bus will drop you at Grand Central Terminal (41st Street between Park and Lexington Avenues), Port Authority Bus Terminal (42nd Street and Eighth Avenue), or Penn Station (34th Street and Eighth Avenue).

Bus information: Olympia Airport Express, *212-964-6233, www.olympiabus. com.*

Bottom line: a sensible choice, but you still have to get to your hotel. (The $5 additional hotel shuttle service operates between 30th and 65th Streets.)

¢ **Minivan fare:** from Super-Shuttle, $13 to and from hotels; $15 to residential addresses. (It's $22 from residential addresses back to the airport, but that's for the first passenger. Additional passengers in your party are $9 each.) From Newark Airport Express, it's $21 from the airport, $28 round trip, and children under 6 free.

Minivan schedule: by arrangement with Super-Shuttle; every 20 minutes with Newark Airport Express.

Minivan stops: your hotel or residence, just like a taxi, with Super-Shuttle; hotels between 23rd and 63rd Streets with Newark Airport Express.

Minivan information: Super-Shuttle, *1-800-BLUE-VAN* or *212-BLUE-VAN*, *www.supershuttle.com*. Newark Airport Express, *1-877-863-9275*, *www.graylinenewyork.com*.

Bottom line: both good bets if you don't mind sharing.

Combination train/monorail fare: $12 on NJ Transit.

Train/monorail schedule: every 20 minutes on weekdays; every 30 minutes on weekends.

Train/monorail stops: airport monorail stations in each terminal go to the Rail Link station served by Amtrak and NJ Transit. The trains there take you directly to Penn Station.

Public transportation info: Air Train, *1-800-772-2222* or *973-762-5100*, *www.airtrainnewark.com*.

Bottom line: of all the public transportation options from New York area airports, this is the simplest.

Long Island MacArthur Airport

Long Island Islip MacArthur Airport (ISP) isn't particularly convenient for New York visitors, but Southwest Airlines flies there—so some budget-minded travelers consider the extra traveling time worth it.

Taxi fare: taxi service to Manhattan isn't available. You can't get there from here.

Car service fare: $123, including tolls but not tip.

Tipping: same as for taxis (15–20 percent).

Car service information: Colonial Transportation, *631-589-3500*, *www.colonialtransportation.com*.

Bottom line: expensive. And the drive will probably take an hour and a half. But if you saved enough money on the airfare, why not?

¢ **Bus fare:** $27, plus a taxi fare to Ronkonkoma (about 15 minutes away).

Bus schedule: varies by season.

Bus stops: numerous stops in Manhattan, as far north as 86th Street.

Bus information: *Hampton Jitney,* ***631-283-4600,*** *www.hamptonjitney.com.*

Bottom line: a clever solution. The Jitney is the bus that Manhattanites take to go to beach houses and hotels in the Hamptons and Montauk.

¢ **Minivan fare:** no service available.

Train/shuttle fare: about $10 on the Long Island Railroad (LIRR), plus the $5 airport shuttle to the train station.

Train/shuttle schedule: every 20 minutes for the shuttle; hourly trains to Manhattan (more frequent during morning rush hour).

Train stops: the LIRR takes you directly to Penn Station.

Train/shuttle information: for the shuttle, Colonial Transportation, ***631-589-3500,*** *www.colonialtransportation.com.* For the train, Long Island Rail Road, ***516-231-5477,*** *www.lirr.org.*

Bottom line: an efficient and cheaper two-part solution.

Finding Your Bearings

Whether you're coming in over the Triborough Bridge or up from the Lincoln or Midtown Tunnel or arriving some other way altogether, that first view of Manhattan is a thrill. But the second that wears off and you've checked into your hotel and put up your feet for a few minutes, you'll probably want to figure out exactly where you are and how to get from here to there.

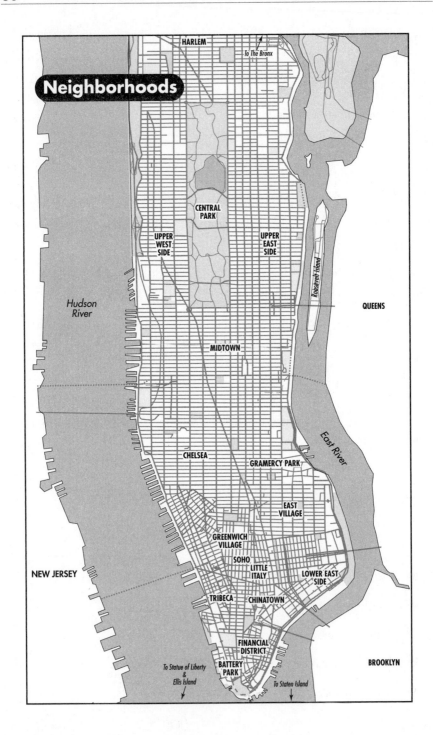

Luckily, in most parts of town this isn't difficult, and you can thank Clinton for that (DeWitt Clinton, that is—a nineteenth-century governor of New York). In 1811, a three-man commission that he set up created an orderly, numbered grid (155 streets and 12 avenues) that keeps Manhattan straight today. (Unfortunately, it was already too late for the lower part of the island, which was and is filled with curvy, twisting streets.)

If you're above 14th Street, all you have to do to navigate around Manhattan is to count, at least in terms of streets, which run east and west and are all numbered. Avenues, which run north and south, and their intersecting streets are partly numbered and partly named. Here are the avenues you'll need to know, going east to west:

- York Avenue (which is Sutton Place for a few blocks in the 50s)
- First Avenue
- Second Avenue
- Third Avenue
- Lexington Avenue
- Park Avenue
- Madison Avenue
- Fifth Avenue
- Sixth Avenue (officially named Avenue of the Americas)
- Seventh Avenue
- Broadway
- Eighth Avenue (which becomes Central Park West)
- Ninth Avenue (which becomes Columbus Avenue)
- Tenth Avenue (which becomes Amsterdam Avenue)
- Eleventh Avenue (which becomes West End Avenue)
- Riverside Drive (which begins on 72nd Street)

Knowing which way traffic runs on each avenue can be helpful when you're trying to get your bearings. When you come up the stairs from the subway, look for the nearest avenue street sign, check out the traffic direction, and you'll know whether you're pointed north (uptown) or south (downtown). Of course, this works better on one-way avenues than on the two-way ones!

- 🍎 York Avenue (two-way)
- 🍎 First Avenue (uptown)
- 🍎 Second Avenue (downtown)
- 🍎 Third Avenue (uptown)
- 🍎 Lexington Avenue (downtown)
- 🍎 Park Avenue (two-way)
- 🍎 Madison Avenue (uptown)
- 🍎 Fifth Avenue (downtown)
- 🍎 Sixth Avenue (uptown)
- 🍎 Seventh Avenue (downtown)
- 🍎 Broadway (two-way)
- 🍎 Eighth Avenue (uptown)
- 🍎 Central Park West (two-way)
- 🍎 Ninth Avenue (downtown)
- 🍎 Columbus Avenue (downtown)
- 🍎 Tenth Avenue (uptown)
- 🍎 Amsterdam Avenue (uptown)
- 🍎 Eleventh Avenue (two-way)
- 🍎 West End Avenue (two-way)
- 🍎 Riverside Drive (two-way)

MANHATTAN? I THOUGHT THIS WAS NEW YORK?

New York City is divided into five boroughs. Manhattan is the best known—the location of the city's most famous sights, such as the Empire State Building, Rockefeller Center, Times Square, and Central Park. Queens has two of the area's major airports and Shea Stadium. The Bronx has the Bronx Zoo and Yankee Stadium. Staten Island has the ferry and splendid isolation. Brooklyn has a bridge, a thriving art scene, a thriving cultural scene, and—for residents old enough to remember the Dodgers—its memories.

Avenue addresses can be tricky. Most of the time, when an avenue address is given, the street that it intersects or the two streets that it lies between is also mentioned (such as, "32 Second Avenue, near Second Street"). If it isn't, just ask, "What's the cross street?" If there's no one to ask, use this formula:

Divide the number in the address by 20, then add or subtract the appropriate number in the following list of the major avenues. (Or even easier, just drop the last digit of the address and divide by two. Close enough.) For example, to find the cross street for 945 Madison Avenue, you divide 945 by 20, which gives you 47.25. Add 27, as the formula directs you, and you get 74.25. In other words, between 74th and 75th Streets.

As the list indicates, there are numerous exceptions to the formula:

Amsterdam Avenue: +59

Broadway: see below

Central Park West: see below

Columbus Avenue: +59

Lexington Avenue: +22

Madison Avenue: +27

Park Avenue: +34

Riverside Drive: see below

West End Avenue: +59

York Avenue: + 4

First Avenue: +3

Second Avenue: +3

Third Avenue: +10

Fifth Avenue: see below

Sixth Avenue: –12

Seventh Avenue: see below

Eighth Avenue: +9

Ninth Avenue: +13

Tenth Avenue: +14

Eleventh Avenue: +15

Broadway: subtract 29 on numbers 756 to 846; subtract 25 on numbers 847 to 953; subtract 31 on numbers above 953

The formula can't be applied to Broadway addresses below 756 because they fall into downtown Manhattan—below the borough's numbered grid.

For Central Park West addresses, divide by 10 (rather than 20) and add 60.

For Riverside Drive addresses, divide by 10 (rather than 20) and add 72 for numbers 1 to 567. Add 78 to numbers above 567.

For Fifth Avenue, the number to add changes several times:

63–108 Fifth Avenue: +11

109–200 Fifth Avenue: +13

201–400 Fifth Avenue: +16

401–600 Fifth Avenue: +18

601–775 Fifth Avenue: +20

For numbers between 776 and 1286, divide by 10 (rather than 20) and subtract 18.

For Seventh Avenue, add 12 to numbers between 1 and 1800. Add 20 to numbers above 1800.

Getting Around the City

All right, I'll admit it. New York City has one problem. Getting around isn't as simple as it is in smaller cities, the suburbs, or the country. But at least we have choices. Here's what you need to know about subways, buses, and taxis.

The Subway: Fast but Flawed

Say what you will about the New York subway system: the stations are dirty, cramped, and crowded. The trains are noisy. The maps are unreadable. Nevertheless, the subway is the fastest way to get around town. If your time in the city is limited, that matters.

There are at least a couple of dozen subway lines, going to the northern reaches of the Bronx, the easternmost boulevards of Queens, and the distant beaches (Brighton, Rockaway, and so on) of Brooklyn. But for the moment, let's deal with just a few.

If you're traveling on the East Side, you'll just need to know the Lexington IRT line (the 4, 5, and 6 trains). The 4 and 5 are express trains. The 6 is a local, stopping at all stations. This line will take you from the Upper East Side (museums at the 86th and 77th Street stations) to Midtown (Bloomingdale's at the 59th Street stop and Grand Central at 42nd Street) to the eastern side of Greenwich Village (Bleecker Street) and SoHo (Spring Street) right into the downtown Financial District (the local stops at City Hall, but the express goes all the way down to Bowling Green on the tip of the island).

Subway stories: If you travel during nonrush hours, you may even get a seat.

Traveling on the West Side, you'll just need to know the Broadway IRT line (the 1, 2, and 3 trains). The 2 and 3 are express trains. The 1 is a local, stopping at all stations. (See how it works the same way as on the East Side?) This line will take you from Harlem (125th Street stop) through the residential Upper West Side to Lincoln Center (66th Street), Times Square (42nd Street), Penn Station (34th Street), Chelsea (23rd Street), the Village (Christopher Street), SoHo (Houston Street), TriBeCa (Canal, Franklin, and Chambers Street stations), past the World Trade Center site, and all the way to the South Ferry stop (also at the tip of the island).

If you want an easy way to go from the East Side to the West Side or vice-versa, take the S train at 42nd Street. This is a one-stop shuttle between Times Square and Grand Central. The trip takes less than two minutes.

Taking the subway for the first time can be daunting, but it's a relatively simple game. Look for the station signs, and before going down the stairs make sure that the station you're entering goes in the right direction (uptown versus downtown). You can buy a MetroCard from one of the automated machines or from the attendant at many token booths (but note that some booths have turned into information/hospitality centers instead). The fare is $2, but if you buy a $20 MetroCard you'll get credit for $23. Don't ask me how you're going to take advantage of a bonus that amounts to an extra ride and a half.

Slide the MetroCard at the turnstile, and don't be discouraged if it doesn't register the first time (the scanner will read "Swipe again"). There's something about the wrist action that takes practice.

Doors open and close automatically on the trains. If you want to avoid horrific crowds and being pressed against your fellow passengers like sardines, avoid rush-hour travel (roughly 8 to 10 A.M. and 5 to 7 P.M.). Keep an eye on your handbag or wallet. Don't make eye contact with people who seem slightly deranged. Have a good time.

Oh, and if you have trouble understanding the announcements on the public address system in subway stations, welcome to the club.

The Bus: Slow but Scenic

If you're in a rush, the New York City bus system is probably not the way to go. But if you have some time and you'd rather travel aboveground than below, by all means take the bus.

The fare is the same as the subway ($2). You can pay by MetroCard or with exact change. That means coins, however, and they don't take half dollars or pennies (picky, picky!). So, you might as well spring for the MetroCard. And if just one bus can't get where you want to go, you can transfer free—either to the subway or to another bus.

The bus is a lot better at going crosstown than the subway is. There are crosstown buses at all the major two-way streets (14th, 23rd, 34th, 42nd, 57th, 72nd, 79th, and 86th) and at some relatively minor one-way streets (49th–50th and 67th–68th, for instance). But just as many bus routes run north and south. Pick an avenue that runs in the direction you want to travel, go to it, and you're sure to find a bus stop (usually complete with shelter and route map) within two or three blocks.

Sit (if you're lucky), and enjoy the ride. This is the closest thing to a free sightseeing trip the city has to offer. There's time to look in store windows, admire architecture at close range, and people watch—all while you rest your feet (and do your deep-breathing exercises, if you want).

When you're ready to get off, press the yellow tape on the wall. If you've done it properly, a cheery bell will ring and the "stop requested" sign will light up at the front of the bus. Be sure to do it early on; the best time is right after the bus has started moving again after the stop before yours. The powers that be like it if you exit through the back doors, but if you're sitting closer to the front, the world won't end if you exit (promptly, please, so new passengers can board) through the front.

Taxis: Expensive but Easy

New York City wouldn't be New York City without that long blur of moving yellow on every avenue. There are about 13,000 licensed yellow cabs on the streets of the city, but when it's raining or when you've just gotten out of the theater, you will feel sure of only one thing: there aren't enough.

People don't call cabs in New York; they hail them. Fortunately, this is not difficult. Just step off the curb and raise your right arm somewhere between a 45-degree and 90-degree angle when you see a free taxi coming. Then, step back slightly as the driver pulls over, and hop in.

You can recognize an available taxi by the lighted word "taxi" on its roof. (The light goes off when a passenger gets into the cab and the meter is turned on.) However, if the words "off" and "duty" are also lit, forget it. That means the driver is on his (the vast majority of New York taxi drivers are men) way home or somewhere else and doesn't want to be bothered with a fare en route.

THE 4 P.M. CRUNCH

If there's any way to avoid it, don't go looking for a taxi at or around 4 P.M. That's when the drivers' shifts change, and while you may see many cabs on the street, most will have their "off duty" signs lit. This is a good time of day to use mass transit. Or stop for a long, leisurely cup of tea.

Fighting other people for a cab is one of the ugly sides of New York life that you may want to avoid. Should you find yourself in this situation, it's considered perfectly appropriate to offer or ask to share. "By any chance, are you headed to the East Side?" (or whatever) is the way to go about it. Then, the first person who reaches his or her destination estimates what the total fare (plus tip) is going to be and pays the other passenger that half with a big thank you. It's equally appropriate to chat or to maintain a pleasant silence during the shared portion of the ride.

Like the rest of humanity, taxi drivers' friendliness ranges from joyous to non-existent. Whatever the case, on your part, a simple "Hi" and an announcement of your destination will suffice. In general, New Yorkers don't give the exact address to which they're going. Instead, they give the intersection. That is, instead of asking to go to 780 West End Avenue, ask for "West End and 98th" (you've determined beforehand what the cross street is, of course). Instead of announcing "470 West 24th Street," you tell the driver you're going to "24th and 10th." (The driver may ask you to confirm that you mean 10th Avenue, in this particular case, because there's also a 10th Street in Manhattan.)

As you approach your destination, the driver may ask which corner you want. If you know, just say "The near left," "The far left," "The near right," or "The far right." If you don't know, it's okay to say, "I'm not sure. Anywhere is fine." Then, you'll figure it out after you get out of the cab.

They're always coming up with new ways to make the ride more … something. Don't even ask longtime New Yorkers about the years of the "fasten your seat belt" announcements recorded by celebrities. (Although I always enjoyed the one starring Elmo of *Sesame Street*.) The latest innovation is television screens with news broadcasts and other programming.

If anything goes wrong, take note of your driver's name and license number (posted on the dashboard). And even if nothing goes wrong, ask for and keep your receipt. If you leave something in the taxi and have this information, you might actually get your item(s) back.

In many taxis, you can now pay by credit card. You just swipe your card (right next to the TV screen on the seat back) and add the tip right on the screen.

Sadly, taxis are expensive. The fare starts at $2.50 the minute the driver turns on the meter and goes up 40 cents every $1/5$ mile, which is about four blocks. There's also a $1 rush-hour surcharge between 4 and 8 P.M. Mondays through Fridays and a 50-cent nighttime surcharge between 8 P.M. and 6 A.M. At regular times, a ride from a residential neighborhood to Midtown or vice-versa can easily run $15 (including a tip of 15 percent or so).

THAT CAB ISN'T YELLOW!

In some parts of town, you'll find what locals refer to as gypsy cabs. These are nonlicensed taxis and may be, in car terms, anything from a beaten-up station wagon to a handsome black sedan. Most gypsy-cab drivers are honest, but their cars have no meters—which means you have to agree to a fare up front ("I'm going to 34th and Fifth. Is $10 okay?") and hope for the best.

Walking: Highly Recommended

There is, of course, one way to avoid subway crowds, bus-lane pokiness, and high taxi fares. Just step out the front door of your hotel and put one foot in front of the other. To do it properly, see "Walking Like a New Yorker" (Chapter 1).

Obviously, walking is great exercise. But even if you're not in fabulous shape (and have no interest in spending your vacation or business trip starting on a fitness program), you can do a lot of your city traveling on foot. Just take breaks every 10 blocks or so. And remember, if you get tired, all you have to do is hop on the next bus that passes by.

Driving: Please Don't

Traffic moves slowly in Manhattan—sometimes painfully slowly. It's almost impossible to find a parking place on the street in the busy parts of town, and parking garages are expensive. There should be plenty of lanes on the avenues for free-flowing traffic, but delivery trucks are everywhere and taxi drivers are all around you, looking for and picking up fares. Side streets are narrow, and it's easy to find yourself blocked on one side by a garbage truck making its daily rounds or a moving van in the middle of a job. But if you absolutely insist on bringing your car into Manhattan or renting a car here, see "Driving Like a New Yorker" (Chapter 1).

Welcome to the 'Hoods

When New Yorkers traveling the country or the world meet one another for the first time, the first thing they tend to say is "Oh, you're from New York. What part?" That's because every neighborhood in New York City has its own special character and helps us define the people who live there. Knowing about those neighborhoods can also help you enjoy New York City more.

Midtown

In any other city, this would be called downtown. This part of town, which runs unofficially from 34th Street to 59th Street and from river to river, is where you'll find most of the big stores (from Macy's to Bloomingdale's), the big office buildings, the grand hotels, and many of the sights that visitors want to see.

Times Square, Rockefeller Center, Radio City Music Hall, the Empire State Building, the Chrysler Building, St. Patrick's Cathedral, and the United Nations are all here—as is the stretch of Fifth Avenue known for elegant shopping.

Some businesses have moved a bit south in recent years, but this is still the heart of the book publishing industry, magazine publishing (both Condé Nast and Hearst have relatively new buildings), television (ABC, CBS, NBC, MTV, Fox, and so on), and an assortment of other industries.

The fashion industry is here, too, in an area in the West 30s known to those who work there and those who don't as the Garment District. The buildings may not look glamorous from the outside, but there's a lot of gorgeous high fashion being created inside.

Midtown is not known as a residential area, but a few parts of the area, such as Murray Hill in the East 30s, are exceptions. So is Hell's Kitchen in the West 40s—a neighborhood that once lived up to its scary name but is now becoming fashionable. And more and more high-rise apartment buildings are going up in the West 50s.

The Upper East Side

For a very long time, the Upper East Side has been the city's most expensive, most prestigious residential neighborhood. The 10021 ZIP code is home to elegant prewar Fifth Avenue apartments with Central Park views, equally elegant apartment buildings on Park Avenue, and—as far east as you can go without getting wet—the enviable river-view apartments of Sutton Place and East End Avenue. (The mayor's official residence, Gracie Mansion, is in the 80s overlooking the East River.)

Holiday style: At Christmastime, trees in Central Park and other parts of Manhattan are covered with lights.

At one time, this was the "old money" side of town—dotted with private mansions where the Astors, Vanderbilts, and Morgans lived like royalty. But most of those huge private homes have been torn down, divided into apartments, or turned into museums or embassies.

Although the Upper East Side is generally a residential area, there are a few very elegant hotels in the neighborhood and some of the city's biggest, best-known museums (including the Metropolitan, the Guggenheim, the Whitney, and the Frick).

The Upper West Side

Once the poor cousin of the neighborhood on the other side of Central Park, the Upper West Side came into its own in the late twentieth century and is now one of the most desirable parts of the city—partly because of some re-markable century-old apartment buildings that draw the rich, famous, and creative.

The best addresses are on Central Park West, West End Avenue, and Riverside Drive. (Just as on the East Side, a view of a park or a river is highly prized.)

The Upper West Side has only one major museum, the American Museum of Natural History, but it has a lot of things the East Side doesn't—an Ivy League university (Columbia, which is on the Upper Upper West Side, or Morningside Heights), the city's most important performing arts complex (Lincoln Center), and the closest thing Manhattan has to a shopping mall (the upscale shops at the Time Warner Center).

Harlem

Harlem, which has been called the cultural capital of black America, begins at different points depending on how far east or west you're standing. On parts of the East Side, Spanish Harlem begins not far above 96th Street. On the West Side, it begins higher—just above Columbia University—around 118th Street.

Named for Haarlem, a city in the Netherlands, this neighborhood began as a Dutch farming settlement and just grew. The Harlem Renaissance, a flour-ishing of African-American arts, took place here in the 1920s and 1930s, but there is another going on now. Although the neighborhood has suffered from high crime rates, it's becoming safer, fashionable, and (inevitably) more expensive.

Sights in Harlem include the Apollo Theater, the Schomburg Center for Black Culture, and 125th Street, the neighborhood's main thoroughfare.

Chelsea

Chelsea, which lies in the West 20s between Greenwich Village and Midtown, has been a fashionable residential area for many decades. But in recent years, it has also become a major art center with hundreds of galleries—many of which moved from SoHo (that area became too expensive) to the far west reaches of this neighborhood.

Chelsea has had a large gay population for a while, too, but lots of heterosexual singles and families have begun to move in.

People assume that Chelsea is named for the London neighborhood, but it's actually the name of the eighteenth-century country estate that once stood there. The estate was owned by the family of Clement Clarke Moore, a theology professor best known as the author of "A Visit from St. Nicholas."

Chelsea Piers, a huge entertainment and sports complex, now stands where great ocean liners once docked. Chelsea Market, a complex of bakeries, eateries, and shops (food, flowers, wine, and so on), is in the old National Biscuit Company buildings.

Granted, Chelsea Market is down on 16th Street, but the more fashionable Chelsea becomes the more its boundaries seem to stretch. Now, any place above 14th Street and below 34th Street claims to be part of the neighborhood.

Gramercy Park

A century ago, this was the city's most elegant address. And this tiny enclave in the East Teens is still one of Manhattan's loveliest spots—especially the nineteenth-century townhouses surrounding the pretty little locked park that gives this section its name. (If you live there, you get a key.)

Greenwich Village

The Village (no self-respecting New Yorker refers to the place by its full name) has had a reputation for being artsy and Bohemian (at least, since the mid-nineteenth century). The beatniks, hippies, and punks are gone, but this neighborhood, which runs roughly from Houston Street to 14th Street and from Fifth Avenue to the Hudson River, still has a little edge of counterculture in the air.

Very few starving artists, poets, or political radicals live here, though. It has gotten much too expensive for that. The Village is a relatively tranquil residential area (particularly the far west part of it) that just happens to be dotted with picturesque streets and charming restaurants.

New York University is here, right next to Washington Square Park. And just at the northern edge, the Meat Packing District (of all places) has turned into the hottest restaurant, hotel, and club scene in town.

SoHo

The name SoHo stands for South of Houston Street, and that's exactly where you'll find it. As with many neighborhoods, its boundaries are debated—but in general, SoHo runs from Houston to Canal Streets and from Lafayette Street on the east to Varick Street on the west.

Fifty years ago, this was an old industrial area—somewhere between dying and dead. But by the 1970s, struggling artists had discovered its huge loft spaces with great light (enormous windows) in old factory buildings.

At the time, rents were cheap—but the artists made the area hip. Affluent Manhattanites looking for the next hot place liked the reverse chic of the nineteenth-century cast-iron buildings and cobblestone streets (a few are still around), and pretty soon SoHo was fashionable, expensive, and crowded.

That's how you'll find the area today, with chic hotels, trendy restaurants, way-upscale designer boutiques, museums, and yes … art galleries here and there.

TriBeCa

People seemed to like saying SoHo so much that they decided to coin a name in the same way for the neighborhood just south of it. The name TriBeCa (pronounced try-BECK-uh) stands for Triangle Below Canal, although the neighborhood isn't even vaguely triangular. It's small, it's fashionable, and it's all that stands between the Village, SoHo, and the Financial District. Roughly, the neighborhood covers the area from Canal to Vesey Streets and from the Hudson River to Broadway.

TriBeCa has a similar history to SoHo's. It was commercial in the late nineteenth and early twentieth centuries (dry goods, food distribution, and so on), and the great old buildings were discovered by artists who were followed by hip singles and eventually by affluent families.

After the terrorist attacks of September 11, TriBeCa, which sat in the shadow of the World Trade Center, was a troubled neighborhood that people felt might go permanently downhill. But thanks to community effort and some influential neighbors (such as Robert De Niro), the place is better than ever—with new apartments, thriving businesses, and fabulous restaurants. It even has its own film festival.

Chinatown

Chinatown is home to many of the Chinese and Chinese Americans in New York (although there are thriving Chinese neighborhoods in Queens, too) as well as major tourist attractions. This tiny section of downtown Manhattan, just north of City Hall, is worth visiting for its restaurants, shops, exotic fish markets, and absolutely authentic atmosphere.

Little Italy

This area used to be bigger, and it used to be a real neighborhood where Italian immigrants and Italian Americans lived. But over the years, Little Italy has shrunk (to a few blocks of Mulberry Street, chockablock with restaurants and cafés)—and most Italian Americans have moved elsewhere. Even the big San Gennaro festival in September is a shadow of its former self.

NAME THAT NEIGHBORHOOD

You may hear the names of some other, smaller neighborhoods. They may be odd names, but the explanations are simple: NoLita means North of Little Italy. NoHo is North of Houston Street. And Dumbo is Down Under the Manhattan Bridge Overpass.

East Village/Lower East Side

For a long time, this entire area above SoHo and east of Greenwich Village proper was one big neighborhood with a history of immigrants living in extremely close quarters in tenements. Then, in the 1960s, the northwest corner of the Lower East Side went psychedelic. The neighborhood became the East Village, and it gradually gentrified—with hippie-oriented restaurants, boutiques, and theater growing more upscale.

But now, the other sections of the Lower East Side—formerly known for bargain shopping on and around Orchard Street—are also beginning to gentrify. Today, Kosher bakeries and delis stand alongside with upscale shops and apartments.

Financial District/Wall Street

This is the oldest part of Manhattan, where the Dutch explorers settled and set up shop as fur traders. Wall Street, the name synonymous with American high finance, is called that because there was a 2,300-foot wall there built by the Dutch in the 1600s.

What you have today is a combination of narrow, winding streets that were laid out centuries ago and towering skyscrapers where bankers, brokers, and other high-powered types keep the economy spinning (more or less). It's all a little claustrophobic but highly energizing.

Not that long ago, no one lived in this part of Manhattan—and it was dead after 5 P.M. (or as soon as the workers finished their cocktails and headed home), but that changed with the creation of Battery Park City, the 92-acre planned community. Now, the Financial District is much more a 24–7 kind of place.

From a tourist's point of view, there are plenty of sights to see, including the Stock Exchange, the World Trade Center site, South Street Seaport, the Staten Island Ferry, and—glittering in the water just beyond Battery Park—the Statue of Liberty.

We'll revisit these neighborhoods in the chapters ahead. And we'll branch out to neighborhoods in Brooklyn, Queens, the Bronx, and Staten Island, with sightseeing and restaurant recommendations there.

Part

2

The East Side

This area has Park Avenue, Fifth Avenue, and Sutton Place—not to mention the Empire State Building, the United Nations, world-famous stores, and more than a few great museums. This section will introduce you to the East Side—its neighborhoods, hotels, restaurants, sights, and more—and all the good reasons you'll want to spend time there.

Chapter

5

Getting Comfortable on the East Side

In This Chapter

- 🍎 Discovering the East Side's neighborhoods
- 🍎 East Side hotels for every budget
- 🍎 Three gorgeous walks—one of them through Central Park

The lyrics "East Side, West Side, all around the town," written back in 1894, carry the best-known and most important geography lesson about New York: that much of the city (by which we mean Manhattan) is divided in two. Anything east of Fifth Avenue is the East Side; anything west of it is the West Side. The East Side has a longtime reputation for wealth and culture (in the olden days, the Upper East Side was referred to as the silk-stocking district). And although other areas in the city have become equally fashionable in their own ways, this part of town—from the newly revitalized Madison Square area to Museum Mile—still has a special air about it. The names Fifth Avenue, Park Avenue, and Sutton Place still convey the same aura that they did throughout the twentieth century.

Finding Your Bearings on the East Side

Most Manhattan neighborhoods are a little amorphous as to where they begin and end. For the purposes of this chapter, we'll refer to the area from 23rd Street to 30th Street as Madison Square. (The Flatiron Building, which marks the center of the Flatiron District, is right on the southwestern border of this area but will be discussed in the Downtown chapter.) We'll call roughly 30th Street to 59th Street Midtown and 60th to 96th Streets the Upper East Side. But there are neighborhoods within neighborhoods, as you'll see.

Midtown

If you're staying in an East Side hotel, chances are that you're in Midtown. Much of Midtown East is filled with large stores (including Saks and Bloomingdale's) and tall office buildings, particularly on the innermost avenues (Fifth and Madison). The main branch of the New York Public Library is at Fifth Avenue and 42nd Street. The campus of the United Nations stands in the 40s, overlooking the East River.

But plenty of people live in this area. **Murray Hill,** named for the estate of an eighteenth-century Quaker shipping tycoon, is a handsome, increasingly expensive residential neighborhood. It runs roughly from 33rd to 39th and from Lexington Avenue to Fifth.

Just east of Murray Hill is **Kips Bay,** named for Jacobus Kip, a seventeenth-century Dutch farmer and a bay that was long ago reclaimed. Kips Bay, which runs from the East River to Lexington and from 23rd to 34th Streets, is a mix of residential and institutional areas. A New York University medical building is here, as is Bellevue Hospital Center.

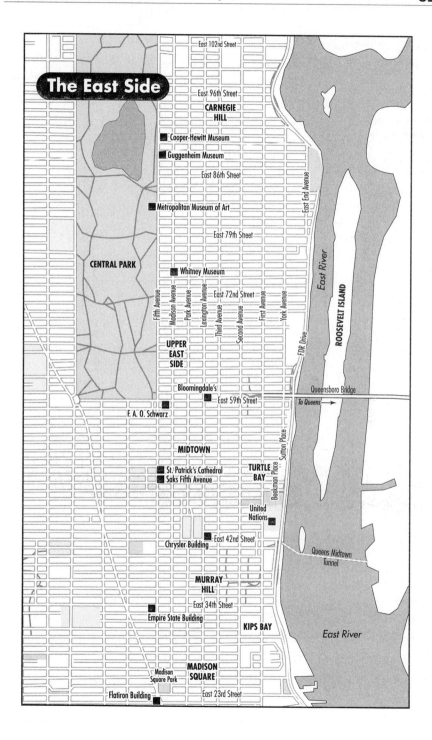

The East Side

East 102nd Street

East 96th Street

CARNEGIE HILL

Cooper-Hewitt Museum

Guggenheim Museum

East 86th Street

Metropolitan Museum of Art

East 79th Street

CENTRAL PARK

Whitney Museum

Fifth Avenue

Madison Avenue

Park Avenue

Lexington Avenue

Third Avenue

Second Avenue

First Avenue

York Avenue

East End Avenue

East 72nd Street

East River

ROOSEVELT ISLAND

FDR Drive

UPPER EAST SIDE

Bloomingdale's

East 59th Street

Queensboro Bridge

F. A. O. Schwarz

To Queens

MIDTOWN

Sutton Place

St. Patrick's Cathedral

Saks Fifth Avenue

TURTLE BAY

Beekman Place

United Nations

Chrysler Building

East 42nd Street

Queens Midtown Tunnel

MURRAY HILL

East 34th Street

Empire State Building

KIPS BAY

East River

Madison Square Park

MADISON SQUARE

Flatiron Building

East 23rd Street

And just above Kips Bay is **Turtle Bay,** running down the easternmost stretches (Third Avenue to the East River) of 43rd to 53rd Streets or so. The United Nations stands on the site of the original bay. The Ford Foundation is here, on 42nd Street. Tudor City, one of the city's most distinctive (and desirable) residential neighborhoods (a city within a city), was built in the 1920s. It runs along First and Second Avenues from 40th to 43rd Streets.

The most desirable address of all in Turtle Bay is Beekman Place, which runs only from 49th to 51st Streets. The rich and famous have lived here, including John D. Rockefeller III and Gloria Vanderbilt. And just above Beekman Place, running up to 59th Street and the border of Midtown, is the equally prestigious address Sutton Place.

GET THEE TO BELLEVUE

In centuries past, Londoners might suggest that a mentally disturbed person be "sent away to Bedlam" (a distortion of the name Bethlem, the world's oldest psychiatric hospital). New Yorkers say, "You're going to end up in Bellevue." The Bellevue Hospital Center, on First Avenue, has been a pioneer in the treatment of mental illness, but its specialists are known for other kinds of medical care, too, including obstetrics, cardiovascular work, and microsurgery.

Upper East Side

Expensive apartments, upscale shops, and a smattering of luxurious hotels make up most of the Upper East Side. The priciest and most prestigious addresses are on Fifth, Madison, and Park Avenues. In general, the Upper East Side is a residential neighborhood, on both the broad avenues and the narrow, tree-lined streets, but it's also the home of many of the city's best-known museums. The Metropolitan, the Guggenheim, and Cooper-Hewitt are among those located on Fifth Avenue in the 80s and 90s—a stretch known as Museum Mile.

Once the home of block after block of private mansions, the Upper East Side has become an area of handsome apartment buildings instead. But a number of those mansions remain, transformed into apartments or now housing museums, schools, or consulates.

Carnegie Hill, which runs roughly from Third Avenue to Fifth and from 86th to 98th Streets, is named for Andrew Carnegie's mansion—built in 1901 at Fifth Avenue and 91st Street (now the Cooper-Hewitt National Design Museum). Carnegie Hill is becoming known more and more as a separate neighborhood.

Madison Square

The first thing to know about the emerging **Madison Square** neighborhood is that this is not where you'll find Madison Square Garden. The first one was built there back in 1879, but by the time the third one went up (in 1925), it had left the neighborhood and moved slightly uptown (the current one is in the West 30s).

But **Madison Square Park** was once the center of an elegant residential neighborhood (Theodore Roosevelt lived there, as did the author Edith Wharton). And now that the park has been restored to its original beauty, elegant apartment buildings are sprouting up—and this is the real clue—so are chic restaurants.

East Side Hotels

There are interesting, often elegant places to stay in just about every part of the East Side, from the Madison Square area to the nicest parts of the residential neighborhoods uptown.

Affinia Dumont   Midtown $ $ $

A number of New York City hotels accept pets, but how many of them give your dog a welcome walk? That's probably one of the reasons the Affinia Dumont is Trip Advisor readers' favorite property in its price category. Fitness is another special emphasis here. For extra money, you can even rent a suite with your own private gym. For the budget-minded, there is a fitness center, a day spa, and a choice of eight pillows, depending on your body's needs. Other features include high-speed Internet access, room service, kitchenettes, and contemporary furnishings. *150 East 34th Street (between Third and Lexington Avenues), New York, NY 10016.* **212-481-7600** *or* **1-866-246-2203.** *www. affinia.com.*

Beekman Tower Hotel   Midtown $ $

The Beekman, an Art Deco treasure from 1928, started life as the Pan-Hellenic Tower—a residence for sorority women. Today, it offers 194 traditionally furnished suites, all with kitchens and wireless Internet access. There is a fitness center, and pets are allowed. Room service is available, but you'll probably want to visit the 26th-floor Top of the Tower Bar and Lounge for a meal at least once. *3 Mitchell Place (49th Street at First Avenue), New York, NY 10017.* **212-355-7300.** *www.beekmanhotel.com.*

Bentley Hotel   Upper East Side $ $

The Bentley is right on the dividing line of the business and residential sections of the East Side. It's in a former office building, which has advantages: oversize windows, some overlooking the 59th Street Bridge. There's a rooftop restaurant and bar, not to mention around-the-clock cappuccino in the lobby. *500 East 62nd Street (east of First Avenue), New York, NY 10021.* **212-644-6000** *or* **1-888-969-0069.** *www.bentleyhotelnewyork.com.*

HOW $295 A NIGHT BECOMES $350

As if New York hotels aren't expensive enough already, management is required to charge sales tax on rooms—and on top of that, hotel taxes. Those extras can add up to more than a 20 percent increase in the price of your stay.

The Carlton   Madison Square $ $ $ $

Formerly the Seville, this hotel, built in 1904, makes a real impression with a three-story lobby with a waterfall. The 316 rooms, many with Empire State

Building views, have Frette linens, marble baths, and lighted magnifying make-up mirrors. The house restaurant, Country, is stunning. *88 Madison Avenue (at 29th Street), New York, NY 10016.* **212-532-4100.** *www.carltonhotelny.com.*

The Carlyle   Upper East Side $ $ $ $ $

The elegant Carlyle has been around since 1930 and can claim as past guests the Prince and Princess of Wales, various kings and queens, and every U.S. president since Harry Truman. The 187 rooms and suites are done in traditional furnishings with a hint of Art Deco, and many have Central Park views. The hotel accepts pets and has elevator operators. In addition to the formal hotel restaurant, there's the famous Café Carlyle, the heavenly Bemelmans Bar, and a brand-new spa (2008 opening) (maybe by the time you arrive). *35 East 76th Street (off Madison Avenue), New York, NY 10021.* **212-744-1600.** *www.thecarlyle.com.*

Courtyard New York Manhattan/
Midtown East   Midtown $ $

This Marriott property, located on the higher floors of a former office building, gets good reviews from Trip Advisor readers and has all the necessities, including high-speed Internet access in all 312 rooms, a breakfast restaurant, a bar, and a fitness center. *866 Third Avenue (between 52nd and 53rd Streets), New York, NY 10022.* **212-644-1300** *or* **1-800-894-6380.** *www.marriott.com.*

FAMILIAR NAME, SCARY PRICE

There are thousands of hotels in Manhattan, and some of them do belong to the chains that you may know from other cities. There are Sheratons and Hiltons and Marriotts and even Holiday Inns. Just be sure to check prices carefully. These companies' New York properties are often considerably more expensive than the ones in Cleveland, Houston, or Seattle.

Doubletree Metropolitan   Midtown $ $ $

There's not a lot of mid-century Moderne design in New York, so it's good that the Metropolitan had its '60s tropical Deco exterior restored. Inside, there are 755 rooms with slate bathrooms and high-speed Internet access. The hotel also has a restaurant, a lounge, room service, and an exercise room. *569 Lexington Avenue (at 51st Street), New York, NY 10022.* **212-752-7000** *or* **1-800-836-6471.** *www.metropolitanhotelnyc.com.*

₵ Fitzpatrick Grand Central   Midtown $ $

The 155-room Fitzpatrick is quite a buy. Rooms have canopied beds (well, semi-canopied), mini fridges, and terrycloth bathrobes. There's 24-hour room service, and Grand Central Terminal is literally right around the corner. *141 East 44th Street (at Lexington Avenue), New York, NY 10017.* **212-351-6800** *or* **1-800-367-7701.** *www.fitzpatrickhotels.com.*

Four Seasons Hotel   Midtown $ $ $ $ $

"Ice-cold elegance" is the term one architecture critic used to describe the Four Seasons when it opened in 1993. If the limestone lobby with its 33-foot ceilings doesn't impress you, you can't be impressed. The hotel is 52 stories tall, so the views from many of the 368 rooms and suites are knockouts. The rooms are sleeker and more contemporary than many Four Seasons properties, but the fabulous bathrooms (which are worth $200 a night all by themselves) are the same. There is a major spa, and the house restaurant is L'Atelier de Joël Robuchon. *57 East 57th Street (between Park and Madison Avenues), New York, NY 10022.* **212-758-5700** *or* **1-800-819-5053.** *www.fourseasons.com.*

MAYBE THERE ARE EIGHT SEASONS

Sometimes in New York, you have to be very careful about specifying names. A comment such as, "Meet me at the Met," out of context, could refer to the Metropolitan Museum of Art or the Metropolitan Opera House. The same is true for the Four Seasons. The hotel on East 57th Street and the restaurant on East 52nd are both elegant and expensive, but they're not related. So give the taxi driver the address as well as the name.

Hotel Giraffe   Madison Square $\boxed{\$}\boxed{\$}\boxed{\$}\boxed{\$}$

You can travel back in time a little at the Giraffe. Almost one third of its 73 rooms are suites decorated in the style of the '20s and '30s. The hotel's early Moderne style includes leather headboards, quilted satin bedspreads, and black-and-white period photos. There's a breakfast buffet, a cappuccino bar, and wine and cheese every night. It's also a smoke-free property. *365 Park Avenue South (at 26th Street), New York, NY 10016.* **212-685-7700** *or* **1-877-296-0009.** *www.hotelgiraffe.com.*

Hotel Thirty Thirty   Madison Square $\boxed{\$}\boxed{\$}\boxed{\$}$

In more genteel days, this was the Martha Washington Hotel for women (see Barbara Parkins in early scenes of *Valley of the Dolls*). But it has changed considerably and become quite popular, with 253 rooms with clean, light, traditional decor. There is a restaurant, a cocktail bar, voice mail, and a data port, and your pet can stay with you. *30 East 30th Street (between Park and Madison Avenues), New York, NY 10016.* **212-689-1600** *or* **1-800-804-4480.** *www.thirtythirty-nyc.com.*

Hotel Wales   Upper East Side $\boxed{\$}\boxed{\$}\boxed{\$}$

The Wales has a great location in the upper end of the Upper East Side—very neighborhoody and close to museums. Built in 1901 and completely renovated in recent years, it has 88 handsome rooms and suites with a nice touch: fresh flowers. The place is also pet-friendly. There's a rooftop terrace. And room service is from the popular restaurant Sarabeth's (downstairs). *1295 Madison Avenue (at 92nd Street), New York, NY 10128.* **212-876-6000** *or* **1-866-WALES-HOTEL.** *www.waleshotel.com.*

The Library Hotel   Midtown $\boxed{\$}\boxed{\$}\boxed{\$}$

This place not only looks like a library, it also actually has books—about 6,000 of them, arranged by the Dewey Decimal System—in its guest rooms. This smoke-free hotel has 60 rooms with tailored décor, wireless Internet access, a rooftop bar, and wine and cheese every day at cocktail hour. Here's a nice touch: The Library doesn't just offer a DVD collection. Its DVDs are the American Film Institute's top 100 films of the twentieth century. *299 Madison Avenue (at 41st Street), New York, NY 10017.* **212-983-4500** *or* **1-877-793-7323.** *www.libraryhotel.com.*

Hotel row: The southern end of Central Park faces both Fifth Avenue and Central Park South.

The Lowell   Upper East Side $ $ $ $ $

The Lowell has real Old World elegance. It doesn't hurt that about half the 70 rooms and suites have wood-burning fireplaces and another quarter have terraces. Most rooms have full kitchens, in case you feel like grocery shopping and whipping up a meal at home. Zelda and Scott Fitzgerald used to spend time here, it's said. But the place probably didn't have the second-floor fitness center then. *28 East 63rd Street (between Park and Madison Avenues), New York, NY 10022.* **212-838-1400** *or* **1-800-221-4444.** *www.kiwicollection.com.*

The Mark Hotel   Upper East Side $ $ $ $ $

The Dalai Lama has been known to stay at the Mark, so you know it must have good vibes. Sadly, one third of the building has now been given over to co-op apartments, but 118 hotel rooms are left and the place has been done over in French modern style (or at least by modern Frenchmen). It was a lovely hotel before and is expected to be even more glamorous now. It also has Bar Mark, a branch of Saint Ambroeus, and a Frédéric Fekkai hair salon. *25 East 77th Street (between Fifth and Madison Avenues), New York, NY 10021.* **212-744-4300.** *www.themarkhotel.com.*

CO-OPS AND CONDOS

These days, most three-year-old children know what a condo (short for condominium) is. New York City has a number of condos, but another form of apartment ownership—the co-op—is more popular here. People who own co-ops don't own their individual apartments per se; instead, they own a percentage of the property, which is the cooperative (say, 2 percent in a building with 50 apartments of equal size). Co-op boards, whose job is to approve new owners, can be very picky. Movie actors and rock stars are always being turned down.

The New York Palace   Midtown $ $ $ $

Set in the old Villard Mansion with gates and courtyard intact, the Palace has what must be the glitziest (in a good way) hotel exterior in the city. And the location is unbeatable. You can't get any closer to Saks Fifth Avenue or Rockefeller Center, and you have a view of St. Patrick's Cathedral from the spa and fitness center. The guest room features include all the little luxuries plus three telephone lines (good for business travelers), high-speed Internet access, and a full-size desk. This hotel also has two restaurants, a bar, and some spectacular staircases. *455 Madison Avenue (at 50th Street), New York, NY 10022.* **212-888-7000.** *www.newyorkpalace.com.*

The Pierre   Midtown (northern edge) $ $ $ $ $

The Pierre, which shut down in 2008 for a $100 million renovation, is still interesting to pass by and take a peek at. Just think of a 41-story French chateau built in 1930 and the olden days when the likes of Audrey Hepburn and Frank Sinatra used to hang out here. The co-op apartments and the grand ballroom remain open. *2 East 61st Street (at Fifth Avenue), New York, NY 10065.* **212-940-8111.** *www.tajhotels.com.*

The Plaza Athenée   Upper East Side $ $ $ $ $

If you're looking for a little corner of Paris in New York, consider that parts of the penultimate episode of *Sex and the City* (set in Paris) were shot here, at the restaurant Arabelle and the romantic Bar Seine. The lobby is very grand, with marble floors and murals. The 149 rooms and suites are decorated in traditional European style. Many have balconies or glass-enclosed terraces. *37 East 64th Street (at Madison Avenue), New York, NY 10065. 212-734-9100. www.plaza-athenee.com.*

The Regency   Upper East Side $ $ $

Just as Park Avenue is turning from tall office buildings to elegant apartment buildings, there's the Regency—looking all shiny and inviting. The guest rooms are handsomely furnished with lots of mahogany and silk. There's a fitness center, a dog-walking service, a place for drinks and a bite, and—above all—Feinstein's at the Regency for some of the best cabaret in town. *540 Park Avenue (at 61st Street), New York, NY 10021. 212-759-4100. www.loewshotels.com.*

St. Regis Hotel   Midtown $ $ $ $ $

Some places have it all: more than 250 rooms and suites with custom-made furnishings, antiques, and silk wall coverings; marble baths; a fitness center and spa; and a butler on every floor, all in a landmarked 1904 Beaux Arts building. Oh, and the latest addition is the famed chef Alain Ducasse's restaurant Adour. *2 East 55th Street (at Fifth Avenue), New York, NY 10022. 212-753-4500. www.starwoodhotels.com.*

WHAT IS BEAUX ARTS ANYWAY?

You'll find a lot of Beaux Arts architectural influence in New York, from Grand Central Terminal to turn-of-the-last-century private homes. The style, popular between 1885 and 1920, is a sort of eclectic neoclassical look, highly ornamented, and heavy on the balustrades, pilasters, columns, and garlands.

The Waldorf-Astoria   Midtown $ $ $ $ $

Its name long ago became a synonym for an elegant place for the wealthy. The Waldorf, which opened on the current site in 1931, still holds its head high—covering an entire city block and offering 1,245 rooms and suites with Art Deco motifs and marble baths. Restaurants and lounge include the Bull & Bear, Peacock Alley, Sir Harry's Bar, Oscar's, and Inagiku. And there's a fitness center. Brad Pitt and Angelina Jolie lived in the super-exclusive annex, the Waldorf Towers, for a while. *301 Park Avenue (at 49th Street), New York, NY 10022.* **212-355-3000** *or* **1-800-WALDORF.** *www.hiltonfamilynewyork.com.*

You're not in New York anymore: The United Nation Secretariat and the rest of the UN campus are technically international territory.

Fabulous Walks, From River to Park

One great thing about walking in New York City is that you always seem to be passing something interesting. With these three walking itineraries, you'll know exactly what landmarks you're passing.

Millionaire's Row

Start at 92nd Street and Fifth Avenue. The **Jewish Museum** (1109 Fifth) is housed in a French Renaissance mansion that belonged to the banker-philanthropist Felix Warburg.

Walk one block south to the **Cooper-Hewitt Museum** (2 East 91st Street). It's in a mansion built for Andrew Carnegie in 1901. Right across the street is the **Convent of the Sacred Heart** (1 East 91st Street), housed in the 1918 Otto Kahn mansion, one of the largest private houses ever built in Manhattan, and the 1901 James A. Burden Jr. mansion, considered perhaps the finest Beaux Arts townhouse in the city.

Pass the **Church of the Heavenly Rest** (2 East 90th Street) and move on to the **National Academy** (1083 Fifth Avenue, between 89th and 90th Streets). The 1913 academy building once belonged to Archer Milton Huntington, a railroad heir.

Go three more blocks and you'll find the **Neue Galerie** (1048 Fifth Avenue, at 86th Street), once the home of Mrs. Cornelius Vanderbilt III.

Give at least a passing glance to **1040 Fifth Avenue** (between 85th and 86th Streets). It's not a former Gilded Age mansion, but it was the longtime home of Jacqueline Kennedy Onassis and her children.

As the **Metropolitan Museum of Art** looms on the Central Park side of the avenue, we come across the **Duke Semans house** (1009 Fifth at 82nd Street), a turn-of-the-century Beaux Arts mansion that belonged first to the tobacco magnate Benjamin N. Duke, then to his brother James. It's now privately owned again.

Nearby, **Goethe House** is a home built for a wealthy stockbroker in 1906. At 81st Street (995 Fifth Avenue), the former **Stanhope Hotel** has been turned into an apartment building. Nearby 991 Fifth was built in 1900 for a steel magnate.

The **Ukrainian Institute** (2 East 79th Street) was formerly the Isaac and Mary Fletcher mansion, and a reclusive descendant of Peter Stuyvesant, the city's last Dutch director-general, lived here until 1953. Nearby, 972 Fifth Avenue (also at 79th Street) is the former Payne and Helen Hay Whitney mansion, built in the first decade of the twentieth century.

The 1912 limestone mansion at 1 East 78th Street is where James B. Duke moved (from 82nd Street) and lived with his daughter Doris.

Continue south on Fifth Avenue. The **Commonwealth Fund's** neoclassical 1908 building (1 East 75th Street) belonged to Edward S. Harkness, a partner in Standard Oil. And finally, we reach the **Frick Collection** (1 East 70th Street) in a 1914 home built for Henry Clay Frick, a Pittsburgh steel tycoon. The house became a museum in 1935.

Distance: Approximately 1 mile

Grand Central Turnaround

Start at **Grand Central Terminal.** Take the 42nd Street exit and cross the street to admire the 1913 Beaux Arts façade.

Turn right and walk to Lexington Avenue. The **Chrysler Building** is across the street to your left, but you'll get a better view later. Between Lexington and Third Avenues, you'll see the attention-getting **Trylon Towers** (three tall pyramid-like glass and steel forms) of the **Chrysler Center,** now occupied by a chain restaurant. The skyscraper office building to your right is the **Socony-Mobil Building** (circa 1956)—best appreciated from a distance.

On the next block, you'll see the striking Art Deco **Daily News Building** (circa 1930). (The newspaper itself moved away in the 1990s, but the name remains.) Between Second and First Avenues, you'll find the **Church of the Covenant,** a small red brick Presbyterian church that began as a mission school in 1871.

Go up the steps just ahead and turn left at the top to enter **Tudor City,** a grand 1920s housing development that has become a highly desirable address. There are some nice **East River** views from here. On 43rd Street, look west and you'll have a lovely view of the **Chrysler Building** through (and above) the trees.

Now take the stairs down to First Avenue, cross the street, and for the next several blocks you'll be passing the **United Nations.** Straight ahead at 48th Street is one of the entrances to **866 U.N. Plaza,** the super-exclusive apartment building where Johnny Carson and Truman Capote once lived (not together).

One more block and you're at the **Beekman Tower Hotel,** an Art Deco (1928) landmark. Turn right and walk one block to **Beekman Place.** Turn left and stroll along these quiet, moneyed streets, where both the fictional Auntie Mame and the real woman who inspired her lived.

On 51st Street, turn left and head back toward the commercial part of the East 50s. On the northwest corner of 51st Street and First Avenue, you'll see an apartment building with a drugstore on the ground floor. This spot is where James Beekman's original mansion, **Mount Pleasant,** stood (1763–1874) and where Nathan Hale was imprisoned during the Revolutionary War.

Continue west four blocks to Park Avenue. Turn right and you'll soon see two important mid-twentieth-century office buildings standing across from each other: the **Seagram's Building** (375 Park Avenue) and **Lever House** (390 Park Avenue), both completed in the 1950s.

Turn back and walk south. **St. Bartholomew's Church** (1919) is between 50th and 51st Streets on the east side of the avenue. The **Waldorf-Astoria Hotel** is on the next block. And you've come full circle. **Grand Central** is straight ahead.

Distance: Approximately 2 miles.

The Best of Central Park

Start at **Grand Army Plaza,** that little island on Fifth Avenue between 59th and 60th Streets. You'll recognize it by the statue of Gen. William Tecumseh Sherman.

Enter the park at the nearest spot and walk slightly downhill to the **Pond,** a peaceful spot below street level surrounded by a wall of trees. At the pond's northeast corner, you'll see **Gapstow Bridge** (1896), a stone structure that offers a great view of the Plaza Hotel.

Just northeast of the bridge you'll find **Wollman Rink,** a relatively recent addition to the park (1949). In winter, this is the city's most romantic spot for ice skating. In summer, in-line skaters take over and an amusement park sprouts up.

Straight ahead (north), that little building that looks like something from a fairy tale is the **Dairy** (1870). Once, it actually supplied milk to park visitors; today, it's a visitors' information center.

Now, make a right (east) and check out the **Arsenal** (1851), a mini-castle that once served as a munitions depot. Now, it's the park commissioner's office. The **Children's Zoo** is just north of it.

Make a sharp left and go north until you hit the **Sheep Meadow,** a huge expanse of green where sheep actually did graze until 1934. (The **Tavern on the Green** restaurant, nearby, was the original sheepfold.) Today, the Sheep Meadow is used mostly by sunbathers.

Retrace your steps and go slightly east until you see the **Mall,** a grand elm-shaded promenade with several statues of literary figures on the southern end. Head north. Toward the end you'll pass the **Naumberg Bandshell,** where musicians from John Phillip Sousa to the Grateful Dead have performed.

At the end of the Mall, you'll be facing gorgeous **Bethesda Terrace.** Take one of the two stone staircases down and admire **Bethesda Fountain;** its central statue, Angel of Waters (1873); and the 22-acre **Lake** beyond. If you're taking this walk in nice weather, the lake is probably filled with people in rowboats.

Exit Bethesda Terrace on the other end, forking right, and you'll find yourself at the **Loeb Boathouse** (1954, replacing the original from 1874), which also houses the **Boathouse Café.**

At the boathouse, make a sharp right and you'll soon arrive at **Conservatory Water,** a lovely spot famous for its popularity with model boat owners. You'll pass a statue of Hans Christian Andersen at the area's western edge. Make your exit, past the Alice in Wonderland statue on the northern end, onto Fifth Avenue around 76th Street.

Distance: Approximately 1 mile.

If you take all three of these walks and remember a lot of the landmark names, you'll be way ahead of many New Yorkers. And after all that walking, you can afford to have a big, gooey dessert at dinner.

Chapter **6**

Enjoying
the East Side

In This Chapter

- All kinds of great East Side restaurants
- The East Side's best shopping streets
- Sights to see, heavy on the museums
- Great places to go after dark
- Seeing the East Side in just one day

If you're spending a large part of your New York visit on the East Side, you have a great deal of choice about what to see and do. There are amazing restaurants at every price level and some of the world's great art in very different museums housed in memorable buildings. Not to mention dozens of places for a satisfying shopping spree and elegant settings for some of the most glamorous cocktail hours you will ever enjoy. Cheers!

Great East Side Dining

In general, restaurants where a dinner for one person costs an average of $80 or more are listed in the Expensive category. Those with average prices of approximately $40 to $80 are in the Moderate category. Those under $40 are in the Affordable section. But of course exactly what you order can increase or decrease the check considerably.

Expensive

Adour Alain Ducasse   Midtown   French $ $ $

The St. Regis Hotel is the site of Monsieur Ducasse's newest attempt to conquer New York. The reviews are in, and the place is a hit, particularly the lamb, the striped bass, the apple soufflé, and the computerized wine list. A five-course tasting menu is $110, but there are bar snacks from $9 to $13. *2 East 55th Street (at Fifth Avenue), New York, NY 10022.* **212-710-2277.** *www.alain-ducasse.com.*

Aquavit   Midtown   Scandinavian $ $ $

Often named on lists of the best restaurants in New York, Aquavit does the chef's native Scandinavia proud. Start with the herring platter (even if you think you don't like herring), then move on to the main courses like hot smoked trout, grilled hanger steak, chili-dusted halibut, or rack of lamb. *65 East 55th Street (between Madison and Park Avenues), New York, NY 10022.* **212-307-7311.** *www.aquavit.org.*

Arabelle   Upper East Side   French $ $ $

The Plaza Athenée's house restaurant is a beautiful gold-domed room with brass and Murano glass chandeliers. The menu has plenty of variety (halibut, cod, risotto, lamb, chicken, sirloin steak), and the place does weekend brunch. If you're filthy rich or feel like a real splurge, order the $215 Osetra caviar appetizer. *37 East 64th Street (at Madison Avenue), New York, NY 10021.* **212-606-4647.** *www.arabellerestaurant.com.*

Aureole   Upper East Side   American $ $ $

After two decades in its tasteful brownstone, filled with towers of flowers, Aureole is revered as a refreshingly civilized dining experience. The American menu includes truffled Amish chicken, butter-poached Maine lobster, pepper-crusted calves' liver, and olive-poached tuna. If you're on a budget, take note: there's a prix fixe lunch. *34 East 61st Street (between Madison and Park Avenues), New York, NY 10021.* **212-319-1660.** *www.charliepalmer.com.*

HOW DOES PRIX FIXE WORK?

Ordering a prix fixe (pronounce it pree fix or pree feex, depending on how French you want to be) lunch or dinner can be an economical way to eat at normally very expensive restaurants. Normally the prix fixe menu page will offer a choice of three appetizers, three entrees, and three desserts, and you can have one of each for a pre-set price, normally considerably less than ordering three courses á la carte (from the rest of the menu).

Café Boulud   Upper East Side   French $ $ $

"A neighborhood bistro for billionaires" is how one Zagat's contributor described this elegant spot. The billionaires (and those with lesser net worths) will find a wood-paneled dining room and a diverse menu that includes Thai-marinated lobster, mushroom risotto, roasted venison saddle, and roasted monkfish. *20 East 76th Street (between Fifth and Madison Avenues), New York, NY 10021.* **212-772-2600.** *www.danielnyc.com.*

Country   Madison Square   French $ $ $

The New York Times critic gave it three stars. Country, the Carlton Hotel's superb house restaurant, is really two restaurants: the casual café downstairs (with bistro food and some dishes that aren't particularly French, like gnocchi with broccoli and pancetta) and the more formal dining room upstairs (where blanquette de veau and a foie gras and pigeon terrine have been on the menu).

The dining room is also drop-dead gorgeous, topped by a Tiffany stained-glass dome, circa 1904. *90 Madison Avenue (at 29th Street), New York, NY 10016.* **212-889-7100.** *www.countryinnewyork.com.*

Daniel   Upper East Side   French $ $ $

If you have only one spectacular meal in New York, save your pennies and let this be the one. Daniel's Venetian Renaissance dining room sets the mood. And then the glorious seasonal menu comes through. Have the white truffles in fall, the black ones in winter, asparagus in the spring, and chanterelles or sweet corn in the summer. For the (relatively) budget-minded, there's a three-course prix fixe for $98. *60 East 65th Street (between Madison and Park Avenues), New York, NY 10065.* **212-288-0033.** *www.danielnyc.com.*

Felidia   Midtown   Italian $ $ $

Felidia's pretty townhouse setting, with soft yellow walls and all that mahogany, is nice, but it's the northeastern Italian food that has kept New Yorkers coming back here for more than a quarter-century. The restaurant is very good with game (e.g., quail saltimbocca). Other favorites include fusilli with pork ribs, grilled octopus, sautéed rock shrimp, risotto (which kind depends on the season), and tiramisu. *243 East 58th Street (between Second and Third Avenues), New York, NY 10022.* **212-758-1479.** *www.lidiasitaly.com.*

The Four Seasons   Midtown   American $ $ $

The Four Seasons opened in 1959, and shortly thereafter the power lunch was invented. Roughly half a century later, the place is still going strong. The Pool Room is the larger and more glamorous of the two dining rooms, but at lunchtime the rich and powerful prefer the smaller Grill Room, where they can have Kobe burgers for $49 each. The seasonal menu can include a little of everything, from vegetable won tons to Long Island duck. *99 East 52nd Street (between Park and Lexington Avenues), New York, NY 10022.* **212-754-9494.** *www.fourseasonsrestaurant.com.*

La Grenouille   Midtown   French $ $ $

La Grenouille (pronounced la grahn-WEE, it just means "the frog") seems to have been a part of New York forever (really, only since 1962), welcoming the fashionable and the well financed into its beautiful dining room, always bedecked with flowers. This is the place for a classic French lunch or dinner. You could have Dover sole or frog's legs or quenelles de brochet, with oeufs à la neige for dessert. No cell phone use allowed, by the way, which is one way they keep things so civilized. *3 East 52nd Street (between Fifth and Madison Avenues), New York, NY 10022.* *212-752-1495.* *www.la-grenouille.com.*

L'Atelier De Joël Robuchon   Midtown   French $ $ $

A place at the counter is the most desirable seating in the Four Seasons Hotel's highly praised New French (i.e., with an Asian touch) restaurant. You could take one of the tables in the black and red lacquer dining room instead, but then you wouldn't be able to see into the kitchen to watch them whipping up your truffled mashed potatoes, crispy langoustine, or quail with foie gras. *57 East 57th Street (between Madison and Park Avenues), New York, NY 10022.* *212-350-6658.* *www.fourseasons.com.*

Le Cirque   Midtown   French/Italian $ $ $

This location, in the Bloomberg office building, is the third incarnation of Le Cirque, which some critics say is coasting on its once superb reputation. But it's still glitzy, with shining ebony walls, and it's still snobbish. *The New York Times* critic liked the langoustine with curry and the trout amandine. A $145 tasting menu starts with scrambled eggs and caviar. *151 East 58th Street (between Lexington and Third Avenues), New York, NY 10022.* *212-644-0202.* *www.lecirque.com.*

Oceana   Midtown   American/Seafood $ $ $

The kitchen at Oceana, where the dining room is designed to look like a yacht, does all manner of wonderful things with seafood. There's gravlax, Maine sea urchin, baby octopus, steamed grouper, Arctic char, and taro-wrapped dorado. The lobster salad and loup de mer are particularly recommended. *55 East 54th Street (between Madison and Park Avenues), New York, NY 10022.* *212-759-5941.* *www.oceanarestaurant.com.*

Peacock Alley   Midtown   American $ $ $

If the idea of sitting in the main lobby of the Waldorf-Astoria and watching all the people go by appeals to you, so will Peacock Alley. You can have an expensive meal (grilled sirloin, Chilean turbot, bouillabaisse, etc.) in this historic but recently renovated lobby restaurant, but you could also just have a drink and one of the small plates the menu offers. Consider a club sandwich for $15, the charcuterie platter for $19, or sashimi or lobster tacos for $14. *301 Park Avenue (between 49th and 50th Streets), New York, NY 10017.* **212-872-4920.** *www.peacockalleyrestaurant.com.*

Sparks   Midtown   American/Steak 💲💲💲

Take a trip back to mid-twentieth-century New York, when men were men and a proper steak dinner began with two martinis. Sparks (established in 1966) is a fairly casual place, considering all the antiques and artwork, and both the food and the wine list have won accolades. Restaurant critics recommend the shrimp cocktail, asparagus vinaigrette, prime sirloin, and cheesecake. *210 East 46th Street (between Second and Third Avenues), New York, NY 10017.* **212-687-4855.** *www.sparkssteakhouse.com.*

Moderate

A Voce   Madison Square   Italian 💲💲

In warm weather, there's a lovely outdoor dining area. Indoors, the look is all stainless steel, lacquer, and leather. A Voce received three stars from *The New York Times*, and the wine list has been praised by *Wine Spectator.* Try the duck meatballs, the black truffle spaghetti, or the pappardelle with lamb Bolognese. *41 Madison Avenue (at 26th Street), New York, NY 10010.* **212-545-8555.** *www. avocerestaurant.com.*

Blue Smoke   Madison Square   Barbecue 💲💲

A barbecue restaurant with culinary chic? At Blue Smoke, you can order deviled eggs as an appetizer, then have sherry-herb mushrooms as a side dish. There are five kinds of ribs on the menu, right alongside seared yellowfin tuna with arugula and radicchio. And there's a jazz club in the basement. *116 East 27th Street (between Park and Lexington Avenues), New York, NY 10016.* **212-447-7733.** *www.bluesmoke.com.*

🖼 The Boathouse   Central Park   American 💲💲

One of the most romantic restaurants in New York is in the middle of Central Park, at the northeastern end of the lake that passes by Bethesda Fountain.

Have lunch or dinner on the deck here, and you can watch ducks, swans, rowboaters, and the occasional gondolier. At lunch you could start with the goat-cheese cake or a foie gras terrine, then move on to salmon or roast chicken or an all-American hamburger. The dinner menu adds a few specialties, like a veal rib chop and Dover sole. *Park Drive North and 72nd Street (enter on Fifth Avenue), New York, NY 10021. 212-517-2233. www.thecentralparkboathouse.com.*

Bull & Bear   Midtown   American/Steak 💲 💲

This old-school steakhouse inside the Waldorf-Astoria reopened in 2007 after a big refurbishment. But it still has an old-school menu, including prime rib, tournedos, New York strip steak and filet mignon (perhaps with onion soup to start?). The menu offers seafood, too. *570 Lexington Avenue (at 49th Street), New York, NY 10017. 212-872-1275. www.bullandbearsteakhouse.com.*

Candle 79   Upper East Side   Vegetarian 💲 💲

The chic veggie fare here includes porcini-chive-crusted tofu, soffrito seared seitan, and house-made gnocchi. *154 East 79th Street (between Lexington and Third Avenues), New York, NY 10021. 212-537-7179. www.candlecafe.com.*

Erminia   Upper East Side   Italian 💲 💲

This very tiny, very romantic place is tucked away in a neighborhoody part of the Upper East Side. Critics recommend the home-made pastas, the veal chop, and the tiramisu. *250 East 83rd Street (between Second and Third Avenues), New York, NY 10028. 212-879-4284.*

Inagiku   Midtown   Japanese 💲 💲

Although it has a separate entrance, Inagiku is part of the Waldorf-Astoria. And it feels like a hotel restaurant, albeit a particularly good one. Sashimi, tempura, chicken teriyaki, and black cod are among the favorites of the regulars, who are a mix of American visitors and Japanese business travelers. *111 East 49th Street (between Lexington and Park Avenues), New York, NY 10017. 212-355-0440. www.inagiku.com.*

JoJo   Upper East Side   French 💲 💲

This little bistro, in a townhouse on a side street, has earned three stars from *The New York Times* restaurant critic and a highly coveted Michelin star. The place is also a neighborhood institution, with its wide-ranging menu, from peekytoe crab to short-rib vinaigrette. *160 East 64th Street (between Lexington and Third Avenues) New York, NY 10021.* **212-223-5656.** *www.jean-georges.com.*

¢ La Mangeoire   Midtown   French 💲💲

With its stucco walls and terra cotta floors, La Mangeoire really does have the feel of a country house in Provence. The menu helps foster the illusion, with fish soup, an onion tart, chicken breast salad, grilled loup de mer, and steak au poivre. And for the budget- or weight-conscious, "small plates" of every dish are offered, for about one-third less than the regular serving. *1008 Second Avenue (between 53rd and 54th Streets), New York, NY 10022.* **212-759-7086.** *www.lamangeoire.com.*

Le Refuge   Upper East Side   French 💲💲

This intimate little townhouse bistro (very convenient to the Metropolitan Museum) does feel like a real getaway from the bustling city around it. The look is rustic, and the menu is right on target. Possibilities include duck liver terrine, a frisée salad with caramelized apples, lamb chops with rosemary sauce, steak frites Bearnaise, and swordfish provençal. *166 East 82nd Street (between Lexington and Third Avenues), New York, NY 10021.* **212-861-4505.** *www.lerefugenyc.com.*

Maya   Upper East Side   Mexican 💲💲

This busy upscale spot specializes in updates of old Mexican classics like chicken enchiladas, mole poblano, chipotle shrimp and braised lamb shank. Not to mention margaritas. *1191 First Avenue (between 64th and 65th Streets), New York, NY 10021.* **212-585-1818.** *www.modernmexican.com.*

Metrazur   Midtown   American 💲💲

There are two restaurants on the balconies of Grand Central with great views of the starry ceiling and the main concourse below. This one's menu ranges from Caesar salads to risotto. There's a large, popular bar area, too. *Grand Central Terminal (42nd Street and Park Avenue entrance), East Balcony, New York, NY 10017.* **212-687-4600.** *www.charliepalmer.com.*

Michael Jordan's Midtown American/Steak $\boxed{\$}$ $\boxed{\$}$

The full name is Michael Jordan's The Steak House NYC. It's also on a Grand Central balcony overlooking the main concourse, and when it opened it surprised everyone by actually having great steaks (porterhouse, strip, rib-eye, sirloin, you name it). And you get the fabulous view. *Grand Central Terminal (42nd and Vanderbilt Avenue entrance), West Balcony, New York, NY 10017.* ***212-655-2300.*** *www.theglaziergroup.com.*

Mr. K'S Midtown Chinese $\boxed{\$}$ $\boxed{\$}$

The palatial Mr. K's has an Art Deco look (to match the 1931 office building where it makes its home). The menu is strictly Chinese, all kinds of it, from Peking, Shanghai, Canton, and Szechuan. Critics love the spring rolls, the Mongolian lamb, and the Peking duck. *570 Lexington Avenue (at 51st Street), New York, NY 10022.* ***212-583-1668.*** *www.mrks.com.*

Oyster Bar Midtown American/Seafood $\boxed{\$}$ $\boxed{\$}$

The red-checked tablecloths! The crazy-busy lunch counter! The vaulted ceilings! A visit to the Grand Central Oyster Bar and Restaurant, serving shellfish and stews on the lower level of the terminal since 1913, is a true New York experience. The menu is ridiculously long, ranging from the obvious (oysters and clams) to snapper, swordfish, and old-fashioned fish and chips. The regulars go for lunch and order the simplest things on the menu (raw oysters and the oyster pan roast), plus a little something from the impressive wine and beer list. *Grand Central Terminal (42nd Street and Vanderbilt Avenue entrance), Lower Level, New York, NY 10017.* ***212-490-6650.*** *www.oysterbarny.com.*

Pampano Midtown Mexican $\boxed{\$}$ $\boxed{\$}$

Shrimp empanadas, red snapper quesadillas, cilantro-ginger tuna, and lobster tacos are among the favorites at this highly rated Midtown spot. Mexican coastal dishes are the specialty. *209 East 49th Street (between Second and Third Avenues), New York, NY 10017.* ***212-751-4545.*** *www.modernmexican.com.*

Payard Bistro Upper East Side French $\boxed{\$}$ $\boxed{\$}$

What a good idea, combining a bistro and a patisserie! No wonder Payard pays so much attention to desserts (pecan tart, fruit napoleon, old-fashioned chocolate soufflé). Main courses here are inventive, too, like the "coq au vin" made with wild boar. *1032 Lexington Avenue (between 73rd and 74th Streets), New York, NY 10021.* *212-717-5252.* *www.payard.com.*

Sfoglia   Upper East Side   Italian 💲💲

The critically praised Sfoglia specializes in Northern Italian cuisine and encourages traditional Italian five-course meals, from antipasto to dessert. They make this easier by offering all the pastas (usually the second course) in large or small sizes. There's an all-Italian wine list. *1402 Lexington Avenue (at 92nd Street), New York, NY 10028.* *212-831-1402.* *www.sfogliarestaurant.com.*

Shun Lee Palace   Midtown   Chinese 💲💲

New Yorkers who like their Chinese food in formal, elegant, even opulent surroundings have been coming to Shun Lee for many decades. There's a huge menu, with both familiar and unfamiliar dishes side by side: wonton soup, prawns on banana leaves with curry sauce, orange beef, and Szechuan rack of lamb. *155 East 55th Street (between Third and Lexington Avenues), New York, NY 10022.* *212-371-8844.* *www.shunleepalace.com.*

Sushi Seki   Upper East Side   Japanese 💲💲

Aside from virtual masterpieces of sushi artistry, Sushi Seki offers an impressive selection of sake and is open until the wee hours of the morning. The really serious aficionados prefer to sit at the bar rather than the dining room. *1143 First Avenue (between 62nd and 63rd Streets), New York, NY 10021.* *212-371-0238.*

Tabla   Madison Square   American 💲💲

This colorful, fashionable restaurant takes American cuisine and adds Indian ingredients, like shrimp with brown basmati pilaf and roasted chili curry or lamb with cracked-wheat pilaf, pine nuts, barberries, and saffron. People seem either to love it or hate it. *11 Madison Avenue (at 25th Street), New York, NY 10010.* *212-889-0667.* *www.tablany.com.*

Tse Yang   Midtown   Chinese 💲💲

Tse Yang is Chinese by way of Paris, where the original restaurant by this name began. So you'll find frog's legs on this lavish restaurant's menu, but you'll also find shredded pork, Szechuan chicken, and Peking duck. *34 East*

51st Street (between Madison and Park Avenues), New York, NY 10022. 212-688-5447. www.tseyang.citysearch.com.

Vong Midtown   French/Thai $ $

The first New York Michelin guide gave it a coveted star. This showy restaurant in what New Yorkers call the Lipstick Building offers some highly praised fusion dishes, like crab spring rolls and rabbit curry. *200 East 54th Street (at Third Avenue), New York, NY 10022. 212-486-9592. www.jean-georges.com.*

Zarela Midtown   Mexican $ $

It's always fiesta time at Zarela (although the party is usually a little quieter in the second-floor dining room than it is downstairs). The food is inventive too, taking salmon, trout, shrimp, tuna steak and the like and doing wonderful things with peppery spices and poblano, chipotle, and jalapeño sauces. But Americans' traditional favorites are on the menu, too: you can start the meal with guacamole or the chili relleno of the day. *953 Second Avenue (between 50th and 51st Streets), New York, NY 10022. 212-644-6740. www.zarela.com.*

Affordable, With or Without Atmosphere

Café S. F. A. Midtown   American $

There you are, shopping your heart out at Saks, and you realize it's lunchtime—or teatime. Anyway, you need a break. On the 8th floor of the store, you'll find a lovely little restaurant with a diverse menu, including an outstanding Mandarin chicken salad, and some pleasant wines by the glass. There's a counter, if you're in a hurry, and some lucky people will get the tables that overlook Rockefeller Center. *611 Fifth Avenue (between 49th and 50th Street), New York, NY 10017. 212-940-4080.*

Candle Café Upper East Side   Vegetarian $

This popular neighborhood spot started out as a juice bar and health food café. Now it offers a full-fledged menu including cashew-crusted tofu, wild mushroom risotto, and seitan tamales. *1307 Third Avenue (between 74th and 75th Streets), New York, NY 10021. 212-472-0970. www.candlecafe.com.*

Gobo   Upper East Side   Vegetarian $

Gobo offers affordable vegetarian food in a cozy, almost serene setting.
Consider the eggplant brandade, the avocado tartare, or the grilled seitan on
skewers. *1426 Third Avenue (at 81st Street), New York, NY 10028.* **212-288-
4686.** *www.goborestaurant.com.*

Itzocan   Upper East Side   Mexican/French $

This cozy Mexican place, on the edge of Spanish Harlem, has a definite
French accent. Dishes include a duck confit and mushroom quesadilla with
brie and greens and roast chicken with tomatillo sauce. At dessert time, you
can go either way—with a tequila lime tart or crème brûlée. *1575 Lexington
Avenue (at 101st Street), New York, NY 10029.* **212-423-0255.**

J. G. Melon   Upper East Side   American $

Forbes magazine once called Melon's "cramped, dark, and delicious." It's a
proudly casual neighborhood hangout that has been around since the customers
were called swinging singles. There are sandwiches, salads, and omelettes on the
menu, but hamburgers are the specialty. Some people think theirs is one of the
best in town. *1291 Third Avenue (at 74th Street), New York, NY 10021.* **212-744-
0585.**

¢ Phoenix Garden   Midtown   Chinese $

The canopy says "authentic Cantonese," and that's what this longtime favorite
(it moved uptown from Chinatown in 1992) takes pride in serving. Salt and
pepper shrimp is one of its specialties. No credit cards. *242 East 40th Street
(between Second and Third Avenues), New York, NY 10013.* **212-988-6666.** *www.
thephoenixgarden.com.*

P. J. Clarke's   Midtown   American $

There are two other locations in the city, but this is the real P. J. Clarke's, in
the same location since 1884, on a block where everything else was torn down
to make room for skyscrapers. Here are some great things about the king of
pub food: A burger is under $10. There's a raw bar. Thursday is meat loaf day.
You can order a wedge of iceberg lettuce or broccoli rabe. The kitchen is open
till 3 A.M. *915 Third Avenue (at 55th Street), New York, NY 10022.* **212-317-
1616.** *www.pjclarkes.com.*

Sarabeth's   Upper East Side   American $\boxed{\$}$

If you pass Sarabeth's at breakfast or brunch time, you may see a long line on the sidewalk out front. The place is wildly popular. But they do lunch and dinner, too. Expect a country-kitchen atmosphere and lots of comfort food, from the cream of tomato soup to the chicken pot pie. *1295 Madison Avenue (at 92nd Street), New York, NY 10028.* **212-410-7335.** *www.sarabeth.com.*

Shopping: This Is the Place

The East Side hasn't always been the place to shop in New York. Back in the nineteenth century, there was a part of town known as Ladies' Mile. It stretched from Union Square, at fourteenth Street, to Madison Square Park, in the 20s, and from Sixth Avenue to Broadway. All the big department stores were there, some still around (like Macy's and Lord & Taylor), some gone (A. T. Stewart, Best & Company).

But in the twentieth century and the beginning of the 21st, if a part of town had to be designated the equivalent of Ladies' Mile, a Midtown stretch of Fifth Avenue would probably win, and upper Madison Avenue would come in a very close second. These are the most potentially rewarding places to begin your shopping adventures in the city.

Fifth Avenue

On a 10-block stretch of Fifth Avenue, running from 59th to 49th Street, you will find more than two dozen stores, most of them glamorous in their own ways.

The **Apple Store** is a big glass box, standing like a temple to technology (or like the pyramid at the Louvre), in front of the General Motors Building. The shopping floor is downstairs. *767 Fifth Avenue (at 59th Street),* **212-336-1440.**

Shop and run: Just off the main concourse of Grand Central Terminal, stores sell clothing, books, food, wine, and a lot more.

FAO Schwarz, the world's most famous toy store, is on the same block, on the lobby level of the GM Building. At holiday time, there can be a line to get inside, but it tends to move fast. *767 Fifth Avenue (at 58th Street),* **212-644-9400.**

Bergdorf Goodman and its men's-store annex face each other on the next block. Bergdorf is one of the most elegant names on Fifth Avenue, and you can find great fashions, fashion accessories, and home accessories here, not all of them outrageously priced. *754 Fifth Avenue (at 58th Street),* **212-753-7300.**

A SLIGHT DETOUR

Lord & Taylor lies outside the core 10 blocks of Fifth Avenue shopping, but it's worth a detour. Founded in 1826, it was the first big store to move to Fifth Avenue and the first to do special Christmas window displays (theirs are still considered among the best). The store has a reassuringly old-fashioned feel, but it has undergone a renaissance of sorts in recent years, and it's a more than worthwhile destination for women's, men's, and children's fashions as well as gifts. *424 Fifth Avenue (between 38th and 39th Streets), New York, NY 10016.* **212-391-3344.** *www.lordandtaylor.com.*

Walking downtown (south), **Tiffany & Company** is on the next corner. Even if you're not planning a major jewelry purchase, the store is an enjoyable browsing experience and there are some affordable gifts upstairs. *727 Fifth Avenue (at 57th Street),* **212-755-8000.**

Go one more block, and the mood changes. You're in front of the **Disney Store,** which has aisles and aisles of Mickey Mouse, *Lion King,* and other Disney-character merchandise. Fifth Avenue ain't what it used to be, but this is a highly popular shopping destination. *711 Fifth Avenue (between 55th and 56th Streets),* **212-702-0702.**

But **Henri Bendel** is across the street, selling trendy women's fashions, accessories, and gifts since 1895. *712 Fifth Avenue (at 56th Street),* **212-247-1100.**

Takashimaya, the New York branch of the Japanese department store and an oasis of serenity, is almost two blocks south. From the floral department on the ground floor through the fashion floors up to the fifth-floor bedroom department, Takashimaya sells gorgeous merchandise in an almost tranquilizing atmosphere. *693 Fifth Avenue (between 54th and 55th Streets),* **212-350-0100.**

At 52nd Street, there's another establishment you wouldn't have seen on the old Fifth Avenue: the **NBA Store.** It sells jerseys, footwear, collectibles, artwork, and other merchandise bearing the name of or connected with every National Basketball Association team there is. The store also has a half-court shooting area and video games. *666 Fifth Avenue (at 52nd Street),* **212-515-6221.**

A branch of **H&M,** specializing in affordable fashions, is one block away. *640 Fifth Avenue (at 51st Street),* **646-473-1164.**

And finally we reach **Saks Fifth Avenue,** the grande dame of the avenue, with men's, women's, and children's fashions; accessories; gifts; and a day spa. *611 Fifth Avenue (between 49th and 50th Streets),* **212-753-4000.**

Rockefeller Center is across the street, with its own shops, including **Teuscher,** the Swiss chocolate makers, on the plaza.

Right next door to Saks is **American Girl Place,** a phenomenal center of doll culture. Little-girl dolls, doll fashions, and doll accessories are on sale, along with little-girl clothes to match their dolls'. The store also houses a restaurant, a doll hair salon, and a theater. *609 Fifth Avenue (at 49th Street),* **212-247-5223.**

And we haven't even mentioned Cartier, Van Cleef & Arpels, Fendi, Prada, Bulgari, Harry Winston, Ferragamo, Fortunoff, H. Stern, Gucci, and Brooks Brothers, all in this same 10-block area.

BEHIND THE BIG BROWN BAG

The Bloomingdale's historians like to say that it all began with the hoop skirt, a trendy little item in the 1860s, when Joseph and Lyman Bloomingdale had a ladies' notions store on the Lower East Side of Manhattan. By the time Bloomingdale's moved to its present location (1886), Lexington Avenue at 59th Street, the Bloomingdale brothers' business had evolved into a department store. A century later, although it had never bothered moving to Fifth Avenue or Madison, it was the hottest store in town.

If its chic quotient has dipped a little in recent years, Bloomie's, as its fans call it, hasn't noticed and just goes on being confident and fashionable. You'll see its distinctive Big (and Little and Medium) Brown Bag, all over town.

Shoppers will find fashion designers from Eileen Fisher to Gianni Versace, from Lilly Pulitzer to Juicy Couture. The men's store, the housewares department, and the white sales are all highly regarded. And the elegant model rooms on the furniture floor are still an excellent source of decorating ideas. (Years ago, a friend of mine just bought an entire room, figuring the store's designers knew better than she and her husband did how to put it all together.)

1000 Lexington Avenue (at 59th Street), New York, NY 10022. **212-705-2000.** *www.bloomingdales.com.*

Madison Avenue

Fifth Avenue shopping is mostly in Midtown, but Madison Avenue's center of designer shops goes in the direction of the residential part of the city. The most spectacular stretch is between 59th and 72nd Streets.

Bottega Veneta, maker of luxurious (and expensive) Italian leather goods, is at 59th Street, marking the beginning of this shopping district. *635 Madison Avenue (at 59th Street),* **212-371-5511.**

Crate & Barrel, with its casual kitchenware and housewares and furniture, stands on the northwest corner and is one of the last affordable stores you'll see. *650 Madison Avenue (at 59th Street), 212-368-0011.*

There is an **Ann Taylor** shop across the way, with pretty much the same women's fashions you'll find in every branch across the nation. *645 Madison Avenue (at 59th Street), 212-832-2010.*

If this part of Madison Avenue were a mall, **Barneys New York** would be the anchor store. What Barneys has is high fashion for men and women—and lots of attitude. Its celebrity clientele and irreverent holiday windows reflect that. *660 Madison Avenue (between 60th and 61st Street), 212-826-8900.*

There is also a daunting **Calvin Klein** store. It's true of much of this neighborhood that some stores are just a little too glamorous for comfort, calling for a certain amount of financial and/or social confidence before a shopper can even walk in the door. *654 Madison Avenue (at 60th Street), 212-292-9000.*

DKNY, with Donna Karan's great-looking fashions, feels a little warmer but still very upscale. *655 Madison Avenue (at 60th Street), 212-223-3569.*

If you're in the market for absolutely gorgeous silver or crystal, drop in at **Christofle.** Nobody does it better. *680 Madison Avenue (at 62nd Street), 212-308-9390.*

Another pocket of affordability opens at the **Timberland** store, where any member of the family might find great boots or shoes. *709 Madison Avenue (at 63rd Street), 212-754-0434.*

A few blocks north, **Fred Leighton** has diamonds and estate jewelry and other baubles. *773 Madison Avenue (at 66th Street), 212-288-1872.*

You'll find statement-making Italian fashions at **Gianni Versace.** *815 Madison Avenue (at 68th Street), 212-744-6868.* The same is true of **Dolce & Gabbana.** *825 Madison Avenue (at 69th Street), 212-249-4100.*

Gorgeous Italian bed linens are the attraction at **Pratesi.** *829 Madison Avenue (at 69th Street), 212-288-2315.*

As you enter the East 70s, pause to honor the grand old man of American fashion. **Ralph Lauren**'s elegant boutique is in a chateau-like Gilded Age mansion on the corner. *867 Madison Avenue (at 72nd Street)*, **212-434-8000.**

Other stores in the area include Valentino, Armani, Emanuel Ungaro, Moschino, Pierre Deux, Georg Jensen, and Yves Saint Laurent.

East Side Sights, A to Z

When it comes to sightseeing, the East Side's museums, churches, and architecture are its greatest assets. Visiting them, you may accidentally pick up a little New York City history along the way.

Asia Society and Museum   Upper East Side

The idea behind Asia Society's art collection and performing arts programs is the promotion of understanding between the United States and Asia. Past events have included a Balinese dance-lesson event for children and exhibitions of the work of the Chinese artist Zhang Huan and artworks from Kashmir. *725 Park Avenue (at 70th Street), New York, NY 10021. Open Tuesdays–Thursdays and Saturdays–Sundays 11 A.M.–6 P.M., Fridays 11 A.M.–9 P.M. Closed Mondays. Adults $10, students and children under 16 $5.* **212-288-6400.** *www.asiasociety.org.*

Carl Schurz Park   Upper East Side

This 14.9-acre park, overlooking the Hell's Gate section of the East River, includes what were the grounds of Gracie Mansion (the official residence of the Mayor of New York) and goes right up to its front door. Its namesake (1829–1906) was a German soldier, statesman, and journalist. The Peter Pan statue here was originally done for the old Paramount Theater. *East End Avenue to the East River, 84th to 90th Streets, New York, NY 10028. www.nycgovparks.org.*

Central Park   Midtown/Upper East Side

All hail, Frederick Law Olmsted and Calvert Vaux, the men who transformed 843 acres (6 percent of all of Manhattan) of swampy land into what many consider the most beautiful urban park in the world. Since 1873, New Yorkers have flocked to the park, which has 36 bridges and arches, 21 playgrounds, and 52 fountains, monuments, and sculptures. See as much of it as you have time for, starting with Bethesda Fountain and the Lake, the Pond, the Zoo, Belvedere Castle, Sheep Meadow, Conservatory Water, the Ramble, and the tiny spot known as Strawberry Fields, dedicated to John Lennon. *59th Street to 110th Street, Fifth Avenue to Central Park West, New York, NY 10022. Open daily 6 A.M.–1 A.M.* **212-360-2726** *(for tours) or* **212-310-6600.** *www.centralparknyc. org.*

Chrysler Building   Midtown

Everything great about Art Deco is reflected in this 1930 office building. At 1,046 feet (and 77 stories), it's the third tallest structure in New York and the tallest brick building in the world. The observatory has been closed for years, but you can appreciate the building's terraced crown, its stainless steel eagle gargoyles, its triangular windows, and its replicas of Chrysler hood ornaments and radiator caps from a distance. The lobby is worth visiting for the mural and the fabulous Art Deco elevator doors. *405 Lexington Avenue (at 42nd Street), New York, NY 10017.*

Cooper-Hewitt Museum   Upper East Side

Founded in 1897 and housed in Andrew Carnegie's old Fifth Avenue mansion, the Cooper-Hewitt National Design Museum has a collection of some 250,000 design objects. They range from a Barcelona chair to a mid-eighteenth-century board game. And they fall into categories including drawings, prints, product design, graphic design, decorative arts, textiles, and wall coverings. The museum is part of the Smithsonian Institution. *2 East 91st Street (at Fifth Avenue), New York, NY 10128. Mondays-Thursdays 10 A.M.–5 P.M., Fridays 10 A.M.–9 P.M., Saturdays 10 A.M.–6 P.M., Sundays noon–6 P.M. Adults $15, students $10, children under 12 free.* **212-849-8400.** *www.cooperhewitt.org.*

Empire State Building   Midtown

Once again the tallest building in New York (since the destruction of the World Trade Center towers in 2001), the Empire State Building is on most visitors' short list of sights to see. They say that on a clear day you can see five states from the 86th-floor observatory. But sometimes it seems you have to stand in line forever to get there. These days you can actually buy your way to the front of the lines now with an express pass for $41.52, more than twice the regular adult admission. The building is 1,250 feet (102 stories) high and was completed in 1931. *350 Fifth Avenue (between 33rd and 34th Streets), New York, NY 10017. Open daily 8 A.M.–2 A.M. Adults $17.61, children 12–17 years old $15.76, children 6–11 $12.07, children 5 and under free.* **212-736-3100** *or* **1-877-NYC-VIEW.** *www.esbnyc.com.*

WHAT DO PURPLE AND YELLOW MEAN?

Three levels of floodlights at the top of the Empire State Building are constantly changing colors, to pay tribute to a holiday (red, white, and blue for President's Day, for instance) or something as esoteric as a dog show (purple, purple and yellow for the Westminster Kennel Club Show). If you can't figure out why the lights are a particular color while you're visiting, go to "lighting schedule" at the building's website (www.esbnyc.com) to find out.

Frick Collection   Upper East Side

My favorite of all of New York's museums, the Frick really does almost feel like visiting the house of a very rich friend with an amazing art collection. Housed in the 1914 mansion of the industrialist Henry Clay Frick (1849–1919), it can compete with many of the great and much larger institutions. The collection includes works by Rembrandt, Vermeer, Degas, Goya, Whistler, Titian, El Greco, Holbein, Turner, Boucher, Watteau, and Bellini and a whole room of Fragonards. *1 East 70th Street (at Fifth Avenue), New York, NY 10021. Tuesdays–Saturdays 10 A.M.–6 P.M., Sundays 11 A.M.–5 P.M. Closed Mondays. Adults $15, students $5.* **212-288-0700.** *www.frick.org.*

Gracie Mansion   Upper East Side

Archibald Gracie built his country house in 1799, back when the northern reaches of New York City were around 14th Street. By the time it became the official residence of New York's mayors, it was right in the middle of an affluent residential neighborhood. The architecture is Federal and the décor nineteenth century. *Official visitors to the city stay here. East End Avenue and 88th Street, New York, NY 10128. Tours on Wednesdays at 10 A.M., 11 A.M., 1 P.M., and 2 P.M. Adults $7, students free. 212-570-4773 (tour reservations). www.nyc. gov.*

Grand Central Terminal   Midtown

People call it Grand Central Station, but since it's the terminus of rail lines, not a station along the way, it's properly called a terminal. And since its restoration in the 1990s, it's become a lot more than a place to catch a commuter train. Opened in 1913, Grand Central is a thing of grandeur, with Beaux Arts architeeture, grand staircases, 75-foot-tall windows, and its star-studded ceiling. There are also restaurants, a large food market, and a bevy of shops. Pick up a map at the "I Love New York" information window in the Main Concourse. And there are tours on Wednesdays, sponsored by the Municipal Arts Society. *Park Avenue and 42nd Street, New York, NY 10017. Suggested donation for tours: $10. 212-340-2345 (for tours) or 212-935-3960. www.grandcentralterminal.com.*

Guggenheim Museum   Upper East Side

The Solomon R. Guggenheim Museum is one of the few art institutions that is talked about more for its building than for its collection. But that's the effect Frank Lloyd Wright's inverted ziggurat design, sometimes described as resembling a nautilus shell or a piece of white ribbon unfurling, has had on people since the museum opened in 1959. It is a very different museum experience, starting at the top of the building and moving down the gently sloping continuous ramp, back to the ground floor. Along the way you'll find works by Picasso, Chagall, Mondrian, and Kandinsky, among others. *1071 Fifth Avenue (at 89th Street), New York, NY 10128. Saturdays–Wednesdays 10 A.M.–5:45 P.M., Fridays 10 A.M.–7:45 P.M. Closed Thursdays. Adults $18, students $15, children under 12 free. 212-423-3500. www.guggenheim.org.*

Jewish Museum   Upper East Side

Torah decorations, Hanukkah lamps, a fourth-century glass vessel, and Richard Avedon photographs are among the 28,000 objects in the collection of the Jewish Museum, whose purpose is to explore Jewish culture and history through art. Housed in the old Felix Warburg mansion, the museum also features works by Chagall and a film and video department, the National Jewish Archive of Broadcasting. *1109 Fifth Avenue (at 92nd Street), New York, NY 10128. Saturdays–Wednesdays 11 A.M.–5:45 P.M., Thursdays 11 A.M.–8 P.M. Closed Fridays. Adults $12, students $7.50, children under 12 free.* **212-423-3200.** *www.jewishmuseum.org.*

The Little Church Around the Corner   Murray Hill

It's Episcopalian and its real name is the Church of the Transfiguration, but it's been known by its nickname since 1870 when another church refused to hold a funeral there because the deceased was an actor. But, they said, there was a "little church around the corner" that might do "that sort of thing." The 1849 English neo-Gothic church, complete with English garden, has had a special connection with actors ever since. The sanctuary, with its brass pulpit, Venetian mosaic rondels, and white marble parapet, is worth seeing, too. *1 East 29th Street (at Fifth Avenue), New York, NY 10016.* **212-684-6770.** *www.littlechurch.org.*

Marble Collegiate Church   Murray Hill

A statue of Dr. Norman Vincent Peale stands out front. Peale, the author of *The Power of Positive Thinking*, was pastor at Marble Collegiate for 52 years. The church, dedicated in 1854, was built from solid blocks of marble and has Tiffany stained-glass windows and a 215-foot spire topped with a Dutch-style weather vane. This was originally the Collegiate Reformed Protestant Dutch Church of the City of New York. *Fifth Avenue at 29th Street, New York, NY 10001. Sanctuary open for viewing on weekdays 10 A.M.–noon and 2 P.M.–4 P.M.* **212-686-2770.** *www.marblechurch.org.*

Metropolitan Museum of Art   Upper East Side

At this, the grandest of all New York's museums, you name it and they've got it: medieval, modern, Greek, Roman, Egyptian, Islamic, and ancient near Eastern art; European and American painting and sculpture; decorative arts; arms and armor; and five centuries' worth of fashions and accessories at the Costume Institute. *1000 Fifth Avenue (at 82nd Street), New York, NY 10028. Tuesdays–Thursdays and Sundays 9:30 A.M.–5:30 P.M., Fridays and Saturdays 9:30 A.M. to 9 P.M. Closed Mondays. Adults $20, students $10, children under 12 free.* **212-535-7710.** *www.metmuseum.org.*

Morgan Museum & Library   Murray Hill

This Italian Renaissance–style palazzo started out as the private library of the financier Pierpont Morgan (1837–1913), adjacent to his home. Today it's one of the city's most treasured museums, with a collection of artistic, literary, and musical works that includes a 1455 Gutenberg Bible and works by Mozart, Rubens, and Thoreau. *225 Madison Avenue (at 36th Street), New York, NY 10016. Tuesdays–Thursdays 10:30 A.M.–5 P.M., Fridays 10:30 A.M.–9 P.M., Saturday 10 A.M.–6 P.M., Sundays 11 A.M.–6 P.M. Closed Mondays. Adults $12, students and children under 16 $8.* **212-685-0008.** *www.morganlibrary.org/.*

Mount Vernon Hotel Museum   Upper East Side

Mount Vernon, one of the oldest buildings in New York, was built in 1799 as a carriage house and became a hotel in 1826. Weary city residents would take a stagecoach or a steamboat up to what was then the country and get away from it all. Eight furnished period rooms are open for viewing. *421 East 61st Street (between First and York Avenues), New York, NY 10065. Tuesdays–Saturdays 11 A.M.–4 P.M. (In June and July, till 9 P.M. on Tuesdays.) Closed the month of August. Adults $8, students $7, children under 12 free.* **212-838-6878.** *www.mvhm. org.*

Museo Del Barrio   Upper East Side

Sure, there are paintings, prints, sculptures, photographs, and films here, but there are also dolls, nativity scenes, musical instruments, and masks. The museum's specialty is the art and culture of the Caribbean and Latin American, from the pre-Columbian era to the present. *1230 Fifth Avenue (at 104th Street), New York, NY 10029. Wednesdays–Sundays 11 A.M.–5 P.M. Adults $6, students $4, children under 12 free.* **212-831-7272.** *www.elmuseo.org.*

Museum of the City of New York   Upper East Side

If you love New York, this museum is a must during your visit. There are more than 1.5 million objects and images connected with the city, including fashions, furniture, and textiles as far back as the seventeenth century, theater memorabilia dating back to the eighteenth century, toys dating as far back as the colonial period, paintings, sculptures, prints, photographs, and decorative arts.

1220 Fifth Avenue (at 103rd Street), New York, NY 10029. Tuesdays–Sundays 10 A.M.–5 P.M. Closed Mondays, except holidays. Adults $9, students $5, children under 12 free. 212-534-1672. www.mcny.org.

National Academy Museum   Upper East Side

The National Academy houses a remarkable collection of nineteenth- and twentieth-century American art, including works by John Singer Sargent, Childe Hassam, Thomas Eakins, Cass Gilbert, Winslow Homer, and Jasper Johns, covering schools of art from the Federal period to abstraction and magic realism. Housed in the old Huntington mansion since 1942, the museum is affiliated with the School of Fine Arts at 5 East 89th Street. *1083 Fifth Avenue (at 89th Street), New York, NY 10128. Tuesdays–Thursdays 10 A.M.–5 P.M., Fridays 10 A.M.–6 P.M., Saturdays–Sundays 11 A.M.–6 P.M. Closed Mondays. Adults $10, students $5, children under 12 free. 212-369-4880. www.nationalacademy.org.*

Neue Galerie New York   Upper East Side

Fans of early-twentieth-century German and Austrian art—and that includes decorative and applied arts—will be in heaven here. The artists represented include Gustav Klimt, Egon Schiele, Vasily Kandinsky, Paul Klee, Marcel Breuer, and Ludwig Mies van der Rohe. The mansion that houses the museum was once the home of Mrs. Cornelius Vanderbilt III. *1048 Fifth Avenue (at 86th Street), New York, NY 10028. Saturdays–Mondays and Thursdays 11 A.M.– 6 P.M., Fridays 11 A.M.–9 P.M. Adults $15, students $10, children under 12 not admitted. 212-628-6200. www.neuegalerie.org.*

New York Public Library   Midtown

The lions guarding the front steps are nicknamed Patience and Fortitude. They have been guarding the main branch of the library, now the Humanities and Social Sciences Library, since this grand Beaux Arts building was dedicated in 1911, on the site of the old reservoir. The city's research libraries now house 43.6 million items, 15.6 million of them books. There are 86 branches of the lending library. *Fifth Avenue and 42nd Street, New York, NY 10018. Mondays and Thursdays–Saturdays 11 A.M.–6 P.M., Tuesdays–Wednesdays 11 A.M.– 7:30 P.M., Sundays 1 P.M.–5 P.M. Guided tours 11 A.M. and 2 P.M. Mondays– Saturdays and 2 P.M. Sundays, beginning at the entrance to Gottesman Hall, First Floor. 212-930-0830. www.nypl.org.*

Roosevelt Island Tram   Midtown

Roosevelt Island, which lies across the East River and was redeveloped as a residential neighborhood in the 1970s, has sights to see. There's a nineteenth-century lighthouse, a chapel from the same period, the ruins of both a psychiatric hospital and another medical building, sports playing fields, and picnic rounds. But what people seem to love is the trip over, on the little red aerial tram. It takes about four minutes and offers great city views from 250 feet above the river. *Second Avenue and 59th Street, New York, NY 10044. Every 15 minutes, more often during rush hour. Adults $2 one-way, students $2 round-trip. 212-832-4540 or 212-832-4555. www.rioc.com.*

St. Bartholomew's Church   Midtown

If you doubt that St. Bart's, which is Episcopal, has a distinguished history, consider that Leopold Stokowski was once the choir director. The church was founded in 1835, but this limestone and brick building was dedicated in 1918, partly Romanesque to match the portal (which was brought over from the old church on Madison Avenue) and partly Byzantine. Fans of old movies will recall that in *Arthur* Dudley Moore's character left his fiancée at the altar here, abandoning her for Liza Minnelli. *Park Avenue between 50th and 51st Streets, New York, NY 10022. 212-378-0200. www.stbarts.org.*

St. Patrick's Cathedral   Midtown

It's the largest Gothic-style Roman Catholic cathedral in the country and quite an impressive sight, of white marble with its spires rising 330 feet above street level. St. Patrick's was dedicated in 1879, and since then the skyscrapers of Midtown have grown up around it. Next door to Saks Fifth Avenue and across the street from Rockefeller Center, the church is sometimes crowded with more tourists than worshippers. *Fifth Avenue between 50th and 51st Streets, New York, NY 10022. 212-753-2261. www.stpatrickscathedral.org.*

Temple Emanu-El   Upper East Side

Completed in 1929 and restored between 2004 and 2006, Temple Emanu-El is the largest synagogue in the world, with room for some 2,500 worshippers. Besides the stunning interior space of the sanctuary, the Romanesque limestone building has Byzantine elements, huge bronze doors, a multicolored ceiling, and a stained-glass window with a giant Star of David at its center. The temple also houses a museum (admission is free) dedicated to Jewish life and the congregation's history. *1 East 65th Street (at Fifth Avenue), New York, NY 20032. Visitors welcome Sundays–Thursdays 10 A.M.–4:30 P.M.* **212-744-1400.** *www.emanuelnyc.org.*

United Nations   Midtown

Technically you leave the United States when you enter the UN headquarters, identifiable by the flags of its member nations along First Avenue. You're in international territory here. The complex, which was completed in 1952, consists of the Secretariat (which looks a little like a 39-story version of the monolith in *2001: A Space Odyssey*), the General Assembly, the Conference Building, and the Dag Hammarskjold Library. There's a lovely garden open to visitors, too. *First Avenue and 42nd to 46th Streets, New York, NY 10017. Mondays–Thursdays 9:30 A.M.–4:45 P.M., weekends and holidays 10 A.M.–4:30 P.M. Adults $11.50, high school and college students $7.50, students in grades 1–8 $8.50, children under 5 not permitted.* **212-963-1234.** *www.un.org.*

Whitney Museum   Upper East Side

The Whitney Museum of American Art is named for its founder, Gertrude Vanderbilt Whitney, who got its permanent collection started in 1931. Artists represented here include Edward Hopper, Thomas Hart Benton, Alexander Calder, Marsden Hartley, and Georgia O'Keeffe. The Whitney Biennial (held in 2008, 2010, etc.) is a major event in the art world. *945 Madison Avenue (at 75th Street), New York, NY 10021. Wednesdays–Thursdays and Saturdays–Sundays 11 A.M.–6 P.M., Fridays 1 P.M.–9 P.M. Closed Mondays and Tuesdays.* **212-570-3614.** *www.whitney.org.*

Fabulous Cocktail Hours

From Midtown to the Upper East Side, there are truly some fabulous places to have a drink before dinner or at the end of an enjoyably busy day. But prices are relatively high; you're paying for atmosphere much of the time. And there may be a dress code (e.g., jackets for gentlemen, tie optional, at the Four Seasons). With the exception of the Boathouse's bar, these are not places to pop into when you're in your T-shirts, shorts, and sneakers.

Bar Seine   Upper East Side

Maybe it's the velvet curtains or the onyx sconces or the perfect lighting or all the animal-print fabrics, but the romantic Bar Seine, inside the Plaza-Athenée Hotel, is very close to the perfect New York cocktail spot. And while you're sitting in this Moroccan fantasy world, you can order something from Arabelle, the hotel restaurant, to go with your drinks. Maybe it's the leather floor. *37 East 64th Street (at Madison Avenue), New York, NY 10021.* **212-734-9100.**

Bemelmans Bar   Upper East Side

If Bemelmans isn't glamorous enough for you in its quiet, tasteful, slightly playful way, you may be impossible to please. Named for Ludwig Bemelmans, the Austrian-born artist who created the *Madeline* children's books, Bemelmans is in an intimate corner of the Carlyle Hotel accented by Bemelmans Central Park mural (which includes rabbits having a picnic). The bar is black granite, the ceiling is covered with gold leaf, and the service is lovely. Bar snacks and light meals are served. There is entertainment in the evenings. And on weekends, there are special Madeline teas, complete with a storyteller and hot fudge sundaes on the menu. *35 East 76th Street (at Madison Avenue), New York, NY 10021.* **212-744-1600.**

Boathouse Bar & Grill   Central Park

You may have to wait in line, depending on how early you arrive, but it's worth a little inconvenience to enjoy a cool drink at the Boathouse's small outdoor bar right on the lake. Have an apple martini or a glass of Pinot Grigio. Have a bite, too, maybe the fruit and cheese platter, the fried calamari, or the grilled shrimp. Pretend you're a guest star in *Sex and the City. Park Drive North and 72nd Street (enter at Fifth Avenue), New York, NY 10021. Open April–November 11 A.M.–11 P.M., weather permitting.* **212-517-2233.** *www.thecentralparkboathouse. com.*

Campbell Apartment   Midtown

Back in 1923, John W. Campbell, president of the Credit Clearing House, took a private office at Grand Central Terminal and used it in the evenings for entertaining. Today his place has been restored, with lots of dark wood, dim lights, and 20-foot ceilings, and turned into a very elegant cocktail bar with a private entrance from outdoors. The signature cocktail is Prohibition Punch (which involves rum, champagne, and Grand Marnier). If you want a seat, avoid commuters' rush hours. *15 Vanderbilt Avenue (at 43rd Street), New York, NY 10017.* **212-953-0409.**

Four Seasons Bar   Midtown

That's the restaurant, not the hotel. As cocktail hour approaches, the chic Grill Room turns into the bar room. It's a beautiful, spacious setting, highlighted by the square wooden bar up front. Snacks from the restaurant menu are available. *99 East 52nd Street (between Park and Lexington Avenues), New York, NY 10021.* **212-754-9494.**

Top of the Tower   Midtown

On the 26th floor of the Beekman Tower Hotel, just a few blocks up from the United Nations, is one of the most gorgeous views in the city. Top of the Tower is a great Art Deco space with city-skyline views at tables facing west and East River views at tables facing east. To add to the romantic atmosphere, there is piano music most nights. Breakfast, lunch, and dinner are served here, but Top of the Tower is known more for its setting than its food. *3 Mitchell Place (First Avenue at 49th Street), New York, NY 10017.* **212-980-4796.**

Entertainment and Nightlife

When East Siders want nightlife, they usually go downtown or at least crosstown. But the entertainment venues on this side of Central Park are very special ones.

Café Carlyle   Upper East Side

Someone once called Café Carlyle's appeal "vintage chic," and that's right on target. The room—renovated in 2007 with new banquettes, mirrored columns, gold wallpaper, and a brand-new sound system—feels like an elegant nightclub from the '50s. The pianist and singer Bobby Short was the headliner here for decades, and his fans were afraid that after his death in 2005, the club might decline. But it's been attracting top names like Judy Collins, Elaine Stritch, Eartha Kitt, Barbara Cook, and Woody Allen and carrying on beautifully. *35 East 76th Street (entrance on Madison Avenue), New York, NY 10021.* **212-576-2232.** *www.thecarlyle.com.*

*Between the lions: The New York Public
Library at Fifth Avenue and 42nd Street.*

Feinstein's at the Regency   Upper East Side

Feinstein's is a relative newcomer, having opened in 1999. The club's namesake, Michael Feinstein, this generation's most noted interpreter of Gershwin's
music, does concerts at holiday time. During the year, performers like Betty
Buckley, Patti LuPone, Chita Rivera, Christine Ebersole, Peter Gallagher,
and Robert Klein appear. *540 Park Avenue (at 61st Street), New York, NY 10021.*
212-339-4095. *www.feinsteinsattheregency.com.*

Jazz Standard   Madison Square

This basement club in the East 20s presents shows by artists like Frank Cata-
lano, New York Voices, and Mike Holober & the Gotham Jazz Orchestra.
There's no food or drink minimum, probably because management figures
you won't be able to resist ordering barbecue from Blue Smoke, the restaurant
upstairs. On Sunday afternoons during the school year, there's a Jazz for Kids
program. *116 East 27th Street, New York, NY 10016.* ***212-576-2232.*** *www.
jazzstandard.net.*

92nd Street Y Upper East Side

The real grand old man of East Side entertainment is the 92nd Street Y, which started out doing free adult education in the 1870s. Today the Y is sort of a big-city cultural and community center serving all New Yorkers (and interested visitors) with a dizzying array of programs. Among them are lectures, panel discussions, concerts, readings, and dance performances. Guests are notable people from film, theater, music, art, dance, and public affairs. In the past you might have seen Paul McCartney, Stephen Sondheim, Barbara Walters, Oliver Stone, Margaret Thatcher, Nora Ephron, John Irving, or the lovely panel discussion that I moderated with John Waters and Broadway cast members from *Hairspray*. *1395 Lexington Avenue (at 92nd Street), New York, NY 10128. 212-415-5500. www.92y.org.*

Plan My Trip: One-Day East Side Itinerary

Even if you have only one day to devote to this side of town, you can squeeze in a lot of culture, sightseeing, and leisurely meals.

9 A.M. Breakfast:	Start the day with a homey breakfast at **Sarabeth's** on Madison Avenue. Before you leave, pick up some house-brand preserves or granola as gifts for everyone back home.
10 A.M.–1 P.M.:	Spend the morning at the **Metropolitan Museum of Art.** Check the newspapers or the museum's website to see if there's a special exhibition you want to check out. If not, choose just one or two areas to concentrate on (you can't do it all in one day, much less one morning). One possibility is the Egyptian Art galleries, followed by the Medieval Art section, which is nearby on the first floor.
1 P.M.–2:30 P.M. Lunch:	Have a seafood lunch at the famous **Oyster Bar** on the lower level of **Grand Central Terminal.** It's a good opportunity to take a look around the terminal itself and appreciate the architecture and the shops.

2:30 P.M.–5 P.M.:	Walk over to Fifth Avenue and head north into the prime shopping neighborhood, starting at 49th Street. You can take a peek at **Rockefeller Center** and **St. Patrick's Cathedral** before you go into Saks.
5 P.M.–6:15 P.M. Cocktails:	Head east to the **Top of the Tower** on the 26th floor of the Beekman Place Hotel for cocktails with a spectacular view.
6:15 P.M.–8 P.M.:	Time to go back to the hotel for a break and a little rest before dinner.
8 P.M.–Whenever. Dinner:	Have a leisurely Italian dinner at **A Voce.** If the weather is nice, ask for a table outdoors. This is your chance to check out the changing Madison Square area.

If you do have more time, check out a batch of other daily itineraries in Chapter 11. They're tailored to various parts of the city and various tastes.

Side Trip: A Day in Queens

Many air travelers arrive in the borough of Queens—both Kennedy and LaGuardia airports are there—and never set foot in it again until their departure. Maybe they feel they know the borough already, as the home of the narrow-minded sitcom character Archie Bunker from *All in the Family.* But Queens is much more. It's a rich, vibrant part of the city, worth a visit if you have the time.

Sights

Chinatown   Flushing

The second largest Chinatown in New York City also has many Korean residents. The neighborhood offers herbal medicine shops, Asian grocers, Chinese bookstores, and bubble-tea cafes mixed in with the McDonald's and Starbucks branches. Try wandering around Roosevelt Avenue, 39th Avenue, and Main Street. There's even a mall. *Subway: No. 7 to Main Street/Flushing. Bus: Numerous lines, including the 12, 13, 14, 65, and 66. www.queens.about.com.*

Flushing Meadows Corona Park   Flushing

Here we have a 1,255-acre site with an art museum, wildlife center, playground, lake, picnic grounds, and ball fields (not to mention Shea Stadium and a major tennis center). But the star of the show is the Unisphere, the 140-foot stainless steel globe from the 1964 World's Fair. However, you'll probably notice it your first day, on the way into the city from the airport. *111 54th Avenue, Flushing, NY 11365. Subway: No. 7 to Willets Point/Shea Stadium. Bus: Q48 to Roosevelt Avenue and Willets Point.* **718-760-6565.** *www.nycgovparks.org.*

Museum of the Moving Image   Astoria

Bad news: This terrific museum, next to Kaufman Astoria Studios, may still be closed for renovations when you visit. That means the film and television artifacts, the audiovisual materials, and the interactive installations are unavailable. But the museum will still be sponsoring film screenings and events throughout the city. *35th Avenue at 36th Street, Astoria, NY 11106.* **718-784-0077.** *www.movingimage.us.*

Noguchi Museum   Long Island City

The works of the sculptor Isamu Noguchi (1904–1988) in metal, wood, and clay are the focus of this worthwhile museum. There are also models for some of his larger projects. *9-01 33rd Road (at Vernon Boulevard), Long Island City, NY 11106. Subway: F to Queensbridge/21st Street. Tram: Roosevelt Island Tram plus 25-cent shuttle bus to Roosevelt Island Bridge. Saturdays–Sundays 11 A.M.– 6 P.M., Wednesdays–Fridays 10 A.M.–5 P.M. Closed Mondays and Tuesdays. Adults $10, students $5, children under 12 free.* **718-204-7088.** *www.noguchi.org.*

P. S. 1 Contemporary Art Center   Long Island City

As its name suggests, the P. S. 1 building was once a public school. Today it's the largest noncollecting contemporary art museum anywhere. But it has numerous long-term installations, including James Turrell's "Meeting" and Richard Artschwager's "blips." In the summer, there's a music festival called Warm Up. *22-25 Jackson Avenue (at 46th Avenue), Long Island City, NY 11101. Thursdays–Mondays 12 P.M.–6 P.M. Closed Tuesdays and Wednesdays. Subway: E or V to 23rd Street/Ely Avenue, 7 to 45th Road/Courthouse Square or G to 21st Street/ Van Alst. Bus: Q67 to Jackson and 46th Avenue or B61 to 46th Avenue. Adults $5,* *students $2. (Free with a Museum of Modern Art ticket bought within the last 30 days.)* **718-784-2084.** *www.ps1.org.*

Shea Stadium   Flushing

The home of the New York Mets since 1964, Shea is much newer than Yankee Stadium but just as beloved by baseball fans. Visitors are allowed to watch batting practice, starting two and a half hours before game time. *123-01 Roosevelt Avenue, Flushing, NY 11368. Subway: No. 7 to Willets Point/Shea Stadium. The E, F, Q, R, and V trains all connect with the 7 at 74th Street-Broadway/Roosevelt Avenue.* **718-507-METS.** *www.mets.mlb.com.*

Restaurants

Park Side   Corona   Italian $ $

Dinnertime at Park Side has been compared to a scene from the Mafia movie *Goodfellas.* It has also been described as existing in a time warp, but obviously plenty of people enjoy the illusion of being back in the old days. *The New York Magazine* critic liked the grill fish and veal dishes. *107-01 Corona Avenue (at 51st Street), Corona, NY 11368.* **718-271-9274.** *www.parksiderestaurant.com.*

WALKING WITH YOUR DESSERT

After dinner, you could have a true Queens experience by paying a visit to Lemon Ice King of Corona. The Italian-style ices here come in many flavors (including peanut butter), but lemon is the classic. There are no tables, but you'll want to stroll with your dessert anyway. Lemon Ice King is near Flushing Meadows Corona Park, Shea Stadium, and the restaurant Park Side. *52-02 108th Street (at 52nd Avenue), Corona, NY 11368. 10 A.M.–12 midnight.* **718-699-5133.**

Taverna Kyclades   Astoria   Greek $ $

There are some 21 seafood choices on the menu here, and the specialty of the house is a dish containing stuffed clams, stuffed shrimp, lobster tail, filet of sole, and scallops. There are meat dishes, too, including a pork kabob and grilled quail. And in case that doesn't sound Greek enough for you, appetizers include stuffed grape leaves and pan-fried cheese. *33-07 Ditmars Boulevard (between 33rd and 35th Streets), Astoria, NY 11105.* **718-545-8666.** *www. tavernakyclades.com.*

Trattoria L'Incontro   Astoria   Italian 💲💲

Declared one of the best Italian restaurants in New York, L'Incontro offers a wide-ranging menu, including pastas (among them, old-fashioned spaghetti and meatballs), risottos, and individual pizzas. The signature dish is Mezza Luna ravioli. There's music with dinner on Tuesday, Wednesday, Thursday, and Sunday nights. *21-76 31st Street, Astoria, NY 11105.* **718-721-3532.** *www. trattorialincontro.com.*

Water's Edge   Long Island City   American 💲💲

A spectacular view of the Midtown Manhattan skyline is the attraction here. To go with it, there's a piano lounge with wood-burning fireplace, a promenade for outdoor dining in good weather, and a three-course prix fixe dinner with more than the usual number of choices (including rack of lamb, Arctic salmon, Long Island duckling, and grilled sirloin). *On the East River at 44th Drive, Long Island City, NY 11101. By sea: free shuttle from 34th Street pier.* **718-482-0033.** *www.watersedgenyc.com.*

Archie Bunker never had it so good. Now it's time to go back to Manhattan and explore the city on the other side of the park.

Part **3**

The West Side

No one can truly see New York City without spending time on the West Side. Times Square, Lincoln Center, and the lights of Broadway are among its best-known assets. It's also the route of the Macy's Thanksgiving Day Parade. This section details some noteworthy places to stay and eat, as well as things to do and see, from busy Sixth Avenue to the grand Hudson River.

Getting Comfortable on the West Side

In This Chapter

- ❦ Finding your way around
- ❦ West Side hotels, old and new
- ❦ Three scenic sightseeing walks

If the only thing that comes to mind when you think of Manhattan's West Side is the classic Broadway musical *West Side Story*, about street gangs and forbidden love, you have some pleasant surprises in store. Close to a half century has passed since Hollywood shot the 1961 movie version in New York. Today, the West Side streets where the Jets and the Sharks and Natalie Wood and Richard Beymer sang and danced are considerably more glamorous. In fact, Lincoln

Center—the city's premier performing arts center—stands there in all its marble-fountain glory.

So let the Upper East Siders say what they will about the elegance of Park and Fifth Avenues. The West Side has plenty to brag about, from Herald Square (maybe you've heard of a little store called Macy's) down on 34th Street to a beautiful urban corner of the Ivy League (that would be Columbia University) roughly five miles north, with Broadway, Times Square, and some very fashionable residential neighborhoods in between.

Finding Your Bearings on the West Side

You know already that Manhattan is divided by Fifth Avenue, so if you are even an inch west of Fifth, you are technically on the West Side. That means the **Plaza** (which is now half hotel, half apartment building) is on the West Side, but **FAO Schwarz,** just across the street, is on the East Side. Technically, all of **Central Park** is on the West Side, but when people talk about this side of town, they normally mean the Theater District and the residential Upper West Side, with Columbus Circle in between.

Below that, the best-known thoroughfare is 34th Street, where you'll find **Macy's** (stretching from Sixth to Seventh Avenues), **Madison Square Garden** and **Penn Station** (from Seventh to Eighth), and the **Javits Convention Center** (all the way over on 11th Avenue).

AULD LANG MISERY

If you enjoy being cold, crushed (by thousands of fellow tourists), regimented (the police are understandably determined to maintain order), and standing in one spot for hours for no good reason, by all means go to Times Square on New Year's Eve. Otherwise, get yourself to a nice dinner or small party that night and watch it on TV. Or reserve a nice, warm restaurant table (months in advance, of course) with a view of the crowd below. Or visit New York in November; the Macy's Thanksgiving Day Parade isn't nearly as crazed.

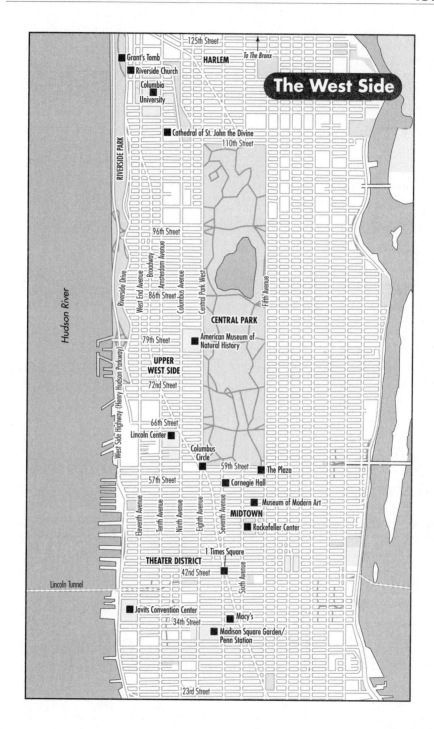

The West Side

Grant's Tomb
Riverside Church
Columbia University
HARLEM
125th Street
To The Bronx

Cathedral of St. John the Divine
110th Street

RIVERSIDE PARK

96th Street

Riverside Drive
West End Avenue
Broadway
Amsterdam Avenue
Columbus Avenue
Central Park West
Fifth Avenue

86th Street

Hudson River

CENTRAL PARK

79th Street
American Museum of Natural History

UPPER WEST SIDE

72nd Street

West Side Highway (Henry Hudson Parkway)

66th Street

Lincoln Center

Columbus Circle

59th Street
The Plaza

57th Street
Carnegie Hall

Eleventh Avenue
Tenth Avenue
Ninth Avenue
Eighth Avenue
Seventh Avenue
Sixth Avenue

Museum of Modern Art
MIDTOWN
Rockefeller Center

1 Times Square

THEATER DISTRICT
42nd Street

Lincoln Tunnel

Javits Convention Center
34th Street
Macy's
Madison Square Garden/ Penn Station

23rd Street

Times Square and the Theater District

That's **Times Square,** by the way, not Time Square (please!). Once known as Longacre Square, it was renamed for *The New York Times* in 1904 when the newspaper moved its offices there, into the tower that is now One Times Square. The newspaper moved half a block away to 229 West 43rd Street in 1913 and then another few blocks—all the way to Eighth Avenue and 41st Street—in 2007, but the name remains.

I was once crossing Broadway on 43rd Street, mere feet from the tower where the Waterford crystal ball falls on New Year's Eve, when I heard an out-of-towner say to his companion, "Let's go and see Times Square and then have dinner." Ever the smart-aleck New Yorker, I offered my help. "This is it," I said, indicating the area with a sweep of my arm. "Enjoy your meal."

If there's an exact spot that can be called Times Square, it is that little island that divides Broadway and Seventh Avenues, where One Times Square stands. But the streets around it, blinking bright with huge electronic ads and video at all hours, are also Times Square. Stand on that island, and you can see, among other things, the studios of MTV and ABC and the lights of Broadway.

You are indeed in the middle of the Theater District. In fact, Times Square and the Theater District are pretty much synonymous—except that there are Broadway theaters as far north as 51st Street.

Columbus Circle

Head north from Times Square and you'll find yourself at what has become one of the city's most beautiful intersections: **Columbus Circle.** A statue of Christopher Columbus, who has been standing atop his 70-foot granite columns since 1892, has a new fountain setting (created in 2005) in the traffic circle now surrounded by the Time Warner Center, the Trump International Hotel, and the leafy southwest corner of Central Park.

For years, while the old Coliseum convention center sat empty, this was an undistinguished corner on the edge of Midtown. Since the **Time Warner Center** opened in 2004, it has become a major hub of upscale shopping and dining. (Inside that "shopping mall" are some of the city's fanciest, priciest restaurants.)

Most important, **Lincoln Center** (which includes the Metropolitan Opera House, Avery Fisher Hall, and Juilliard) is just half a dozen blocks north.

WHAT'S IN A NAME?

Off-Broadway theater is a term that has almost nothing to do with geography. It has to do with the size of the theaters (small). Off-Broadway and off-off Broadway theaters can be in the East Village or the far West 40s or almost anywhere (even on Broadway, like the late, lamented Promenade, which operated at Broadway and 76th Street for more than four decades).

The Upper West Side

After Lincoln Center, the most famous building on the Upper West Side is probably the **American Museum of Natural History** (entrance on Central Park West between 79th and 81st Streets), where generations of little New Yorkers have been introduced to dinosaur skeletons, among other things. Between those two landmarks and above them, however, is a residential neighborhood of distinction that is equally popular with families (lots of older buildings with bigger apartment layouts) and actors and musicians (ever so convenient to work, when work is Broadway or Lincoln Center).

Central Park West, West End Avenue, and Riverside Avenue are the premier residential avenues, and charming townhouses and brownstone apartment buildings still line most of the side streets.

West End, by the way, was named for London's Theater District; it was originally planned as a commercial avenue, while Broadway was expected to be the residential avenue. Things turned out just the opposite.

Residents of West End and Riverside have a long walk (well, four blocks) to Central Park, but they have their own gorgeous stretch of urban nature. **Riverside Park** runs from 72nd to 158th Streets alongside the Hudson River.

Around 116th Street in a neighborhood known as **Morningside Heights,** the campus of **Columbia University,** founded in 1754, begins. This neighborhood has other major attractions: the **Cathedral of St. John the Divine** (Amsterdam Avenue between 110th and 113th Streets), **Riverside Church** (Riverside Avenue between 120th and 122nd Streets), and **Grant's Tomb** (across from Riverside Church).

Just above and to the east of Columbia is **Harlem,** a center of African American culture now thriving commercially, too. The main thoroughfare is 125th Street, where you'll find the **Apollo Theater** still going strong.

HOW DO YOU GET TO CARNEGIE HALL?

Just walk up Seventh Avenue (to 57th Street) and turn right. This world-famous concert hall named for Andrew Carnegie has been standing there since 1891, back when this part of town was the suburbs.

West Side Hotels

There are advantages to staying on the West Side. It's easier to get to Lincoln Center or the Theater District. Facing west, you'll get beautiful sunsets over the river. And you can find a hotel of just about any size, style, and price.

Beacon Hotel   Upper West Side $ $

This modest 255-room property is right across the street from Fairway, the ultimate Upper West Side food-shopping experience, and right next door to the Beacon Theater, a venue that draws acts as big and as varied as James Taylor, James Blunt, P. J. Harvey, and Foo Fighters. The Beacon offers wireless Internet, an Equinox fitness center on the premises, and a kitchenette in every room. *2130 Broadway (at 75th Street), New York, NY 10023. **212-787-1100** or **1-800-572-4969.** www.beaconhotel.com.*

Doubletree Guest Suites   Times Square $ $ $ $

You couldn't be more in the middle of things. If you're a fan of the TKTS booth, where New Yorkers and out-of-towners alike stand in line for half-price Broadway theater tickets, this could become your favorite place. The booth is right across the street from this bustling, family-friendly, 460-suite hotel, and the Palace Theater is right downstairs. The one-bedroom suites have sofa beds in the living room, so you can squeeze Mom, Dad, and a couple kids into one. There's a fitness center, wireless access, and in-room "wet bar" (which includes a microwave, coffeemaker, and refrigerator). *1568 Broadway (at 47th Street), New York, NY 10036.* **212-719-1600, 1-877-874-7127,** *or* **1-800-222-TREE.** *www.nyc.doubletreehotels.com.*

Empire Hotel   Just above Columbus Circle $ $ $ $

The neighborhood almost lost this longtime favorite to a condo conversion. But as of 2007, the Empire is back and more elegant than ever—with kitschy zebra-print accessories in the lobby, a rooftop pool (heated, of course), 24-hour room service, a fitness center, and a true lobby bar. And your front door is exactly 50 paces (I counted) from Lincoln Center. *44 West 63rd Street (between Broadway and Amsterdam Avenue), New York, NY 10023.* **212-265-7400.** *www.empirehotelnyc.com.*

Excelsior Hotel   Upper West Side $ $

The location is terrific on a gorgeous residential block (hey, if it's good enough for Jerry Seinfeld …) across the street from the American Museum of Natural History and mere steps from Central Park. The Excelsior, in a landmarked building that went up in 1922 as the Hotel Standish, offers old-fashioned elegance in some 200 rooms and suites—lots of them with museum/park views at moderate prices. It has wireless Internet, a fitness center, and a breakfast room. *45 West 81st Street (between Central Park West and Columbus Avenue), New York, NY 10024.* **212-362-9200.** *www.excelsiorhotelny.com.*

Hilton Times Square   Times Square $ $ $ $

This Hilton is right in the middle of the area's busiest block, on 42nd Street between Broadway and Eighth Avenue. You've got the New Amsterdam Theater, the New Liberty Theater, Madame Tussauds, and the biggest McDonald's in town nearby. Happily, the guest rooms in this 44-story tower start on the 23rd floor, so you're well above the fray. There's wireless Internet, a fitness center, 24-hour room service, and—on the sky-lobby level—a small bar with nice northern views and the restaurant Above. This Hilton is a nonsmoking property, by the way. *234 West 42nd Street, New York, NY 10036.* **212-840-2222** *or* **1-800-HILTONS.** *www. hiltonfamilynewyork.com.*

FEELING TERRIBLY RICH

You don't have to pay $1,000 a night to soak up the atmosphere at New York's most luxurious restaurants. Just go for a drink at the lobby bar of your dream hotel and pretend.

¢ Hotel QT   Times Square $ $

It's a little disconcerting that the front desk is also a newsstand, but in a way, what could be more New York City? It's a small price to pay for affordable rooms in a place done by André Balazs, who designed the ultra-chic Mercer Hotel downtown. Just think of your guest room as a stateroom (the C line has two platform twin beds and two bunk twins) and the entire trip as a cruise. Somehow, they've squeezed in a pool, a sauna, a steam room, and a bar. And there's a DJ, so this probably isn't the place for those who hate nightlife. The place is also pet-friendly, but I'm not sure where you'd put Pooky when you got him there. *125 West 45th Street (near Avenue of the Americas), New York, NY 10036.* **212-354-2323.** *www.hotelqt.com.*

The Lucerne   Upper West Side $ $ $

It looks like a nice prewar (in this case, pre–World War I) apartment building, albeit one with an unusual terra-cotta façade, right off Amsterdam Avenue. And this 184-room property has all the conveniences of real neighborhood living, just two blocks from the legendary gourmet food shop Zabar's and the joys of H&H Bagels. Room service is from the casual-chic Nice Matin, which is right next door. *210 West 79th Street, New York, NY 10024.* **212-875-1000** *or* **1-800-492-8122.** *www.thelucernehotel.com.*

Mandarin Oriental   Columbus Circle $ $ $ $ $

Where to begin? Atop the Time Warner Center, the dazzling 35th-floor lobby leads to a tower of 248 ultra-luxurious guest rooms and suites with floor-to-ceiling windows—all the better to enjoy the Central Park, Hudson River, and skyline views. Naturally, there's a spa, a fitness center, a pool with a view, a fancy restaurant (Asiate), wireless Internet, and 24-hour room service. Sure, for the price of a night in the cheapest room here (38th floor, city view), you could buy a basic laptop or a couple of TV sets. But as someone (probably a New Yorker) once said, "You only live once." *80 Columbus Circle (at 60th Street), New York, NY 10023.* **212-805-8800** *or* **1-800-526-6566.** *www. mandarinoriental.com.*

Marriott Marquis   Times Square $ $ $ $

Everyone seems to end up staying here at one time or another. And no wonder, with its more than 1,900 rooms and suites on 50 floors. Some aspects of this two-decade-old property have lost their charm—among them the bubble elevators; the upper-lobby-level restaurants and lounges, which feel a little like an underused shopping mall food court; and the rotating rooftop restaurant. But the Marriott Marquis is right in the heart of the Theater District. In fact, it has its own Broadway theater, the Marquis, along with its own sushi bar and its own Starbucks.

If you're going at Thanksgiving and want to avoid the crowds on the street, reserve early and request a parade-view room. There's also a fitness center and high-speed Internet. This Marriott is a nonsmoking property. *1535 Broadway (at 45th Street), New York, NY 10036.* **212-704-8930** *or* **1-800-843-4898.** *www. nymarriottmarquis.com.*

UP ON THE ROOF

There's a reason New York City isn't filled with rotating rooftop restaurants. The views aren't that satisfying. If you want a breathtaking view of the Manhattan skyline, have dinner at the River Café in Brooklyn. Anyway, it's unnatural for anything in the city (except rush-hour traffic) to move that slowly.

The Michelangelo — Just north of Times Square — $ $ $ $ $

The lobby is ornate. The 178 elegantly decorated guest rooms and suites are large by New York standards (as are the bathtubs). The Michelangelo likes to bill itself as an Italian villa experience, but the rooms have neoclassical décor and some of the suites are done in country French and Art Deco. There's a fitness center, high-speed Internet, 24-hour room service, and Insieme, a sleek two-menu Italian restaurant. *152 West 51st Street, New York, NY 10019. 212-765-1900 or 1-800-237-0990. www.michelangelohotel.com.*

Your driver is waiting: The larger the hotel, the more likely you are to find a line of taxis at the front door.

The Muse Hotel — Times Square — $ $ $

The Muse is a pleasant boutique hotel on an otherwise slightly cluttered block, with 200 rooms and suites, contemporary furnishings, and various little luxuries. The emphasis seems to be on countering the stresses of New York, with in-room spa services, complimentary yoga accessories, and the like. There's a fitness center, wireless Internet, and District, an American-menu restaurant with a David Rockwell interior. *130 West 46th Street, New York, NY 10036. 212-485-2400 or 1-877-692-6873. www.themusehotel.com.*

The Paramount Hotel — Times Square — $ $ $

If you like white, you will probably love the Paramount's tiny all-white guest rooms, each dominated by one big piece of art. Ask for one of the newly renovated rooms; their amenities include 32-inch flat-screen TVs. The hotel also has a mezzanine restaurant, two bars, and a gourmet takeout place on lobby level. *235 West 46th Street, New York, NY 10036.* **212-764-5500.** *www. nycparamount.com.*

The Plaza   Midtown $ $ $ $ $

The century-old grande dame of New York hotels has been turned into multi-million-dollar apartments. But they left 282 rooms and suites as hotel accommodations. The Palm Court and Oak Room and Bar are back. There's a new champagne bar and the Rose Club, where the Persian Room nightclub used to be. The Plaza offers almost every imaginable luxury, and guests pay dearly for the glory of it all. *768 Fifth Avenue (at 59th Street), New York, NY 10019.* **212-759-3000** *or* **1-800-257-7544.** *www.fairmont.com.*

Trump International
Hotel & Tower   Columbus Circle $ $ $ $ $

An unassuming little lobby leads you to Donald Trump's most recent (1997) hotel undertaking. The rooms, which are on the 3rd to 17th floors, aren't particularly large—but most of them (132 out of 167) are suites with full kitchens and floor-to-ceiling Central Park views. The hotel even provides a telescope so that guests can get a good look at the city (and possibly their neighbors) without leaving their rooms. Guests will also find a 6,000-square-foot fitness center, and the 24-hour room service is from Jean-Georges, a restaurant of note (to say the least). *1 Central Park West (at 60th Street), New York, NY 10023.* **212-299-1000** *or* **1-888-44-TRUMP.** *www.trumpintl.com.*

West End Studios and Hostel   Upper West Side $

If you want to go low budget and are willing to share a bathroom, this 85-room hostel in the middle of a quiet, residential neighborhood and a block from Riverside Park could be for you. Granted, it's farther uptown than you'd ever expect to be. I can vouch for the neighborhood, but that's all *850 West End Avenue (between 101st and 102nd Streets), New York, NY 10025.* **212-662-6000** *or* **1-888-6-HOSTEL.** *www.westendstudios.com.*

Crossroads of the world: News, video, bright lights, and New York's Finest in Times Square.

Fabulous Walks, From River to Park

Here are three walking tours that will help you get to know the West Side.

Times Square to Central Park

Start at 40th Street and Eighth Avenue with a quick look at the new (2007) building of *The New York Times,* at 620 Eighth Avenue, across from **Port Authority,** New York's bustling, decidedly unglamorous bus station.

Head uptown (north) and turn right on 42nd Street, the formerly naughty, bawdy thoroughfare of musical fame that's now a center of family entertainment. Between Eighth Avenue and Broadway you'll pass **Madame Tussauds Wax Museum,** a couple of major theaters, and a gigantic McDonald's.

Turn left on Broadway and you're in the heart of **Times Square.** One Times Square, with the electronic news zipper, is on the island at 43rd Street. The **ABC News** studios are on your right at 44th. The **MTV** studios are on the second floor on your left.

Eat your heart out, Los Angeles: the nighttime Manhattan skyline from Top of the Rock.
(Photo courtesy of Top of the Rock.)

Where "The Godfather" got his start: the Ellis Island Immigration Museum, a quick ferry ride from Manhattan. (Photo © Photodisc.)

Art Deco rules: the lights of the Chrysler Building's top floors standing out in the Midtown skyline. (Photo © Photodisc.)

Patriot act: the Empire State Building showing its colors for the Fourth of July.
(Photo © Photodisc.)

Just call it Sixth: some streets and avenues are so nice they named them twice. (Photo © Photodisc.)

Optical illusion: The streets were never really paved with gold, as immigrants had hoped, but sometimes they look that way. (Photo © Photodisc.)

Angel in America: Bethesda Fountain, unveiled in 1873, in the heart of Central Park.
(Photo © Photodisc.)

On the way to the airport: the Unisphere, a gigantic stainless-steel globe from the 1964
World's Fair, still stands in a Queens park. (Photo © Photodisc.)

Stuart Little boated here: Conservatory Water in Central Park, with Fifth Avenue apartment buildings beyond. (Photo © Photodisc.)

There used to be real sheep here: New Yorkers and visitors relaxing in the Sheep Meadow in Central Park. (Photo © Photodisc.)

French import: the Statue of Liberty presiding over New York Harbor since 1886.
(Photo © Photodisc.)

Turn left at 45th Street for a peek at some major Broadway theaters, including the **Shubert,** which opened in 1913 and where *A Chorus Line* ran for 15 years (1975–1990).

Cross **Shubert Alley,** over to 46th Street, and turn right to go back to Broadway. Now turn left and keep heading uptown. You'll pass the **TKTS** booth on 47th Street, the **Brill Building** (1619 Broadway), once the headquarters of the popular music industry, at 49th Street, and the **Ed Sullivan Theater** (1697 Broadway), home of *The Late Show With David Letterman,* on 53rd Street.

Continue north to 57th Street, which used to be an elegant shopping street but now largely caters to the strictly tourism-minded (not you!). But **Carnegie Hall** is still there, on the southeast corner of Seventh and 57th.

Central Park is two blocks north, just on the other side of **Columbus Circle,** which you'll recognize by its fountain, with the **Time Warner Center** shopping and restaurant complex on your left.

Distance: Approximately 2 miles.

Great Apartment Buildings of the Upper West Side

Start at the corner of Central Park West and 72nd Street, heading uptown. The park is on your right, and the great Victorian Gothic **Dakota** (1 West 72nd Street), built in 1884, is on your left. The building has had a bevy of famous residents, including Leonard Bernstein, Rudolf Nureyev, and Lauren Bacall, but it's probably best known now as the site of the 1968 urban-horror film *Rosemary's Baby* and, sadly, as the site of John Lennon's murder by a fan in December 1980.

Head north on Central Park West, and you'll soon find yourself at the **San Remo** (145 Central Park West, between 74th and 75th Streets). As the city's original twin towers (these have Roman-style temples at the top), this classical building with an Art Deco entrance was built in 1930 and has had numerous celebrity residents. But it's probably most famous for having turned down Madonna when she tried to buy an apartment here.

Continue north, and you'll pass the **American Museum of Natural History** just before you get to the **Beresford** (211 Central Park West, with a main entrance on the avenue and two additional entrances on 81st Street). This Italian Renaissance building went up in 1929 just at the time of the stock market crash that launched the Depression. Past and present tenants include Mike Nichols, Beverly Sills, Helen Gurley Brown, Tony Randall, and Jerry Seinfeld.

Turn left on 81st and walk two blocks over to Broadway, where you'll find **Zabar's,** the food market, at 80th Street. Turn left again, and between 78th and 79th Streets you can't miss the grand courtyard of the **Apthorp,** which goes all the way over to West End Avenue. William Waldorf Astor, who once owned the whole block, planned the Apthorp, which opened in 1908.

Keep heading downtown (south) on Broadway. Just past the incomparable food market **Fairway** (at 74th Street), you'll find the Ansonia between 73rd and 74th. Opened in 1903 as a hotel, this building was once Babe Ruth's home.

Two more blocks south at 171 West 71st Street, you'll find the flamboyant Beaux-Arts **Dorilton,** which was completed in 1902. You're just a few blocks north of **Lincoln Center,** so if you haven't checked it out take a stroll around its four-decade-old performing-arts campus before you go home.

Distance: Approximately 1 mile.

Upper Upper West Side, With Park

Start at Broadway and 95th Street, beside **Symphony Space** (see Chapter 8). Walk west and as you approach West End Avenue, peek through the gate at **Pomander Walk,** one of Manhattan's more unusual housing enclaves. This little mews of two-story Tudor-style houses, most with two apartments each, was built in 1920 and has somehow survived as high-rises have sprouted up all around it.

Next head straight into **Riverside Park.** It's worth going a few blocks out of your way (left, which is south) to see the **Joan of Arc Monument** at 93rd Street and, inside the park, the exquisite **91st Street Garden,** made famous by the romantic final scene of *You've Got Mail,*—the most West Side–celebratory movie ever made.

Now walk north through the park. You'll pass a large dog run around 105th Street, and across from it, if you're visiting in warm weather, the **Hudson Beach Café** (which my friends and I insist on referring to as the Dog Run Café instead). The food's nothing special (burgers, salads, and wine and beer in plastic cups), but the view of the **Hudson River** is glorious.

Turn right and come out of the park somewhere around 110th (if you've come to the tennis courts, you've gone just a few steps too far). Head east a couple of blocks until you come to Broadway. At 112th Street, take note of **Tom's,** a diner whose exterior you may recognize from the sitcom *Seinfeld*. Go one more block east, to Amsterdam, and you've arrived at the **Cathedral of St. John the Divine** and its gardens.

Head back to Broadway and up another few blocks to **Columbia University.** The campus begins at 114th Street and it's worth a short stroll. Head one block (Claremont Avenue) or two (Riverside Drive) west and visit **Riverside Church.** And just across from its front door is **Grant's Tomb.**

Distance: Approximately 2.5 miles.

Now you know your way around three different West Side neighborhoods. When you come back to see specific sights, you'll be an old hand.

Enjoying the West Side

In This Chapter

- Great West Side restaurants, from '21' to Burger Joint
- The best stores and shopping neighborhoods
- A complete guide to West Side sightseeing
- Drinking with the rich and famous (maybe)
- Theater, music, and other nightlife
- Exploring the West Side in just one day

Once you've settled in and feel you have the lay of the land, it's time to take advantage of all the West Side has to offer. Of course, there are way too many places to see and things to do to squeeze it all into one trip, but making your own things-to-see list is part of the fun.

Great West Side Dining

On the West Side, you can eat cheaply (by New York City standards). Or you can splurge at some of the most elegant places in the world. You can also have a great meal without blowing the entire vacation budget. Restaurants in the following expensive category will cost $80 or more (in some cases, a lot more) per person for dinner. At those in the moderate category, dinner for one will run somewhere between $40 and $80. At the restaurants listed as affordable, you can generally have dinner for less than $40.

Expensive

Anthos   Midtown   Greek 💲💲💲

At Anthos, an upscale and elaborate restaurant slightly north and east of the Theater District, you'll find the usual Greek ingredients and dishes on the menu—baklava, feta cheese, avgolemono sauce—but not in the same old ways (or at the same old prices). *36 West 52nd Street (between Fifth and Sixth Avenues), New York, NY 10019.* **212-582-6900.** *www.anthosnyc.com.*

Asiate   Columbus Circle   French/Japanese 💲💲💲

The Mandarin Oriental Hotel's serene, ultra-stylish house restaurant has a floor-to-ceiling 35th-floor view of Central Park, Central Park South, and the East Side skyline beyond. Add an innovative menu of knockout fusion cuisine (think côté de boeuf in Peking duck broth), and you have an evening to remember. *80 Columbus Circle (at 60th Street), New York, NY 10023.* **212-805-8801.** *www.mandarinoriental.com.*

Café des Artistes   Upper West Side   Continental 💲💲💲

Let's face it—this elegant café, which has been around since 1917, is as pretty and as romantic as restaurants come. Café des Artistes's famous pastel murals (naked nymphs romping), mullioned windows, and invitingly diverse menu are a few blocks from Lincoln Center, just off the lobby of an apartment building that used to be the Hotel des Artistes. It's the perfect place for Dover sole or pot au feu. *1 West 67th Street (off Central Park West), New York, NY 10023.* **212-877-3500.** *www.cafenyc.com.*

Estiatorio Milos   Midtown   Greek $ $ $

The specialty here is Greek seafood—octopus, calamari, loup de mer, sardines—and the reviews are outstanding. *125 West 55th Street (between Sixth and Seventh Avenues), New York, NY 10019, 212-245-7400. www.milos.ca.*

Gordon Ramsay at
the London   Theater District   French $ $ $

The dining room is icily elegant. The chef is a celebrity. And the place, in the London NYC Hotel, had barely opened before it had two stars from the very first American edition of the Michelin restaurant guide. You'd better make reservations a month or two in advance. Expect wine sauces, caviar sauces, foie gras, and truffles in the consommé. *151 West 54th Street, New York, NY 10019. 212-468-8888. www.gordonramsay.com.*

Insieme   Theater District   Italian $ $ $

Pronounce it een-see-EM-ay, the way the Italians do. This sleek dining room, right off the lobby of the ornate Michelangelo Hotel and across the street from the Winter Garden Theater, has Italian specialties of all kinds. The restaurant critics' favorites include the bollito misto, veal tartare, shellfish stew, and strawberry tart. *777 Seventh Avenue (at 51st Street), New York, NY 10019. 212-582-1310. www.restaurantinsieme.com.*

Jean Georges   Columbus Circle   Thai-French $ $ $

Jean-Georges Vongerichten's elegant restaurant in the Trump International Hotel and Tower can do no wrong, it seems. *The New York Times* gave it four stars almost a decade after it opened. And Michelin's new American guide gave it three stars (only two other restaurants, Per Se and Le Bernardin, were awarded three). Reserve ahead to enjoy the innovative menu there, which includes Japanese snapper sashimi, duck with cracked almonds, young garlic soup, and Arctic char with porcini mushrooms and garlic. *1 Central Park West (at 60th Street), New York, NY 10023. 212-299-3900. www.jean-georges.com.*

Le Bernardin   Theater District   Seafood $ $ $

A food critic once called Le Bernardin "the restaurant equivalent of old money." Of the three New York restaurants that rated three stars in the very first

American Michelin guide, only this confident West Sider has been around since the 1980s. And it just keeps winning accolades. The décor isn't much, but the menu (which, at a recent glance, included sea urchin caviar and a very upscale surf-and-turf) will make you forget that. *155 West 51st Street (between Sixth and Seventh Avenues), New York, NY 10019.* **212-554-1515.** *www.le-bernardin.com.*

Masa   Columbus Circle   Japanese 💲 💲 💲

It'll cost you an arm and a leg (at press time, the prix fixe per person was $350), but the sushi is said to be a religious experience. The space is minimalist and serene. And at those prices, it should be. *Time Warner Center, New York, NY 10019.* **212-823-9800.** *www.masanyc.com.*

Nobu 57   Midtown   Japanese 💲 💲 💲

The original New York Nobu is in TriBeCa, but if you're not going below 14th Street this trip, this stylish uptown sibling will do just fine. All the chef's signature dishes are here, including the rock shrimp tempura and black cod. *The New York Times* restaurant critic gave it three stars. *40 West 57th Street (between Fifth and Sixth Avenues), New York, NY 10019.* **212-757-3000.** *www.noburestaurants.com.*

Per Se   Columbus Circle   American 💲 💲 💲

If you want to have dinner at this knockout hideaway of grand California cuisine (three stars from Michelin's American guide), tucked away upstairs inside the Time Warner Center, make reservations months ahead and set aside a long, lazy evening to appreciate its greatness. This is not the place for a quick pre-theater bite; the chef's tasting menu, for instance, is nine courses (but you don't have to go that far). Don't let the dishes' witty, deceptively simple names fool you. Macaroni and cheese is something much more elaborate, and the dessert they call a creamsicle isn't. *Time Warner Center, New York, NY 10023.* **212-823-9335.** *www.perseny.com.*

Petrossian   Midtown   Continental 💲 💲 💲

The setting is sumptuous and decadent. The room is hushed. The menu includes smoked salmon, Muscovy duck breast, dozens of choices of champagne, and tons of caviar. It's expensive à la carte, but a prix fixe lunch and dinner put it within the reach of mere mortals. *182 West 58th Street (off Seventh Avenue), New York, NY 10019. 212-245-2214. www.petrossian.com.*

Picholine   Upper West Side   Continental $ $ $

The chef calls this elegant, highly esteemed (three stars from the first American Michelin guide) restaurant French/Mediterranean, but you might find chicken Kiev, venison, or wild mushroom risotto on the constantly changing menu. It's just a few blocks from Lincoln Center. *35 West 64th Street (between Central Park West and Broadway), New York, NY 10023. 212-724-8585. www. picholinenyc.com.*

Porter House New York   Columbus Circle   Steak $ $ $

Porter House is an old-fashioned steak restaurant. You can tell that in many ways but particularly by the desserts (which include coconut layer cake). The dining room has wraparound windows—all the better to show off the Columbus Circle view. *Time Warner Center, New York, NY 10019. 212-823-9500. www.porterhousenewyork.com.*

⚜ Rainbow Grill/Rainbow Room   Midtown   Italian $ $ $

You can't beat the 65th-floor view and the Art Deco ambiance in the Rainbow Grill, which operates like a normal restaurant. (That is, you can make reservations for dinner or just drop in for cocktails.) The Rainbow Room itself, on the same floor, offers dinner and dancing to a big band-style orchestra, but only on certain Friday and Saturday nights. *30 Rockefeller Plaza, New York, NY 10112. 212-632-5100. www.rainbowroom.com.*

Russian Tea Room   Midtown   Russian $ $ $

Ever since the longtime owner left in 1995, the Russian Tea Room has opened, closed, been renovated, opened, and closed again. Who knows what the future will hold, but for now there's a rich menu with caviar omelets, chicken Kiev, eggplant à la russe, and beef stroganoff. And being next door to Carnegie Hall has never hurt. *150 West 57th Street (between Sixth and Seventh Avenue), New York, NY 10019. 212-581-7100. www.russiantearoomnyc.com.*

The Sea Grill   Midtown   Seafood $ $ $

Forget skyline vistas from sky-high floors. The quintessential New York restaurant view is right here at the ground-level Sea Grill, which looks out (in winter) at the ice skaters happily circling the rink at Rockefeller Plaza. But a visit here is just as much about the food; even the side dishes are fancy (such as black truffle mashed potatoes). A recent look at the menu showed bass, cod, grouper, prawns, monkfish, sushi and—appropriately enough—skate. *19 West 49th Street (between Fifth and Sixth Avenues), New York, NY 10020.* **212-332-7610.** *www.theseagrillnyc.com.*

Shun Lee West   Upper West Side   Chinese $ $ $

This gigantic palace has it all—Szechuan, Hunan, and Cantonese—and it's just a hop, skip, and a jump from Lincoln Center. The huge menu (which includes favorites such as orange beef, crispy prawns, and lobster in black bean sauce as well as less traditional dishes) and the gorgeous black lacquer décor make this special-occasion Chinese, but they do deliver. Shun Lee Café next door has dim sum. *43 West 65th Street (between Columbus Avenue and Central Park West), New York, NY 10023.* **212-595-8895.** *www.shunleewest.com.*

Lunch with a view: the daytime Manhattan skyline.

'21' Club   Midtown   Continental $ $ $

A former speakeasy, '21' still feels as if it belongs to some other era—one that you'd like to move to. Whether you have dinner in the cozy bar room downstairs or in the more spacious upstairs dining room, you'll find all the great old-fashioned standards on the menu: Dover sole, steak tartare, and the '21' burger. *21 West 52nd Street (between Fifth and Sixth Avenues), New York, NY 10019.* **212-582-7200.** *www.21club.com.*

Moderate

Angus McIndoe   Theater District   American $\boxed{\$}$ $\boxed{\$}$

Angus—as the Broadway stars, directors, and playwrights who frequent this cozy place call it—sounds Scottish, looks French (bistro style), and tastes American. You can enjoy domestic favorites such as New York strip steak, burgers, swordfish, or any-time-of-day breakfast while catching glimpses of the Broadway notables on their way to their secret upstairs room. (I'm always seated downstairs. You probably will be, too.) *258 West 44th Street (between Broadway and Eighth Avenue), New York, NY 10036.* **212-221-9222.** *www. angusmcindoe.com.*

Becco   Theater District   Italian $\boxed{\$}$ $\boxed{\$}$

A longtime Theater Row favorite, Becco is known for its all-you-can-eat pasta sampler—but it has other hearty Italian favorites. Get a table at the patio out back if you can. *355 West 46th Street (between Eighth and Ninth Avenues), New York, NY 10036.* **212-397-7597.** *www.becconyc.com.*

Bryant Park Grill   Midtown   American $\boxed{\$}$ $\boxed{\$}$

Tucked behind the New York Public Library and facing Bryant Park itself, the Bryant Park Grill has one of the prettiest settings in town. In warm weather, its patio is a fabulous spot for lunch or brunch. The menu includes steaks, pork chops, pasta, salads, and other basic American favorites. There's a children's menu, too. *25 West 40th Street (between Fifth and Sixth Avenues), New York, NY 10018.* **212-840-6500.** *www.arkrestaurants.com.*

Café Luxembourg   Upper West Side   French $\boxed{\$}$ $\boxed{\$}$

This lively Art Deco bistro a few blocks north of Lincoln Center just keeps rolling on. Café Luxembourg has been around since the early '80s, and in New York restaurant years that's venerable. The crowd is lively (okay, sometimes just plain loud) and good-looking. The room is intimate and warm.

The fare (from cassoulet to organic salmon) is just what it's supposed to be. *200 West 70th Street (between Amsterdam and West End Avenues), New York, NY 10023.* **212-873-7411.** *www.cafeluxembourg.com.*

Café Un Deux Trois   Times Square   French $ $

Un Deux Trois looks like a big Parisian brasserie and has a menu to match, with steak frites, beef bourgignon, duck à l'orange, and escargot. It's a popular, pleasant place for a pre-theater (or après-theater) meal. Crayons are provided so the kids (and others) can be creative on the paper tablecloth tops. The name is, of course, the address. *123 West 44th Street (between Sixth Avenue and Broadway), New York, NY 10036.* **212-354-4148.** *www.cafeundeuxtrois.biz.*

District   Theater District   American $ $

The Muse Hotel's house restaurant gives you a choice between serious food (even the club sandwich is ambitious, made with shrimp and pancetta) and just a bite (mini cheeseburgers, small pizzas, and the like). And there's a special late-night menu at the aptly named Mini Bar. *130 West 46th Street (between Sixth and Seventh Avenues), New York, NY 10036.* **212-485-2999.** *www. districtnyc.com.*

Docks   Upper West Side   Seafood $ $

The full name is Docks Oyster Bar and Seafood Grill, but you can get just about anything seafood-related in this popular neighborhood spot (there's an East Side Midtown branch, too). That includes lobster, fish and chips, shrimp, salmon, tuna, crab cakes, sushi, and sashimi. And if you change your mind about the fish thing, there are steaks, burgers, and pasta on the menu, too. *2427 Broadway (between 89th and 90th Streets), New York, NY 10024.* **212-724-5588.** *www.docksoysterbar.com.*

Joe Allen   Theater District   American $ $

You'll find a mix of tourists and real theater people at this beloved brick-walled Restaurant Row tavern, which has been around since 1965. The burgers are famous, as is the meatloaf sandwich—but you could also have steak, chicken, fish, a big salad, or an omelet. If you don't recognize the names of the shows on the theater posters, that's because the theme is big Broadway flops. *326 West 46th Street (between Eighth and Ninth Avenues), New York, NY 10036.* **212-581-6464.** *www.joeallenrestaurant.com.*

Marseille   Times Square   French 💲💲

Over on Ninth Avenue, Marseille is a few steps out of the way for a pre-theater lunch or dinner—but this handsome place is well worth the trip. The menu is French (steak frites, mussels, and the like), but you'll also find Mediterranean, African, and other influences (hummus, gnocchi, veal scallopine, and shrimp beignets). It has a nice bar and nice brunch. *630 Ninth Avenue (at 44th Street), New York, NY 10036.* **212-333-2323.** *www.marseillenyc.com.*

Orso   Theater District   Italian 💲💲

One of the more elegant spots on Restaurant Row, Orso is a lively, fashionable Northern Italian spot, so reserve ahead of time if you're planning pre-theater dinner there. The pastas and small pizzas are popular. You'll also find fancy salads, Tuscan seafood chowder, calf's liver, swordfish, shrimp, gelatos, and sorbets. *322 West 46th Street (between Eighth and Ninth Avenues), New York, NY 10036.* **212-489-7212.** *www.orsorestaurant.com.*

Ouest   Upper West Side   French 💲💲

There's something soothing about settling into one of the red leather booths at this bustling upscale spot, even before the food arrives. Ouest brought haute cuisine to the Upper West Side back in 2001, and it sometimes seems a little taken with itself because of that—but you can't argue with the food, from the seared tuna to the pan-roasted squab. It has a small, usually overcrowded bar. *2315 Broadway (between 83rd and 84th Streets), New York, NY 10024.* **212-580-8700.** *www.ouestny.com.*

Rosa Mexicano   Upper West Side   Mexican 💲💲

The food isn't really the attraction here. It's the striking décor, the convenience to Lincoln Center (across the street, basically), the guacamole, and the margaritas. *61 Columbus Avenue (at 62nd Street), New York, NY 10023.* **212-977-7700.** *www.rosamexicano.com.*

Ruby Foo's   Times Square/Upper West Side   Asian 💲💲

There are two Ruby Foo's, and both are lively, deliberately gaudy places with a menu that's sort of Chinese and sort of pan-Asian. Both are on Broadway but in very different neighborhoods. *1626 Broadway (at 49th Street), New York, NY 10036.* **212-489-5600.** *2182 Broadway (77th Street), New York, NY 10024.* **212-724-6700.** *www.brguestrestaurants.com.*

Telepan   Upper West Side   American $ $

Where else will you find foie gras doughnuts on the menu? The understated, critically praised Telepan and its "greenmarket cuisine" was an immediate hit when it opened in Santa Fe's old location just off Columbus Avenue—a short walk from Lincoln Center—at the end of 2005. You can get meat and potatoes here, but the place is known for its delicious seafood (like the lobster Bolognese). *72 West 69th Street (between Columbus Avenue and Central Park West), New York, NY 10023.* **212-580-4300.** *www.telepan-ny.com.*

Virgil's Real BBQ   Times Square   Southern $ $

All kinds of barbecue (pork, chicken, lamb, ribs, and the like) is the specialty in this bustling, casual theater district spot ideal for a pre-matinée lunch. I personally prefer the grilled catfish, but then it's all about the side dishes anyway (sinfully gloppy mashed potatoes with gravy, collard greens, macaroni and cheese, and the like). And the hush puppies (one serving will feed an entire family) are to die for. *152 West 44th Street, between Sixth Avenue and Broadway.* **212-921-9494** *(212-921-9663 for takeout and delivery). www.virgilsbbq.com.*

Affordable, with and without Atmosphere

Bouchon Bakery   Columbus Circle   American $

It may be right in the middle of the corridor at the Time Warner Center (the third floor), but this is not typical mall food. The chef at fancy Per Se (upstairs) offers shoppers fine sandwiches, salads, soups, quiches, and desserts (including what *New York Magazine* declared the best sticky buns in town). There's a takeout counter, convenient for Central Park picnics across the street. *10 Columbus Circle (at 60th Street), New York, NY 10019.* **212-823-9366.** *www.bouchonbakery.com.*

Burger Joint   Midtown   American $

You have to know where to look to find Burger Joint. It's hidden away in a corner of the lobby of the elegant Parker-Meridien Hotel—a pretend greasy spoon with close to greasy-spoon prices. Basically all they have is burgers and beverages (with grilled cheese sandwiches for vegetarians), but apparently that's enough because the place is usually packed. *119 West 56th Street (off Sixth Avenue), New York, NY 10019.* **212-708-7414.** *www.parkermeridien.com.*

🖼 Café Edison   Theater District   Eclectic 💲

Neil Simon once wrote, "Eating there is like going home to visit Mom." And he, like all of the café's longtime fans, calls it the Polish Tea Room. This charmingly run-down diner off the lobby of the Hotel Edison offers deli sandwiches, matzo ball soup, and other diner dishes with an Eastern European accent. Have a blintz. *228 West 47th Street (between Broadway and Eighth Avenue), New York, NY 10036.* **212-840-5000.** *www.edisonhotelnyc.com.*

Carnegie Deli   Midtown   American 💲

For a casual lunch or midnight snack with real (if slightly self-conscious) New York atmosphere, the Carnegie Deli has almost everything. The menu includes blintzes, burgers, omelets, diner-style plates, cheesecake, and gargantuan sandwiches with names such as Tongue's for the Memory, Nova on Sunday, and Bacon Whoopee. *854 Seventh Avenue (at 55th Street), New York, NY 10019.* **212-757-2245.** *www.carnegiedeli.com.*

Daisy May's BBQ USA   Theater District   Southern 💲

Well, it's on the outskirts of the theater district, anyway. Daisy May's is a little off the beaten path (all the way over on the far side of Eleventh Avenue), but it may be the best barbecue in New York (praised by Zagat's, *The New York Times,* and a lot of people in between). And they deliver. *623 Eleventh Avenue, at 46th Street.* **212-977-1500.** *www.daisymaysbbq.com.*

Gray's Papaya   Upper West Side   American 💲

¢ Okay, it's just a glorified hot dog stand, but there's a reason Gray's Papaya has been around on this same busy city corner (plus, there are two other branches) since 1973. People love these hot dogs and the fruit drinks that are the place's other specialty. Where else are you going to get a yummy lunch, dinner, or midnight snack (it's open 24 hours) for less than $4? *2090 Broadway (at 72nd Street), New York, NY 10024.* **212-799-0243.**

Hell's Kitchen   Theater District   Mexican 💲

Hell's Kitchen (which is also the name of this neighborhood within a neighborhood) serves sophisticated Mexican food in a very casual setting. *New York Magazine* liked the artichoke quesadillas and the coconut flan. Customers seem to like the margaritas and sangria. *679 Ninth Avenue (between 46th and 47th Streets), New York, NY 10036.* **212-997-1588.**

Rack & Soul   Upper West Side   Southern $

Fried chicken and barbecue come with a diverse selection of side dishes, including black-eyed peas, candied yams, stewed okra, and Belgian waffles. And if some members of your party aren't in the mood for down-home cuisine, they can have a chicken, salmon, or shrimp Caesar salad instead. Rack & Soul looks like a coffee shop, and it does do takeout and delivery—but there's wine, beer, a full bar, and comfy red booths. So a leisurely lunch or dinner isn't out of the question. *2818 Broadway (at 109th Street), New York, NY 10025.* **212-222-4800.** *www.rackandsoul.com.*

Shopping (Such as It Is)

Just a few words about the fine shopping in Times Square: there isn't any. You'll find branches of the Gap, Ann Taylor Loft, and Sephora, but that's about it. Mostly, there are souvenir shops—and you don't need any guidance about those.

Macy's

It has to be the best-known store on the West Side—if not in the entire city—thanks to the world-famous Thanksgiving Day Parade, which started back in 1924.

The Herald Square store (there are also nearby branches in Queens, Brooklyn, and Jersey City) has been in that location since 1902 (the original wooden escalators are still in use) and has billed itself as the world's largest department store since the Seventh Avenue addition back in the '20s. (Bring your cell phones or flares. It's exceedingly easy to get lost here.) Macy's is one of New York's few remaining true department stores, and it has merchandise at just about every price level.

151 West 34th Street (between Sixth and Seventh Avenues), New York, NY 10001. **212-695-4400.** *www.macys.com.*

The Shops at Columbus Circle

Manhattanites looked down their noses at shopping malls until this upscale batch of stores opened on the lower floors of the Time Warner Center, mixed in with some of the most elegant restaurants in town.

On the ground floor, you can walk straight into a spacious branch of Williams-Sonoma or take the escalator down to a cavernous Whole Foods for glamorous groceries. There are a mix of expected stores (J. Crew, Borders, Sephora, Coach, Godiva Chocolates, Benetton, and Crabtree & Evelyn) and less typical ones (Davidoff of Geneva, J. W. Cooper, Stuart Weitzman, Swarovski, Thomas Pink, and Wolford).

Columbus Circle at 60th Street, New York, NY 10019. **212-823-6300.** *www. shopsatcolumbuscircle.com.*

Times Square

Ever since the formerly squalid Times Square neighborhood underwent Disneyfication in the 1990s and became a wholesome family destination, stores and other businesses have been coming and going and opening and closing like crazy. But this has yet to result in any notable shopping in the area beyond souvenir shops. However, there are a few exceptions.

The multilevel **Virgin Megastore** (*1540 Broadway, between 45th and 46th Streets*) is indeed mega, loud, and bustling—a convenient spot for CD shopping in all genres.

Toys 'r' Us (*1514 Broadway, at 44th Street*) is just a big toy store, but it achieves specialness with a couple of features. One is a 60-foot-tall indoor Ferris wheel, which children and their adult companions can ride (souvenir photographs of the experience are available, of course). Another is a 20-foot-tall animatronic T-Rex upstairs, which is likely to thrill some young shoppers and terrify others.

Colony Music (*1619 Broadway, at 49th Street*) is one of the great old neighborhood standbys, selling sheet music, karaoke, and CDs of all kinds (Broadway cast albums are a specialty). It's just where it should be, on the ground floor of the Brill Building, where mid twentieth-century pop music was born.

Upper West Side Residential

Columbus Avenue (not to be confused with Columbus Circle), between Central Park West and Amsterdam Avenue, offers a nice mix of chic shops and neighborhood necessities (dry cleaners, liquor stores, and so on).

From the West 60s up to the American Museum of Natural History in the 80s, you'll find the likes of **Betsey Johnson, Laila Rowe, Penny Whistle Toys,** and **DWR** (Design Within Reach).

Over on Broadway just above Lincoln Center, you'll find a nest of familiar stores such as **Pottery Barn, Banana Republic,** and **Bed Bath & Beyond** all in a row. And right in the middle is one of my favorite stores anywhere, **Gracious Home** (*1992 Broadway, at 67th Street*). Don't let the diminutive ground floor fool you, attractive as it may be. Most of the merchandise (bedding, towels, dishes, luggage, cookware, bathroom fixtures, housewares, and hardware of all kinds) is on the two lower levels.

West Side Sights, A to Z

The West Side is chockfull of intriguing museums, beautiful churches, lovely views, and a great deal more. Read on.

American Folk Art Museum   Midtown

More than just quilts and weathervanes, this museum has an impressive collection of eighteenth- to twenty-first-century paintings, drawings, and sculpture and a special section devoted to the outsider artist Henry Darger. *45 West 53rd Street (between Fifth and Sixth Avenues), New York, NY 10019. Open Tuesdays–Thursdays, Saturdays and Sundays 10:30 A.M.–5:30 P.M., and Fridays 10:30 A.M.–7:30 P.M. Adults $9, students $7, children under 12 free.* **212-265-1040.** *www.folkartmuseum.org.*

American Museum of Natural History   Upper West Side

The dinosaurs are still this museum's biggest attraction, but the Rose Center for Earth and Space (which includes the Hayden Planetarium) is a close second. You'll also find the John James Audubon Gallery, the Hall of Human Origins, and dioramas galore. *Central Park West and 79th Street, New York, NY 10024. Open daily 10 A.M.–5:45 P.M. Suggested admission: adults $15, students $11, children under 12 $8.50.* **212-769-5100** *(Advance tickets:* **212-769-5200***).* www. amnh.org.

Cathedral of St. John the Divine   Upper West Side

Someday they'll finish this church. The cornerstone was laid in 1892. The ground was broken for the nave in 1916. Although it's still a work in progress, this partly Romanesque/Byzantine, partly Gothic church for all nations and faiths is one of the city's most worthwhile sights. *1047 Amsterdam Avenue (at 112th Street), New York, NY 10025. Open daily 7 A.M.–6 P.M. Grounds and garden are open during daylight hours. Public tours available. Adults $5, students $4.* **212-316-7490.** www.stjohndivine.org.

Children's Museum of Manhattan   Upper West Side

Kids can drive a fire truck, paint on an art wall, and meet a talking baby dragon. Even the special exhibitions are interactive. When the museum did something on Ancient Greece, young visitors got to climb a giant Trojan horse. Here's a warning, however: this place can be mobbed on weekends. *212 West 83rd Street (between Broadway and Amsterdam Avenue), New York, NY 10024. Open Tuesdays–Sundays 10 A.M.–5 P.M. Adults $9, children $9.* **212-721-1234.** www.cmom.org.

The Cloisters   Upper Upper West Side

This one is a trek—all the way up to Fort Tryon Park (which starts at 192nd Street)—but it's exceedingly worth the trip if you can schedule the time. The Cloisters, a monastery-like getaway dedicated to the art of Medieval Europe, opened in 1938 and is an official branch of the Metropolitan Museum of Art. So, you can take a bus (the M4) a block from the main museum. You get a gorgeous Hudson River view as well. *Fort Tryon Park, New York, NY 10040. Open Tuesday–Sunday 9:30 A.M.–5:15 P.M. (closes half an hour early November to February). Suggested admission is adults $20, students $10, children under 12 free.* **212-923-3700.** www.metmuseum.org/cloisters.

Columbia University   Upper West Side

All the Ivy League schools aren't in New England or in pastoral college towns. Columbia, founded in 1754, is right in the big city—a half-hour subway ride from Times Square. Columbia moved uptown in 1897. The classical-style Low Memorial Library, built two years earlier and known for its huge all-granite dome (the largest in North America), is the most famous building on campus. It's the president's office now, and Pulitzer Prizes are awarded here. *Broadway from 114th to 120th Streets, New York, NY 10027.* **212-854-1754.** *www.columbia. edu.*

Grant's Tomb   Upper West Side

Clearly, 1897 was a big year in this part of town. That's when former President Ulysses S. Grant was buried here (not at West Point, because he wanted to be buried with his wife) in this marble and granite monument, two years after his death. Try to ignore the ugly benches beside it, which give contemporary art a bad name. Look instead for the nearby Tomb of the Amiable Child—a 5-year-old boy who fell to his death over these cliffs and has been lying in this spot since 1797, 100 years longer than Grant. *Riverside Drive and 122nd Street, New York, NY 10027. Open daily 9 A.M.–5 P.M. (until 8:30 P.M. on Wednesdays in July and August). Free. www.grantstomb.org.*

Intrepid Sea, Air, and Space Museum   Midtown West

This huge floating museum (seven decks, 900 feet long) closed from Fall 2006 to Fall 2008 for an equally huge renovation. The Intrepid itself is an aircraft carrier that saw action in World War II's Pacific campaign and in the Vietnam War and was a rescue vessel for NASA. The museum also includes the Growler, an intact strategic diesel-powered submarine, and a British Airways/ Singapore Airlines Concorde, the supersonic plane that regularly crossed the Atlantic in under three hours. *Pier 96 (12th Avenue and 46th Street), New York, NY 10036. Check the website for days, hours, and admission fees. Free guided tours.* **212- 245-0072.** *www.intrepidmuseum.org.*

Jacob K. Javits Convention Center   Midtown

There's absolutely no reason to visit the Javits Center unless you're attending a trade show or other event there, but you can wave to it if you're taking a taxi down Eleventh Avenue. The place is 675,000 square feet, and an expansion (including a hotel) is planned. *655 West 34th Street, New York, NY 10001. www. javitscenter.com.*

Lincoln Center   Upper West Side

Stroll by anytime and admire the Lincoln Center for the Performing Arts, which is really about a dozen different cultural organizations in one. The major buildings surrounding the Revson Fountain in the center are the New York State Theater (home to the New York City Ballet and New York City Opera), the Metropolitan Opera House, Avery Fisher Hall (the first building in the complex to open, as Philharmonic Hall, in 1962), and the Vivian Beaumont Theater. But there are several others, including the distinguished Juilliard School. There's lots of renovation and construction going on there now, but lots of the beautiful glass and travertine 16-acre campus is visible, too. Jazz at Lincoln Center, a few blocks away at the Time Warner Center, is also part of the organization. *Columbus Avenue to Amsterdam Avenue, 61st Street to 65th Street, New York, NY 10023. Guided tours four times a day: adults $13.50, students $10, children under 12 $6. Combined Lincoln Center and Jazz at Lincoln Center tours: adults $20, students $15, children under 12 $8. Ticket information: see website.* **212-875-5350.** *www.lincolncenter.org.*

Madame Tussauds   Times Square

It's easy to make fun of this hokey museum concept imported from London, but it can be fun to stand next to the statues of the greats—dead and alive—if only to get a real feel for how tall, short, fat, or thin they are. (I have a lovely photo of myself with Princess Diana.) *234 West 42nd Street (between Seventh and Eighth Avenues), New York, NY 10036. Open 365 days a year. Mondays–Thursdays 10 A.M.–8 P.M. (to 10 P.M. in summer, Memorial Day to Labor Day), Fridays and Saturdays 10 A.M.–10 P.M. year-round. Adults $29, children 4–12 $26, children under 4 free.* **1-800-246-8872.** *www.nycwax.com.*

Museum of Modern Art   Midtown

New Yorkers call it MoMA (rhymes with Roma), and it's one of the most important, impressive sites in town (especially since its superb 2004 renovation). Some of the truly great works of modern art are here, including Van Gogh's

Starry Night and Picasso's *Demoiselles d'Avignon*. MoMA is also known for its film programs, its spectacular sculpture garden, and—in recent years—its highly elegant restaurant, the Modern (a reserve-ahead splurge). *11 West 53rd Street (between Fifth and Sixth Avenues), New York, NY 10019. Open 10:30 A.M.–5:30 P.M. (to 8 P.M. on Fridays) daily. Closed Tuesdays. Adults $20, students $12, children under 16 free. 212-708-9400. www.moma.org.*

New-York Historical Society   Upper West Side

Fans of this very special museum love that hyphen—a reminder of the way the city's name was punctuated in centuries past. The historical society, in the middle of the residential Upper West Side, has more than 60,000 artifacts and works of art, including landscapes from the Hudson River School, Audubon "Birds of America" watercolors, folk art, and a notable Tiffany lamp collection, with a special emphasis on New York's role in history. *170 Central Park West (between 76th and 77th Streets), New York, NY 10024. Open Sundays 11 A.M.–5:45 P.M., Tuesdays to Saturdays 10 A.M.–6 P.M. (Fridays to 8 P.M.). Closed Mondays. Adults $10, students $6, children 12 and under free. 212-873-3400. www.nyhistory.org.*

Paley Center for Media   Midtown

Formerly the Museum of Television & Radio, this institution, recently re-named for William S. Paley (its founder and the former chairman of CBS), is a great spot for TV fans of all ages. It sponsors special screenings, but its real appeal is its library. Just sit down at a console, alone or with a friend or two, and watch your favorite old TV shows (the museum has more than 140,000 on file), complete with commercials. It's a trip into the past. *25 West 52nd Street (between Fifth and Sixth Avenues), New York, NY 10019. Open daily noon to 6 P.M. (until 8 P.M. on Thursdays). Closed Mondays. Recommended contribution is adults $10, students $8, children under 14 $5. 212-621-6800. www.mtr.org.*

Riverside Church   Upper West Side

Riverside may be a relatively new church (it was dedicated in 1931), but it has some original Renaissance stained-glass windows (sixteenth-century Flemish), French tapestries from the fifteenth to seventeenth centuries, and a Gothic look reminiscent of Chartres Cathedral in France. The church's history is Baptist (John D. Rockefeller Jr. got things started), but it was conceived of and has always been nondenominational. *490 Riverside Drive (120th to 122nd Streets), New York, NY 10027. Claremont Avenue (one block west of Broadway) entrance open daily 7 A.M.–10 P.M. Free guided tours Sundays at 12:15 P.M.* **212-870-6700.** *www.theriversidechurchny.org.*

Riverside Park Upper West Side

It's not as famous as Central Park, but it had the same designer (Frederick Law Olmsted). Originally developed between 1875 and 1910, Riverside Park runs four miles along the Hudson River waterfront, and its three terraced levels have many charms. There's the marina, known as the 79th Street boat basin; the templelike Soldiers and Sailors Monument (dedicated to New Yorkers who served in the Civil War) at 89th Street; a bronze equestrienne statue of Joan of Arc at 93rd Street; the River Run playground at 83rd Street, one of more than a dozen playgrounds in the park where visiting children can burn off some energy; and my favorite spot, the gorgeous 91st Street Garden, where (as '90s movies fans know) Meg Ryan and Tom Hanks had their big romantic finale in *You've Got Mail. Riverside Drive and points west, 72nd to 158th Streets, New York, NY 10115.* **212-870-3070.** *www.riversideparkfund.org or www.nycgovparks.org.*

Schomburg Center Harlem

The Schomburg Center for Research in Black Culture is a branch of the New York Public Library—and a very special one. The manuscripts, archives, rare books, films, sound recordings, photographs, prints, and artifacts cover subjects as diverse as the modern Civil Rights movement, African culture, jazz, slavery, and the Harlem Renaissance. *515 Malcolm X Boulevard (at 135th Street), New York, NY 10037. Various days and hours for various divisions. Arts and Artifacts division open by appointment only.* **212-491-2200.** *www.nypl.org/research/sc/sc.html.*

Funny, I thought they were larger: The Statue of Liberty and other city-landmark souvenirs in a store window.

Times Square

You can't come to New York City without paying at least one visit to Times Square—where the crowd gathers and the ball drops at midnight every New Year's Eve, where the entire world seemed to gather to celebrate the end of World War II, and where the bright lights of Broadway theaters meet the bright lights of digital animated advertising. The area is named for *The New York Times* back when the newspaper had its headquarters in the building where the electronic zipper displays news headlines around the clock. Times Square is now also a major center of communications, with the ABC and MTV television studios and the Reuters news organization's offices all in a cluster and the Condé Nast Building (all the glamorous magazines, from *Vogue* to *Vanity Fair*, and all the well-dressed people who work there) right around the corner on 42nd Street between Sixth and Seventh Avenues. *One Times Square (43rd Street at the intersection of Seventh Avenue and Broadway). Times Square Information Center, Seventh Avenue between 46th and 47th Streets, New York, NY 10036.* ***212-768-1560.*** *www.timessquarenyc.org.*

Top of the Rock   Midtown

For the last few years, this observation deck has been giving the Empire State Building a real run for its money in the sky-high 360-degree view department. Checking out the view from the Empire State Building is still the traditional thing to do, but this 70th-floor view, atop the General Electric Building, has its advantages. One is timed ticketing, so there's considerably less standing in line. The other is a closer view of Central Park—and the ability to look at the Empire State Building itself, which you can't do when you're in it. *30 Rockefeller Plaza (entrance on 50th Street between Fifth and Sixth Avenues), New York, NY 10020. Open daily 8 A.M.–midnight. Adults $17.50, children 6–12 $11.25.* **212-698-2000** *or 1-877-NYC-ROCK. www.topoftherocknyc.com.*

Fabulous Cocktail Hours

Finding a terrific West Side place to have a drink at the end of the day is not that easy. But most of the good places are very special, each in its own way.

Mandarin Oriental Bar   Columbus Circle

Take the elevator to the 35th-floor lobby of the Mandarin Oriental Hotel, walk straight ahead, and there you are in the New York cocktail bar of your dreams. It's spacious and comfortable, and you're overlooking Central Park with the Columbus Circle fountain below and the skyline of Fifth Avenue in the distance. (Okay, it faces east, which is the wrong direction for sunsets—but you can't have everything.) *80 Columbus Circle (at 60th Street), New York, NY 10023,* **212-805-8880.**

The Algonquin   Theater District

Yes, this is the landmarked 1902 hotel where Dorothy Parker, Robert Benchley, and the rest of the Round Table gang sat around at lunch being witty during the '20s and '30s. You could have dinner in that dining room. Or you could have drinks in the hotel's Blue Bar. But the real kick of nostalgia is in the lobby bar, where you can settle into comfy chairs and settees and order something old-fashioned like a Sazerac, a Negroni, or a martini with Lillet. *59 West 44th Street (between Fifth and Sixth Avenues), New York, NY 10036.* **212-840-6800.** *www.algonquinhotel.com.*

Bar 41   Theater District

It's easy to miss this narrow, intimate, low-key hotel bar down the block from *The New York Times* and right next door to the Nederlander Theater. If you're feeling sociable, sit up front near the music speakers. If you're more in the mood for a soulful chat, go for one of the tables in the back. There's a sizeable bar menu with salads, quesadillas, fries, satay, mozzarella sticks, and chicken wings. *Hotel 41, 206 West 41st Street (between Seventh and Eighth Avenues), New York, NY 10036. **212-703-8608.***

Sardi's Theater District

People have been saying for decades that Sardi's, which opened in the 1920s, is just a relic of Broadway's past, but it just keeps marching on. There's a bar upstairs, but the tiny ground-level one (turn left as you enter) is my favorite. It's nothing fancy, but you can soak up all that theatrical history—this is where the Tony Awards were born, you know—and admire some of the celebrity caricatures the place is known for. *234 West 44th Street (between Seventh and Eighth Avenues), New York, NY 10036. **212-221-8440.***

Entertainment and Nightlife, A to Z

The West Side is home to a lot of the city's best-known entertainment venues. Lincoln Center, Carnegie Hall, and the Apollo are just a few. Check it out.

Apollo Theater Harlem

The Apollo's heyday was a long time ago, but for the last few decades, it has been back and going strong with musical and other acts right on Harlem's main street. Wednesday evenings are still amateur night. *253 West 125th Street (between Sixth and Seventh Avenues), New York, NY 10027. **212-531-5305.** www. apollotheater.com.*

Broadway Theater District

The Broadhurst, the Biltmore, the Barrymore, the Booth, the Shubert, the Eugene O'Neill, and the Helen Hayes are just a few of the theaters cozily nestled together in the West 40s and 50s. Live musicals, comedies, and dramas—some of them brand new and some of them revivals—make Broadway one of New York City's most spectacular attractions. Most theaters don't take orders at their box-office numbers, but you can buy tickets by going to the box offices in person, through Telecharge (*www.telecharge.com or **212-239-6200***) or through Ticketmaster (*www.ticketmaster.com or **212-307-4100** or **1-800-755-4000***). Or just drop by the TKTS booth in Times Square. To see what's playing, check out the listings in the arts section of *The New York Times*, *The New Yorker*, or *New York Magazine* or a website like www.broadway.com.

Carnegie Hall   Midtown

Symphony orchestras, chamber ensembles, pianists, violinists, mezzo-sopranos, musical theater casts, and even comedians may turn up on the stage of this grand (the main auditorium seats 2,800 or so) old concert hall. *57th Street and Seventh Avenue, New York, NY 10019.* **212-247-7800.** *www. carnegiehall.org.*

City Center   Midtown

City Center's pride and joy is its "Encores!" series—short runs of new, often star-studded productions of old Broadway shows that deserve revivals. A remarkable number of them go back to Broadway as a result. But then, you might also find ballet, Gilbert & Sullivan operettas, or even flamenco on the City Center Stage. *130 West 56th Street (between Sixth and Seventh Avenues), New York, NY 10019.* **212-247-0430.** *www.nycitycenter.org.*

Lincoln Center   Upper West Side

Opera, ballet, theater, music, and film are the attractions at the mother of all New York performing arts centers. There is no better place to spend an elegant cultural evening, no matter what your tastes (*Tosca, The Nutcracker,* or the New York Film Festival). For programs and schedules, see www.lincolncenter. org. Alice Tully Hall, *1941 Broadway (at 65th Street),* **212-875-5050.** Avery Fisher Hall, *10 Lincoln Center Plaza (Columbus Avenue at 65th Street),* **212-875-5030.** The Juilliard School, *60 Lincoln Center Plaza (65th Street between Amsterdam and Columbus Avenues),* **212-769-7406.** Metropolitan Opera House, *30 Lincoln Center Plaza (Columbus Avenue between 62nd and 65th Streets),* **212-362-6000.** New York State Theater, *20 Lincoln Center Plaza (Columbus Avenue at 63rd Street),* **212-870-5570.** Vivian Beaumont Theater and Mitzi E. Newhouse Theater, *150 West 65th Street (between Broadway and Amsterdam Avenue),* **212-362-7600.** Walter Reade Theater, *165 West 65th Street (between Amsterdam and Columbus Avenues),* **212-875-5600.** There are restaurants at the New York State Theater, the Metropolitan Opera House, and Avery Fisher Hall.

Jazz at Lincoln Center   Columbus Circle

Technically part of Lincoln Center, this venue is a few blocks south in Time Warner Center. There are two theaters and Dizzy's Club Coca-Cola, an intimate jazz club. *Broadway at 60th Street, New York, NY 10023.* **212-258-9800.** *www.Jalc.org.*

Off-Broadway Theater   Theater District

Conveniently enough, some of the city's most interesting off-Broadway theater is just around the corner from Broadway itself. On Theater Row, 42nd Street west of Ninth Avenue, you'll find small theaters including the Beckett, Clurman, Little Shubert, and Playwrights Horizons doing a wide range of theater—some of it quite notable. There are relatively few super-long runs in the world of off-Broadway, but newspaper and magazine listings as well as websites such as www.playbill.com and www.theatermania.com can keep you updated on what's playing now and opening soon.

Symphony Space   Upper West Side

There's something quintessentially Upper West Side about Symphony Space, where you might attend a musical or dance concert, catch an old movie at a film series, watch theater stars or authors do a showcase or a reading, or pop in for a special family program. *Broadway and 95th Street, New York, NY 10025.* **212-864-5400.** *www.symphonyspace.org.*

Town Hall   Midtown

You could drop by Town Hall to see almost any kind of act: a pop singer, a comedian, dance, film, lectures, or even a live radio broadcast of *A Prairie Home Companion. 123 West 43rd Street (between Sixth and Seventh Avenues), New York, NY 10036.* **212-997-1003.** *www.the-townhall-nyc.org.*

Plan Your Trip: One-Day West Side Itinerary

If your time is limited, try this one-day itinerary offering the best of the West Side. That includes a museum visit, shopping, three square meals, and a Broadway show.

One-Day Trip:

9 A.M. Breakfast:
Start with a leisurely breakfast at **Nice Matin** on 79th Street and Amsterdam Avenue.

10 A.M.–Noon:
Spend the morning just a few blocks away at the **American Museum of Natural History.** Choose your favorite part (the meteorites? the dioramas? the space museum?), but whatever you do, don't miss the dinosaurs.

Noon–12:30 P.M.:
Take a scenic stroll. Head out the museum's front door on **Central Park West,** turn right, and enjoy the gorgeous view of the park as you walk south to 72nd Street. Turn west at the **Dakota** apartment building, walk over to Columbus Avenue, and window shop until 80th Street or so.

12:30–2 P.M. Lunch:
Have lunch on **Upper Broadway.** You could pop into the café at **Zabar's** (or just pick up some cheese, salmon, or prepared dishes there).

2–2:30 P.M.:
Take a short stroll around **Lincoln Center** just to admire the buildings and the fountain. If you're planning a night of culture later on, pop into the box office and pick up tickets.

2:30–4:30 P.M.:
Make an afternoon of it at the **Shops at Columbus Circle.** Go crazy with men's and women's fashions, cookware, gourmet food gifts ... you name it. If you feel like a break, stop for a snack or a drink and enjoy the **Central Park** view.

4:30–6:15 P.M.:
Relax, refresh, and get dressed for dinner.

6:15–7:45 P.M. Dinner:
Arrive early for your pre-theater dinner reservations so you can walk a few blocks and appreciate the dazzling lights of **Times Square.** Have a nice dinner at **Orso** or **Becco** on Restaurant Row—a short stroll from many Broadway theaters.

7:45 P.M.–whenever:
Take in a show (it's probably an 8 P.M. curtain, but double check your tickets for the time). Enjoy the bustle. And if it's absolutely impossible to find a taxi when the show lets out, just hop onto a bus or the subway or walk a few blocks in the direction of your hotel. Or duck into the nearest restaurant for a nightcap and a midnight after-theater chat.

The Bronx Is Up

There's a famous zoo, the original Hall of Fame (of any kind), and a pretty successful Major League baseball team. The borough's main boulevard, the Grand Concourse, is a little bit like the Champs Élysées and a little bit Art Deco. And some New Yorkers consider Arthur Avenue the real Little Italy. There are lots of good reasons to visit the Bronx, and it's usually a snap to get there. Just hop on the same subway you've been taking to places in Manhattan and stay on for a few extra stops.

Sights

If you can possibly work it into your schedule, visit the Bronx. There's a lot of history there, as well as some very worthwhile restaurants. And the zoo alone is worth the trip.

Bronx Zoo

They've got the Congo gorilla forest, butterfly garden, bison range, monkey house, giraffe building, sea lion pool, sea bird colony, World of Darkness (nocturnal animals), baboon reserve, camel rides, and more. The Bronx Zoo houses more than 4,000 animals on 265 acres of parkland and has been delighting New Yorkers and their children since 1899. For lunch, there are cafés and snack stands. *Fordham Road and Bronx River Parkway, Bronx, NY 10460. Subway: No. 2 or 5 to East Tremont Avenue/West Farms Square. Bus: BxM11 on Madison Avenue to Bronx River entrance. Spring/summer: Mondays–Fridays 10 A.M.–5 P.M. Weekends and holidays 10 A.M.–5:30 P.M. Fall/winter: daily 10 A.M.– 4:30 P.M. Adults $14, children 3–12 $10, children under 2 free.* **718-367-1010.** *www.bronxzoo.com.*

Edgar Allan Poe Cottage

Poe, the poet and author, lived in this wood-frame 1812 farmhouse the last three years of his life, 1846–1849. He moved out of the city into what was then the country for the health of his wife, who had tuberculosis, but she died there. Three period rooms—a parlor, a bedroom, and the kitchen—are decorated to reflect life in the 1840s. *Poe Park, Grand Concourse at Kingsbridge Road,*

Bronx, NY 10458. Subway: D or 4 to Kingsbridge Road Bus; several lines, including Bx1 and Bx2 to Kingsbridge Road and Bx9 and Bx34 to 194th Street. Saturdays 10 A.M.–4 P.M., Sundays 1 P.M.–5 P.M., and weekdays by appointment. Adults $3, students and children $2. **718-881-8900.** *www.bronxhistoricalsociety.org or www. museumregister.com.*

WHY THEY CALL IT THE BRONX

Jonas Bronck, a Swedish sea captain, was the first European settler in the area when he arrived in 1639. People referred to Bronck's place (or possibly going up to see the Broncks), and the name soon began to be applied to the entire borough.

Hall of Fame for Great Americans

This was the original Hall of Fame before the ones for baseball, rock and roll, or anything else. Founded in 1901 (the neighborhood has changed considerably since then), it's now on the campus of Bronx Community College. The hall features a 630-foot open-air colonnade and 98 bronze busts of notable men and women. The honorees include presidents, inventors, and a few arty types like Walt Whitman and Mark Twain. *West 181st Street and University Avenue, Bronx, NY 10453. Subway: No. 4 to 183rd Street. Free.* **718-289-5161.** *www.bcc.cuny.edu.*

New York Botanical Garden

Start with the Peggy Rockefeller Rose Garden, move on to the rock and native plant gardens, then visit the Enid A. Haupt Conservatory and the Everett Children's Adventure Garden. Think magnolias, daffodils, tulips, lilacs, azaleas, peonies, and two casual restaurants where you can stop and talk about taking time to smell the flowers. *412 Bedford Park Boulevard, Bronx, NY 10458. Subway: B, D, or 4 to Bedford Park Boulevard. Bus: Bx26, east to Mosholu Gate entrance. Tuesdays–Sundays 10 A.M.–6 P.M. (closes at 5 P.M. during parts of winter). Closed Mondays except holidays. Adults $13, students $11, children 2–12 $5 for all* *tours and events; adults $6, students $2, children 2–12 $1 to visit the grounds only. Children under 2 are admitted free.* **718-817-8700.** *www.nybg.org.*

Van Cortlandt House

The National Society of Colonial Dames operates this museum, the mid – eighteenth-century Georgian main house of a large grain plantation and mill. Jacobus Van Cortlandt had the house built in 1848–1849, and his slave-owning son Frederick lived there with his family. Several period rooms, most of them with seventeenth- and eighteenth-century furnishings, include two parlors, a formal dining room, a Colonial Revival kitchen, and a nursery. *Broadway and West 246th Street, Bronx, NY 10451. Subway: No. 1 to 242nd Street/Van Cortlandt Park. Bus: Bx9 to 244th Street. Tuesdays–Fridays 10 A.M.–3 P.M., Saturdays– Sundays 11 A.M.–4 P.M. Closed Mondays, except holidays. Adults $5, students $3, children under 12 free.* **718-543-3344.** *www.vancortlandthouse.org.*

Woodlawn Cemetery

Established in 1963, Woodlawn has many notable residents, but the cemetery has long had a particular connection with music and the entertainment industry. So in addition to the graves of socialite types such as Barbara Hutton and Gertrude Vanderbilt Whitney, you'll find those of Irving Berlin, Duke Ellington, Miles Davis, Lionel Hampton, and George M. Cohan. The administrative office (closed on Sundays) has maps. *Webster Avenue and East 233rd Street, Bronx, NY 10470. Subway: No. 4 to Woodlawn or No. 2 or 5 to 233rd Street.* **718-920-0500.** *www.thewoodlawncemetery.org.*

Yankee Stadium

"The house that Ruth built" (Babe Ruth, as even nonbaseball fans know) opened in 1923 with wooden bleachers and a manually operated wooden scoreboard. A few improvements were made over the years, including lights in 1946 and a complete renovation in the mid-1970s. A new stadium is imminent (maybe open by the time of your visit), but for the time being, there are still tours of the old one. *River Avenue and 161st Street, Bronx, NY 10451. Subway: B, D, or 4 to 161st Street/Yankee Stadium. Bus: Bx6, Bx13, Bx55 to 161st Street/Grand Concourse. Adults $20, children under 14 $15.* **718-293-4300.** *www.yankees.mlb. com.*

Restaurants

The Feeding Tree
Jamaican $

You could try the jerk shrimp or the curried goat at this popular Jamaican place near Yankee Stadium. Their beef patties are famous, but they also make chicken, vegetable, and calaloo patties. Or you could just have fried chicken and potato salad. *892 Gerard Avenue (at East 161st Street), Bronx, NY 10452.* *718-293-5025.*

Jake's Steakhouse
American/Steak $ $

Jake's menu includes steaks, chops, pasta, and surf-and-turf. You could go crazy and have the porterhouse for two ($63). But critics rave most about the rack of pork ribs and the mashed potatoes. *6031 Broadway (at 242nd Street), Bronx, NY 10471.* *718-581-0182.* *www.jakessteakhouse.com.*

Liebman's
Kosher $

Ever wish you could have seen one of those great old Jewish delis back in the 1950s? Its fans consider Liebman's, a family-run operation, very close. A little corned beef, a little chicken soup, maybe some brisket, and you'll feel better. *552 West 235th Street (at Johnson Avenue), Bronx, NY 10463.* *718-548-4534.* *www.liebmansdeli.com.*

Mario's
Italian $ $

A James Beard Award winner, Mario's is known for its Neapolitan-style dishes, including at least 10 ways to do spaghetti. The place has been around since 1919. *2342 Arthur Avenue (between 184th and 185th Streets), Bronx, NY 10458.* *718-584-1188.* *www.mariosrestarthurave.com.*

Roberto's
Italian $ $

The setting, with farmhouse tables, is like some village restaurant in Tuscany. The portions are huge. There are at least a dozen handmade pastas. No wonder there always seems to be a line out front. *603 Crescent Avenue (at Hughes Avenue), Bronx, NY 10458.* *718-733-9503.*

¢ Siam Square

Thai $

The Zagat's guide gave it a rating of 24 for food, which is great for any restaurant and fabulous for one with these prices. It's a pleasant place, too, with nice lighting by which you can enjoy all the "pad" dishes and curries. *564 Kappock Street (right off the Henry Hudson Parkway), Bronx, NY 10463.* **718-432-8200.** *www.siamsq.com.*

Clearly, there are far too many things to do and places to visit on the vibrant West Side. One solution is just to toss a coin. Or stay longer!

Part 4

Downtown

Greenwich Village was the home of early Bohemians, the Beat generation, and then the hippies. SoHo and TriBeCa attracted artists and galleries that later moved to Chelsea. Meanwhile, the Financial District flourished. Somehow, many of the old, narrow streets and historic buildings survived—making this an architecturally rich area. There are even a few places to stay, along with stellar dining and memorable sights in this conglomeration of neighborhoods where the city began and grew.

Chapter 9

Getting Comfortable Downtown

In This Chapter

- Getting to know all the hip Downtown neighborhoods
- Downtown hotels in every price range
- Three walking tours in Chelsea, the Village, and the Financial District

When New Yorkers talk about Downtown, they don't mean the busy business district of their city. (That's Midtown.) They mean the southern part of Manhattan Island, where European settlement began back in the 1620s. Today, everything from Battery Park (at the very tip of Manhattan Island) to Chelsea (in the West 20s) can be considered Downtown. If you're spending a lot of time there, you'll have plenty to keep you busy.

Finding Your Bearings Downtown: The Neighborhoods

Every Downtown neighborhood has its own distinct character and look. But beware: once you get to the Village, that simple numbered grid that has made it so easy to navigate the rest of Manhattan is about to disappear. Instead, you'll find the sometimes winding paths of Bleecker Street, Broome Street, the Bowery, and Maiden Lane. Maybe you should grab a street map.

Chelsea

In the 1700s, **Chelsea** was just the name of Capt. Thomas Clarke's country estate, which stretched from what is now 14th Street to 24th Street and from Eighth Avenue to the Hudson River. Moore's grandson, Clement Clarke Moore, a college professor best known as the author of "A Visit From St. Nicholas" ("'Twas the Night Before Christmas"), divided the estate into lots in the 1830s.

Today, Chelsea is a fashionable neighborhood that has extended its reach considerably beyond the estate's borders. Now, most people would say it reaches up to at least 30th Street and as far east as Sixth Avenue. But its spiritual center is 23rd Street.

You'll find lots of art galleries there, good restaurants, the area's earliest luxury apartment building (**London Terrace,** which opened in 1930 with its own indoor pool), a big entertainment and sports complex (**Chelsea Piers**), and the **General Theological Seminary.**

Once a neighborhood of immigrants, Chelsea now has a large gay population. They don't call Eighth Avenue in the teens and 20s "the boyfriend superhighway" for nothing.

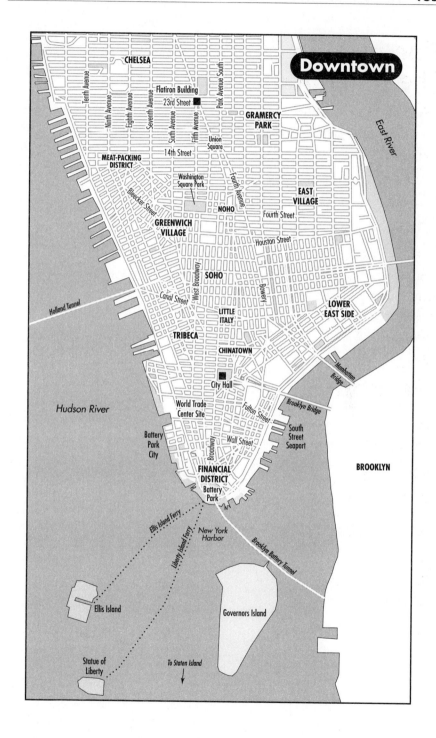

Now it has its own district: The 22-story Flatiron Building, one of the city's tallest skyscrapers when it opened in 1902.

Gramercy Park

If you had visited New York in the 1870s and wanted to see where the rich and famous lived, you would have headed straight for **Gramercy Park** between 20th and 22nd Streets at the foot of Lexington Avenue. In fact, the Gramercy Park Hotel stands on the site of the townhouse where the author Edith Wharton was born (into a very wealthy family).

As the city expanded northward, many of the rich went with it, moving to upper Fifth Avenue and Park Avenue. But Gramercy Park has remained upper-crust and very special. The tiny park itself is private—gated and locked—and only residents of the buildings right around it have keys. And the gorgeous nineteenth-century townhouses remain—most of them still residences of one kind or another.

As in other neighborhoods, the notion of exactly where Gramercy Park begins and ends has been stretched considerably. People from 17th to 22nd Streets like to say they live in it. And areas around the park, from Union Square to

Madison Square, have come up in the world and now offer great restaurants and good shopping.

Union Square

Slightly southwest of Gramercy Park, you'll find **Union Square,** a park that runs from 14th to 17th Streets, where Downtown's Fourth Avenue becomes Park Avenue South. (Its north side faces Broadway.)

This is a historic spot—the site of a huge public demonstration in 1861 at the beginning of the Civil War and the very first Labor Day parade in 1882. Today, with apartment building development and the four-day-a-week greenmarket, Union Square has become fashionable in its own distinctive way.

Meat Packing District

When I moved to New York City, this area really was an old cobblestone street part of town where huge slabs of beef could be seen hanging in old buildings. I knew one young man (an early adapter) who had moved into a rustic loft on Gansevoort Street.

Today, the cobblestones (actually Belgian block) are still there, but Gansevoort and the adjoining blocks would be unrecognizable to the butchers of yesteryear. There are glamorous hotels, exclusive restaurants, and a lineup of the kinds of shops that some of us are afraid to walk into without having had a beauty/fashion makeover.

Technically, this should be just the northwestern corner of the Village—but the **Meat Packing District** has taken on a hip character all its own.

Greenwich Village

In the early 1800s, **Greenwich** was truly a village—completely rural and very separate from New York City, which was still largely confined to the southernmost end of Manhattan. But whenever there was a yellow fever epidemic, New Yorkers would go up to the Village to escape and get some country air. Eventually, they began to move there.

Bohemian culture moved in shortly thereafter. The Village has long had a reputation as the home of daring artists, political rebels, and alternative culture in general. The Beat Generation made its headquarters here in the 1950s.

Few starving artists or old beatniks could afford to live in the Village now. The affluent have taken over most of the nineteenth-century row houses on the beautiful narrow streets (there are high-rise apartment buildings in the neighborhood, but they're in the minority). And statusy fashion designers have taken over many of the little neighborhood shops. But there's still a tinge of counterculture in the air. It has just lost a bit of its edge.

The Village reaches from 13th Street to Houston Street and from the Hudson River to Fifth Avenue, where Washington Square Park stands (surrounded by New York University). The neighborhood still has a lively restaurant and bar scene.

East Village/Lower East Side

All of this area was considered the **Lower East Side** until the 1960s or so. That's when the hippie crowd, who couldn't afford the real Village, moved into the northern part of this neighborhood from Second Avenue all the way over to Avenue D and declared it the **East Village.**

Today, the East Village—which runs roughly from 13th Street to Houston Street—is becoming an expensive place to live. It's also filled with terrific restaurants, clubs, and off-Broadway theater.

What remains as the Lower East Side, below Houston Street, is also having a renaissance of sorts. Just a few years ago, it looked much as it had at the turn of the twentieth century when it was the home of mostly Jewish and Italian immigrants. If uptown New Yorkers ever visited, it was for the discount shopping on Orchard Street.

But that's changing, and a couple of glamorous hotels have opened in the neighborhood. So Orchard, Delancey, Hester, Grand, and Ludlow Streets may soon be the chic places to go.

SoHo

As most people know, **SoHo** stands for south of Houston Street. A hundred years ago, this area—from Houston to Canal Streets north and south and from Crosby Street to West Broadway east to west—was a manufacturing center. But by the 1970s, the factories had vacated hundreds of nineteenth-century cast-iron buildings with huge windows, and struggling artists discovered them and turned them into spacious, light-filled studios. Then, they began moving into them.

Three decades later, those lofts have had fabulous kitchens and bathrooms installed, are filled with expensive furniture, and sell for millions of dollars. Many of the little art galleries that sprang up there have moved to other neighborhoods (mostly Chelsea) where the rents are (or were) lower.

European designer shops line Mercer, Greene, Wooster, and Thompson Streets, Broadway, and West Broadway. Expensive restaurants draw New Yorkers from all over town. The fashionable shop for food at the original Dean & DeLuca. There's even a SoHo Bloomingdale's. At least the architecture remains the same.

NO, NO, NOHO

If SoHo means south of Houston Street, it stands to reason that NoHo means north of Houston Street. Specifically, it's a tiny area too far east to be Greenwich Village and too far west to be the East Village.

TriBeCa

TriBeCa, or the Triangle below Canal Street, lies just south of SoHo. And it picked up where **SoHo** left off, transforming itself into an amorphous area just north of the **Financial District** into a chic neighborhood filled with expensive lofts and trendy restaurants.

TriBeCa runs roughly from Broome Street to Barclay Street and from Broadway to the Hudson River. The area gets more tourists now than in the past because of its proximity to the **World Trade Center** site (and, to a lesser degree, because John F. Kennedy Jr. and his wife, Carolyn Bessette, lived there at 20 North Moore Street, off Varick Street).

THE LITTLE FILM FESTIVAL THAT COULD

Most big-time film festivals are named for cities: Cannes (France), Toronto (Ontario, Canada), Venice (Italy), Berlin (Germany), and New York (New York). But the **TriBeCa Film Festival** is named for a tiny neighborhood—one that barely existed 20 years ago.

Things got underway less than three months after the terrorist attacks of September 11, 2001. TriBeCa, which lies a few blocks north of the World Trade Center site, was suffering. Robert De Niro and a partner stepped up, creating a festival that would act as economic and emotional relief for Downtown in general.

The first festival was held in May 2002, screening some 150 films of all kinds, and the festival has had a high profile in the film industry ever since. If you're planning a visit in May, you could order tickets and be part of it.

Box Office: 15 Laight Straight (between Varick Street and Sixth Avenue). ***646-502-5296.*** *General information* ***212-941-2400.*** *www. tribecafilmfestival.org.*

Little Italy

Little Italy lies east of SoHo, west of the Lower East Side, and right next to **Chinatown.** Most of the Italian immigrants who once lived here and their Italian American descendants have moved on—like everyone else—to the suburbs or to other parts of the city. Mulberry Street remains, though, as the symbolic center of Little Italy—a good place to visit for a pasta-based meal and a yummy Italian dessert.

Chinatown

One of the largest concentrations of Chinese people in the Western Hemi-sphere live in this tiny, bustling neighborhood north of City Hall. (It's a time-honored tradition among New Yorkers to have lunch in **Chinatown** when serving jury duty at nearby courthouses.)

They say it all began with a grocery store on Mott Street in the 1870s, but as more and more immigrants moved here—fleeing anti-Chinese violence in the Western United States—the neighborhood grew to what it is today. There are scads of Chinese restaurants of all kinds, interesting food markets, and small shops.

Financial District

Or ... just call it **Wall Street.** The oldest part of New York has grown into one of the busiest. The narrow streets do feel like canyons with the office sky-scrapers lining them, but there is lots of history here, too.

During most of the twentieth century, no one lived in this part of town. When office workers left at 5 P.M. (or whenever they'd finished operating the banks, brokerage firms, and other businesses), the streets were empty. But that has changed, especially with the building of **Battery Park City** on the west side of this part of town.

This is where you come to get to the **Staten Island Ferry,** see the **Statue of Liberty** in the harbor, visit the **Stock Exchange,** or—sadly—pay your re-spects at the site where the World Trade Center towers once stood, now com-monly referred to as **Ground Zero.**

Great Downtown Hotels

When you decide to make any one of the Downtown neighborhoods your home base, you can be almost certain that you'll wake up in the middle of things. Choices range from hostels and modest guesthouses to drop-dead-gorgeous showplaces offering luxuries galore.

Abingdon Guest House   Greenwich Village $ $

Travel & Leisure magazine said it was like staying at "a friend's place in Connecticut." The *Times of London* gave it a rave review. Abingdon consists of nine rooms in two 1850's Federal-style townhouses on lively Eighth Avenue in the Village. All the rooms are different. Some have fireplaces, canopy beds, and country-house décor. *21 Eighth Avenue (between West 12th and Jane Streets), New York, NY 10014.* **212-243-5384.** *www.abingdonguesthouse.com.*

Blue Moon   Lower East Side $ $ $

Even an old tenement can be turned into a glamorous boutique hotel. Blue Moon, on the cobblestone streets of the Lower East Side, has 22 rooms with period décor, named for celebrities of the 1930s and 1940s (Benny Goodman, Tommy Dorsey), some with the original walnut shutters and window seats. But there are plenty of modern amenities, including free wi-fi. *100 Orchard Street (between Broome and Delancey Streets), New York, NY 10002.* **212-533-9080.** *www.bluemoon-nyc.com.*

NOW YOU KNOW YOUR ABCS

Alphabet City isn't exactly a full-fledged neighborhood, but people sometimes think of it that way. The name just refers to Avenues A, B, C, and D in the East Village, which begin as soon as you walk east of First Avenue. Back in the 1980s, Edward I. Koch, former Mayor of New York, described Alphabet City as "one of those dreary symbols of human failure" that evoke, among other things, despair. Happily, those blocks have improved considerably since then.

¢ Bowery's Whitehouse Hotel of New York   East Village $

Some might disagree on what neighborhood this is (maybe East Village, maybe NoHo). No one would argue that this is anything but a hostel. For the low, low prices, you get a tiny room with a latticework ceiling (in other words, you can hear your neighbors) and shared bathrooms. But you also get air-conditioning, laundry facilities, and wi-fi (although not in your room).

No children allowed. *340 Bowery (between East Second and East Third Streets), New York, NY 10012.* **212-477-5623.** *whitehousehotelofny.com.*

🏛 Chelsea Hotel   Chelsea $ $

It started out as an apartment building in 1883, became a hotel in 1905, and has welcomed guests from Eugene O'Neill and Dylan Thomas to Janis Joplin and Bob Dylan, not to mention Sid Vicious, whose stay ended unpleasantly. The Chelsea is in a class all its own, fashionably seedy and eclectic in every way. But they are bourgeois enough to have cable TV and private bathrooms. *222 West 23rd Street (between Seventh and Eighth Avenues), New York, NY 10011.* **212-243-3700.** *www.hotelchelsea.com.*

Chelsea Pines Inn   Greenwich Village $ $

You don't have to be gay to appreciate this friendly little guesthouse, but it helps. Rooms are named for old movie stars (e.g., Susan Hayward and Rock Hudson), and there's a nice breakfast buffet. The least expensive rooms have semi-private bathrooms. The most expensive have luxuries like flat-screen TV and iPod docks. *317 West 14th Street (between Eighth and Ninth Avenues), New York, NY 10014.* **212-929-1023** *or* **1-888-546-2700.** *www.chelseapinesinn.com.*

Cosmopolitan Hotel   TriBeCa $ $

A hop, skip, and jump from City Hall, the 150-room Cosmopolitan keeps prices down with Ikea-style furniture and bare-minimum services. But you do get satellite TV, private baths, and free wi-fi. *95 West Broadway (at Chambers Street), New York, NY 10007.* **212-566-1900.** *www.cosmohotel.com.*

Duane Street Hotel   TriBeCa $ $ $

Many rooms in this 45-room boutique hotel have floor-to-ceiling windows for spectacular views. There are also 11-foot ceilings, plasma TV, slate baths, room service, wi-fi, premium cable, and a free *Wall Street Journal* every day. The business center is open 24 hours. *130 Duane Street (at Church Street), New York, NY 10013.* **212-964-4600.** *www.duanestreethotel.com.*

East Village Bed & Coffee   East Village $ $

As its name suggests, this popular guest house, just a block from Tompkins Square Park, is a little bit less than a bed and breakfast. And a little bit more.

There are shared baths but lots of friendly charm. *110 Avenue C (at East Seventh Street), New York, NY 10009.* **917-816-0071.** *www.bedandcoffee.com.*

Gramercy Park Hotel   Gramercy Park $ $ $ $ $

Built in 1925, this 185-room grande dame got a complete makeover in 2006, going all rococo with chandeliers and rich Renaissance colors and velvet headboards, tasseled chairs and mahogany liquor cabinets in the guest rooms. But the Gramercy Park also has pretty much every modern amenity you can think of: plasma TVs, CD and DVD players, a fancy fitness center and spa, handsome new bathrooms. Not to mention one restaurant, two bars, and a private roof garden and club. The hotel also lends keys to the park to its guests, which is a big deal. *2 Lexington Avenue (at East 21st Street), New York, NY 10010.* **212-920-3300** *or* **1-866-784-1300.** *www.gramercyparkhotel.com.*

Hampton Inn—Manhattan Seaport   Financial District $ $

This 65-room Hilton property has an interesting location, just south of the Brooklyn Bridge. It offers high-speed Internet access (plus free wi-fi in the lobby), free in-room movie channel, free copies of *USA Today*, and free breakfasts (in an "on the run" bag, if you're late for an appointment). Small pets (25 pounds and under) are allowed. *320 Pearl Street (between Peck Slip and Frankfort Street), New York, NY 10038.* **212-571-4400.** *www.hamptoninn.hilton.com.*

Hotel Gansevoort   Meat Packing District $ $ $ $ $

The ultra-modern, ultra-chic Gansevoort is quite a sight in the city's hippest neighborhood. From the rooftop, with its heated outdoor pool and the bar named Plunge, to the spa that turns into a nightclub, this is the place to be. Many of the 187 rooms have floor-to-ceiling windows with Hudson River views and all the little luxuries, like wi-fi, mini-bars, marble baths, and steam showers. *18 Ninth Avenue (between 13th and Little West 12th Streets), New York, NY 10014.* **212-206-6700.** *www.hotelgansevoort.com.*

The Hotel on Rivington   Lower East Side $ $ $ $

Anyone who thinks the Lower East Side hasn't left its immigrant-and-tenement days behind hasn't seen this 21-story glass tower. Every room has floor-to-ceiling windows, and many have Italian tile baths with steam showers, soaking tubs, and great views. There are also Frette linens, balconies (two-thirds of the rooms), and in-room spa services, from a man's shave to facials and massages. The place is pet-friendly, too. *107 Rivington Street (between Essex and Ludlow Streets), New York, NY 10022.* **212-475-2600.** *www.hotelonrivington. com.*

₵ Hotel 17   Union Square/Gramercy Park $|$

Madonna lived here once. Woody Allen shot the movie *"Manhattan Murder Mystery"* here. One magazine called Hotel 17 "transient chic." This is definitely a budget hotel, with shared bathrooms, but you do get TV, toiletries, and a hair dryer. *225 East 17th Street (between Second and Third Avenues), New York, NY 10003.* **212-475-2845.** *www.hotel17ny.com.*

Inn at Irving Place   Gramercy Park $|$|$|$

Two 1834 brick townhouses make up this 12-room getaway, where the guest rooms are named for the likes of Dvorak and Sarah Bernhardt. The rooms have antique furnishings and fireplaces (decorative only) as well as modern amenities like wi-fi, mini-bars, HBO, VCRs, 24-hour room service, and a free copy of *The New York Times* every morning. Breakfast and afternoon tea are served in Lady Mendl's Tea Salon. *56 Irving Place (between 17th and 18th Streets), New York, NY 10003.* **212-533-4600.** *www.innatirving.com.*

Inn on 23RD Street   Chelsea $|$

As *Elle* magazine wrote (but in French), "charm, charm and nothing but charm" is what this warm, welcoming 14-room property has to offer. You might choose to stay in the 1940s room or the Victorian room, but you'd still have satellite TV, high-speed Internet access (wi-fi in the breakfast room too), and a modern private bath. The Culinary Center of New York holds its cooking classes here. *131 West 23rd Street (between Sixth and Seventh Avenues), New York, NY 10011.* **212-387-2323.** *www.innon23rd.com.*

₵ Larchmont Hotel   Greenwich Village $|$

The bathrooms are down the hall, but you get a robe and slippers, color TV, and air-conditioning for what are, in New York, amazing prices. And the Village location, on a great residential block, can't be beat. *27 West 11th Street (between Fifth and Sixth Avenues), New York, NY 10011.* **212-989-9333.** *www. larchmonthotel.com.*

Maritime Hotel   Chelsea $ $ $ $

You can't miss the Maritime, a tall white building with portholes for windows. Formerly the headquarters of the National Maritime Union and a residence for sailors, the place feels a little like a cruise ship, thanks to those windows and the teak paneling in the guest rooms. The hotel offers free wi-fi, DVD and CD players, room service, mini-bars, an Italian restaurant, a Japanese restaurant, a fitness center, movies on demand, and Nintendo. *363 West 16th Street (between Eighth and Ninth Avenues), New York, NY 10011.* **212-242-4300.** *www.themaritimehotel.com.*

Mercer Hotel   SoHo $ $ $ $ $

Want to know how fashionable the 75-room Mercer is? This is where Russell Crowe allegedly threw a phone at a desk clerk back in 2005. So we know that movie stars appreciate all this minimalist, modernist elegance in a six-story landmark building. There are huge marble bathtubs and a hip restaurant (Mercer Kitchen), 24-hour room service, and private trainers and masseurs and Pilates instructors, if you want them. The staff will even pack and unpack for you. It's so *Upstairs, Downstairs. 147 Mercer Street (at Prince Street), New York, NY 10012.* **212-966-6060.** *www.mercerhotel.com.*

Millenium Hilton   Financial District $ $ $ $

This is a big (565 rooms) hotel that attracts both business travelers and vacationers, with luxuries like marble baths, CD players, a glass-enclosed pool, and 42-inch plasma TVs and amenities like high-speed Internet access, two-line phones, 24-hour room service, and a fitness center. This Hilton pays tribute to the Financial District by calling its bar Liquid Assets. And maybe someday management will learn how to spell millennium. (P.S. You can't get much closer to the World Trade Center site than this, but that may mean construction noise and street closings for some time to come.) *55 Church Street (between Fulton and Dey Streets), New York, NY 10007.* **212-693-2001.** *www.hilton.com.*

Ritz-Carlton Battery Park   Financial District $ $ $ $

No wonder the Art Deco-ish downtown Ritz-Carlton has made so many "best hotels" lists since it opened in 2002. This gorgeous 298-room property, overlooking the harbor (and the Statue of Liberty) at the southwestern tip of the island, can create the illusion of having a resort vacation in the city. Oh, sure, they have a fitness center and a spa and free wi-fi and a DVD library and 24-hour room service. But it's really the combination of Ritz-Carlton style and the location (there are telescopes in harbor-view rooms) that does the trick. *2 West Street (at First Place), New York, NY 10004.* **212-344-0800** *or* **1-800-241-3333.** *www.ritzcarlton.com.*

Sixty Thompson   SoHo $ $ $ $ $

With sleek guest rooms dressed all in neutrals and mini-bars stocked with Dean & DeLuca goodies, this 100-room boutique hotel strives to be "simultaneously timeless and avant-garde" (their words). The amenities include free wi-fi, flat-screen TVs, marble baths, a fitness center, 24-hour concierge service, a fashionable restaurant, an equally fashionable bar, and a private rooftop lounge. *60 Thompson Street (between Spring and Broome Streets), New York, NY 10012.* **1-877-431-0400.** *www.sixtythompson.com.*

SoHo Grand   SoHo $ $ $ $

This stylish 363-room hotel offers oversize windows, flat-screen TVs, wi-fi, DVD players, mini-bars, and a fashionable bar. Not only is the place pet-friendly but they will even provide you with a complimentary pet goldfish upon request. *310 West Broadway (between Grand and Canal Streets), New York, NY 10013.* **212-965-3000.** *www.sohogrand.com.*

SoHo House   Meat Packing District $ $ $ $ $

The thing I like most about SoHo House is that it isn't in SoHo. The thing I like least is its positioning as a private club (lower rates and preferential booking for members). But the location is great, and it's sort of amusing that instead of naming their 24 guest rooms Superior Kings and Deluxe Twins and the like, they call them Playpens, Playrooms, Playhouses, and Playgrounds. There are brick walls, exposed wooden beams, and a rooftop pool that's been on *Sex and the City.* *29 Ninth Avenue (at West 13th Street), New York, NY 10014.* **212-627-9800.** *www.sohohouseny.com.*

Tribeca Grand   TriBeCa $ $ $ $

Modern, minimalist, and tastefully towering with a central atrium, this was the first luxury hotel in the neighborhood. Almost everything seems 24-hour here: room service, the business center, the fitness center. There are also flat-screen TVs, DVD players, wi-fi, and two-line phones. You can get a pet gold-fish here, too. (Did we mention that the two Grand hotels are owned by Hartz Mountain Industries?) *2 Avenue of the Americas (where Church, White, and Walker Streets meet), New York, NY 10013. **212-519-6600.** www.tribecagrand. com.*

Washington Square Hotel   Greenwich Village $ $

This popular smoke-free property, just across from Washington Square Park, gives its guests continental breakfast, a restaurant, a bar, high-speed Internet access, a fitness room, and free wi-fi at the bar. Many of the 160 rooms have been redone in Art Deco style, and even the most basic ones have cable TV, voice mail, and a hair dryer. *103 Waverly Place (at MacDougal Street), New York, NY 10011. **212-777-9515** or **1-800-222-0418.** www.washingtonsquarehotel.com.*

Fabulous Walks, River to River

There's something special about walking Downtown, maybe because it in-cludes the oldest parts of the city and the scale of buildings and streets is smaller. These walks cover Chelsea, Gramercy Park, the Village, and Wall Street.

Gramercy Park to Chelsea

Begin at Lexington and 21st Street, in front of the glamorously redone **Gramercy Park Hotel.** Cross 21st to get a better look at the private park itself. You'll see a quiet place (probably deserted on weekdays, but for the pigeons and a squirrel or two) with trees, bushes, benches, and gravel paths behind a tasteful black-iron fence.

Turn left and go to the end of the park to admire a couple of remarkable build-ings. There's a grande dame of a Gothic Revival apartment building (1906), **36 Gramercy Park East,** guarded by two armed knights in white armor. No. 34, the brick and brownstone building next door, was built in the 1880s.

At the southern end of the park you'll see the **Brotherhood Synagogue** (1859) to your left; **24 Gramercy Park South,** a historic turn-of-the-century co-op building with its nice portico and four columns and two nice red brick town-houses (one for sale the last time I looked). Not that long ago, a four-bedroom at 24 Gramercy Park South had an asking price of $14.5 million.

Cross the street, going west now, and you'll notice that Lexington Avenue has become Irving Place. On this block you'll find the fabulous **16 Gramercy Park South** (built in the 1840s), the **Players Club,** once the home of its founder, Edwin Booth (Edwardian actor and brother of a presidential assassin). The **National Arts Club** is next door at **15 Gramercy Park South,** a Renaissance Revival mansion built in the 1840s but considerably redone a few decades later.

Turn right and cross the street to **Gramercy Park West. No. 4,** where James Harper, a publisher (his company was HarperCollins' ancestor) and one-time mayor of New York, lived, has lovely black wrought-iron gates and veranda. So does **3 Gramercy Park West** next door. Both were built in the 1840s.

Now leave Gramercy Park and walk west on 21st Street. The brownstone church on your right, at Park Avenue South, is **Calvary Episcopal,** a Gothic Revival building dedicated in 1847. Cross Park Avenue South for a better look at it.

Walking west toward Broadway, you'll see a real mix of residential and commercial buildings. At Broadway, you'll see the back of the famous **Flatiron Building** (circa 1902), once the tallest building in the city. Turn right toward 23rd, so you can see the front as well. You'll also get a clear view of the **Empire State Building,** looking north, and **Madison Square Park.**

The next few blocks, walking west on 23rd Street, are fairly short on historical sights. But you will find the **St. Vincent de Paul Church** (unless the plan to demolish it has been carried out) between Sixth and Seventh Avenues on the north side of the street (right). Mass was held in French in this old Greek Revival church. The lovely little hotel **the Inn on 23rd** is right next to it.

Between Seventh and Eighth Avenues, on the left (south), you'll pass the **Chelsea Hotel,** which looks a little seedy but has some amazing literary and show-business history. The front wall is covered with plaques commemorating famous guests.

At Ninth Avenue, you'll see **London Terrace** across the street on your right. Built in 1930, it was the first real luxury apartment building in this neighborhood and is still a prized address. This is where Clement Clarke Moore's family's country estate began, too, running all the way down to 14th Street.

Turn left here and go down to 21st Street. Turn right and you'll see part of the **General Theological Seminary.** Go over to Tenth Avenue, turn left, and come back east on 20th Street. There's a much better view of the seminary's handsome nineteenth-century campus there and a nice block of townhouses across the street from it.

Distance: Approximately 1.5 miles.

A Touch of the Village

Start out by taking the West Side subway (No. 1, 2, or 3) to 14th Street. Take the 13th Street exit and walk west on 13th to Greenwich Avenue, where you'll find one of the cutest little shops in town. **Mxyplyzyk,** named for a character in a Superman comic book, carries all sorts of adorable items (soaps, candles, umbrellas, tote bags, picture frames, lighting, bath items, place mats, various useful objects shaped like dogs).

After doing your window shopping or real shopping, walk south (turn right as you walk out of the store) two blocks to Bank Street. Turn right onto Bank, and you'll find yourself on a typical residential Village side street. But on your left you'll see **Ye Waverly Inn,** once a friendly neighborhood place, now so hot that you practically have to be a close friend of the editor of *Vanity Fair* to get in.

As you approach the corner of Bank and Bleecker Streets, take a quick look at the large apartment building on your right. That's where the very young Lauren Bacall moved (along with her chaperoning mother) when she moved into Manhattan to pursue a modeling career.

Turn left on Bleecker, one of the Village's prettiest streets, with a history of music clubs, then small neighborhood shops full of character. Now it's turned into Madison Avenue Downtown, with an explosion of designer stores.

As you walk southeast (straight ahead), past West 11th, Perry, Charles, West 10th, and Christopher Street, you'll find blocks dominated by high-end stores. There are two (maybe three by now) Ralph Lauren shops, one Marc Jacobs (two others are on West Fourth Street), Lulu Guinness, Cynthia Rowley, James Perse, and Miguelina, not to mention Coach, Tommy Hilfiger, and Juicy Couture.

Do stop, if you're hungry, and pick up a cupcake from **Magnolia Bakery** (Bleecker and West 11th). After Christopher Street (where signs of the old Bohemian Village begin to turn up), go two more blocks, to Barrow Street, then turn left. (Take a quick peek to the right, though. **Greenwich House,** which has produced some very nice off-Broadway things in the past, and **One if by Land, Two if by Sea,** one of the city's most romantic restaurants, are on this block.)

Walk two blocks north on Barrow Street and you'll come to **Sheridan Square.** You'll probably recognize **Village Cigar,** on your left, because it's been photographed and filmed so many times as a symbol of the heart of Greenwich Village. Yes, you will find a whole wall of cigars for sale inside, along with pipes and non-tobacco products such as cough drops and Lifesavers.

Now turn right, just past the little island with the newsstand and the subway station, and check out tiny **Christopher Park.** You'll find two unusual all-white George Segal sculptures—one of a two-man couple, the other of a two-woman couple—a tribute to gay and lesbian rights.

A few yards away (go right on Christopher Street to Nos. 51 and 53), you'll find the **Stonewall Inn,** where the gay rights movement is considered to have begun in 1969. The last time I passed by, Stonewall was still in business with a cheerful sign outside that said "Happy Hour 2–8, *American Idol* Hour 8–9."

On the same block you'll find the **Oscar Wilde Memorial Bookshop,** founded in 1967 and thought to be nation's oldest gay and lesbian bookstore.

Keep going a couple of blocks, and you'll come to a large square, where Christopher Street, Greenwich Avenue, and Sixth Avenue all meet. Look slightly to your left and you'll see what looks like a gorgeous old red brick church with a small community garden in its backyard.

This was originally the **Jefferson Market Courthouse,** built in 1877 and named a few years later the "fifth most beautiful building" in the country. (I guess they made those kinds of lists in the nineteenth century, too.) Today it's a branch of the **Public Library,** and you should cross the street on Sixth Avenue between 9th and 10th Streets to appreciate it fully. But first be sure to read the plaque on the garden gate, explaining all about the **Women's House of Detention,** which once stood where the garden blooms today.

Walk straight ahead (east) one block on Ninth Street, a typical upscale Village residential block. You'll pass 35 West Ninth Street, an apartment building where the poet Marianne Moore lived.

At Fifth Avenue, turn right and you'll see the Washington Arch and all of **Washington Square Park** behind it. If you're lucky, all the renovations and restorations will be completed and you can walk right in and rest your weary feet.

Distance: Approximately 1 mile.

A WORD ABOUT STONEWALL

The gay rights movement is generally considered to have begun with one event on the night of June 27, 1969. That evening, the New York Police Department staged what was described as a "routine raid" on the Stonewall Inn, a gay bar then known for a cross-dressing clientele, on Christopher Street. After decades of harassment, the gay men there had apparently had enough, and they fought back (with bricks, bottles, and other weapons). This led to several days of riots and eventually to a widespread re-evaluation of attitudes toward gay men and women.

Wall Street, All the Way

Start out in front of **120 Wall Street,** an elegant 1931 ziggurat-style skyscraper with a gorgeous black and gold Art Deco entrance. The East River and the Wall Street Ferry Pier are right behind you.

As you head west, inland, straight ahead, remember that Wall Street is named for an actual wall that once stood here. Dutch settlers erected it in the 1650s, both as protection and to mark the northernmost point of what was then New Amsterdam.

Take note that **75 Wall Street,** on your left, is a combination hotel and apartment building (condos). A generation ago, nobody lived on Wall Street. They just worked there, then headed uptown or out of town at the end of the day.

Cross Pearl Street, named because of the mother-of-pearl oyster shells that lined this street back in the seventeenth century. No. 67, on your left, is another apartment building.

At 48 Wall, you'll see the former Bank of New York building. It was completed in 1928, but the bank had actually had its headquarters on this spot since 1797. Today, the building is the newly created **Museum of American Finance.**

55 Wall is the **Cipriani Club and Residences.** You can live there or just join and use the restaurant, bar, library, spa, and other services.

Cross William Street, named for William of Orange. This is a glitzy block, with one of the city's many Trump buildings on your right and the Downtown branch of **Tiffany** sparkling on your left.

Next we come to the **statue of George Washington** on the spot where he was inaugurated in 1789 as first president of the United States. You have to imagine his standing on the balcony of the original Federal Hall. (The **Federal Hall National Monument** behind him wasn't built until 1842.) Today Washington is flanked by two fitness centers.

On the next block, on your left, you can catch a glimpse of the **New York Stock Exchange.** Odds are there will be barriers preventing you (and terrorists) from getting too close. If it's between 9 A.M. and 4 P.M. on a weekday, the American economy is being bounced around inside.

Cross Broadway and your way will be blocked by glorious **Trinity Church,** circa 1846, and its country churchyard, now surrounded by skyscrapers. Take a minute to wander through the graveyard, where Alexander Hamilton, Robert Fulton, and other notables are buried.

Where it all started: An actual wall, built by Dutch settlers in the 17th century, once stood on what is now Wall Street.

Turn right and walk north on Broadway. As you pass Cortlandt Street, turn your head left and you'll see **Century 21,** the popular discount store. At the corner of Broadway and Fulton Street, you'll pass **195 Broadway,** originally the American Telephone & Telegraph Building (1912), with its enormous granite columns and its marble lobby. Today it's a multi-tenant office building.

Just across the street is **St. Paul Chapel** (1766), the oldest public building in New York, which served two functions after the terrorist attacks of September 11. Workers and volunteers used it as a place of refuge. People searching for their loved ones who had been at the World Trade Center posted photographs and messages, which became memorials.

Continue north on Broadway. You'll come to the **Woolworth Building,** the tallest building in the world when it was completed in 1913. Turn right and you're at **City Hall,** a century older (completed in 1812), where the mayor and city council members work.

Now, look straight ahead (east), and there's the magnificent **Brooklyn Bridge** (1883). This might be a good time to take a picture.

Distance: Approximately 2 miles.

Now you see how differently the Downtown neighborhoods are laid out, compared with the East and West Sides farther north. And you've had a history lesson during your walks.

Chapter

10

Enjoying Downtown

In This Chapter

- All kinds of downtown restaurants, from Chelsea to the Battery
- A complete guide to Downtown sightseeing
- A one-day itinerary covering almost all the Downtown neighborhoods
- A quick jaunt to fashionable Brooklyn
- The little-known treasures of Staten Island

There's so much to do in Downtown Manhattan that you may want to choose just one neighborhood to focus on. Or maybe you'll want to concentrate primarily on restaurants, shopping, or historical sights. But if you're feeling ambitious, go ahead and paint all these neighborhoods red. You could work south to north (the Financial District to Chelsea), exactly the way the city grew.

Great Downtown Restaurants

Congratulations! You've arrived at restaurant central. Every New York City neighborhood has a few great places to have a memorable meal, but Downtown is chock full of them.

As in other chapters, restaurants listed in the Expensive category are likely to cost $80 or more per person for an appetizer, a main course, dessert, one drink, and tax. Restaurants in the Moderate category will run somewhere between $40 and $80 per person. Those in the Affordable category should come to $40 or under. But on most menus, you'll find both splurge dishes and bargains—so you can control the cost of your meal to some degree.

Expensive

Annisa   Greenwich Village   American 💲💲💲

This intimate Village restaurant has great fish (including halibut, brook trout, and sable), an excellent wine list with at least 30 choices by the glass, and an inventive menu overall. The zucchini blossoms stuffed with falafel represent the kind of international accents you'll find here. *13 Barrow Street (between Seventh Avenue South and West Fourth Street), New York, NY 10014. **212-741-6699.** www.annisarestaurant.com.*

Babbo   Greenwich Village   Italian 💲💲💲

It's strange to hear rock music blaring in the pretty townhouse that belonged to the genteel Coach House for so many years. But Babbo has been entrenched here for a while, and it's going strong with inventive dishes such as goose liver ravioli, pine nut crostata, and osso buco with saffron orzo. The critics' praises keep coming in. *110 Waverly Place (between MacDougal Street and Sixth Avenue), New York, NY 10011. **212-777-0303.** www.babbonyc.com.*

Bouley   TriBeCa   French 💲💲💲

The very elegant, very subdued Bouley always turns up on the list of the city's most popular restaurants in the Zagat's guide—even if the service isn't flawless. The critic from *The New York Times* liked the smoked trout with avocado and balsamic vinegar and the chocolate brioche pudding. *120 West Broadway (at Duane Street), New York, NY 10013. **212-964-2525.** www.davidbouley.com.*

Buddakan   Chelsea   Asian $ $ $

This place is enormous, flashy, loud, and theatrical—from the dim sum (edamame dumplings, anyone?) to the tempura apple fritter. The dress code is described as "downtown chic, fun, and hip," so the best way to go to Buddakan is probably in a party mood. Have some sake or sparkling wine. Then, try a couple of notable dishes—maybe the mao poe tofu, or fried rice with scallop congée. Plus, now you've seen Chelsea Market. *75 Ninth Avenue (at 15th Street), New York, NY 10011.* **212-989-6699.** *www.buddakannyc.com.*

Chanterelle   TriBeCa   French $ $ $

I had my 40th birthday dinner at Chanterelle, and it was very close to perfect. Since 1979, this very special restaurant has managed to be both exceptional and unpretentious. In a lovely room with custard-colored walls and a fancy tin ceiling, you might try the marinated loin of lamb with rosemary and polenta fries, the New Zealand snapper, or the free-range chicken breast with black trumpet mushrooms. *2 Harrison Street (at Hudson Street), New York, NY 10013.* **212-966-6960.** *www.chanterellenyc.com.*

Craft   Flatiron District   American $ $ $

Craft has an enormous and outstanding porterhouse steak (of course, they also have a separate steakhouse) in its spacious dining room. They do something else unusual, too: they let diners design their own meals by choosing their side dishes. *43 East 19th Street (between Broadway and Park Avenue), New York, NY 10003.* **212-780-0880.** *www.craftrestaurant.com.*

Craftsteak   Chelsea   American/Steak $ $ $

At Craftsteak, you have a lot of choices. Just how much your steak will cost depends on size, cut, age, what it was fed, and where it grew up. The 18-ounce New York strip from California, aged 75 days, for instance, will set you back $71. Oddly, what a lot of people like best about Craftsteak are its side dishes (including nine different kinds of mushrooms) and the desserts. The West Side Highway views arenice, too. *85 Tenth Avenue (at 15th Street), New York, NY 10011.* **212-400-6699.** *www.craftrestaurant.com.*

Cru   Greenwich Village   Mediterranean $ $ $

The wine cellar, they say, has more than 65,000 bottles. And at least 50 wines are available by the glass. Cru is an elegant, clubby place, and the food is as good as the drinks. Favored dishes include the Arctic char, langoustine, quail breast, and turbot. *24 Fifth Avenue (at Ninth Street), New York, NY 10011.* **212-529-1700.** *www.cru-nyc.com.*

Danube   TriBeCa   French/Italian $ $ $

The romantic Danube started out as an Austrian restaurant but changed its mind in the Summer of 2008. It shut down and reopened with a menu that's a mix of French and Italian influences. Almost as important, the place is still absolutely great-looking. *30 Hudson Street (between Duane and Reade Streets), New York, NY 10013.* **212-791-3771.** *www.davidbouley.com.*

Del Posto   Chelsea   Italian $ $ $

The grand, palatial Del Posto was one of only four New York City restaurants to be given two stars in the Michelin Guide. The menu includes plenty of pastas and risottos but also orecchietti with lamb neck sausage, monkfish, and wood-grilled lobster. *85 Tenth Avenue (at 16th Street), New York, NY 10011.* **212-497-8090.** *www.delposto.com.*

Gotham Bar and Grill   Greenwich Village   American $ $ $

Fashionable but not snobbish, the Gotham Bar and Grill has been a favorite of New Yorkers since 1984. The dining room has high ceilings and floor-to-ceiling windows. Notable dishes include roast squab, porcini-crusted halibut, and a masala-spiced chicken breast.

¢ The prix fixe lunch is a bargain. *12 East 12th Street (between Fifth Avenue and University Place), New York, NY 10003.* **212-620-4020.** *www.gothambarandgrill. com.*

Gramercy Tavern   Flatiron District   American $ $ $

Gramercy Tavern may be the perfect restaurant, but don't take my word for it: ask the people at Michelin, Zagat, *The New York Times, Wine Spectator, Gourmet, Forbes,* and *Esquire,* who have given it accolades and stars. One critic explained its charm as "elegant without being formal and comfortable without being casual." The pretty, white-tablecloth dining room has early American antiques and copper sconces. You might try the tuna and beet tartare, the rack of lamb, or the tarte tatin. If you waited too late to call and get a reservation, try the front room or eating at the bar. *42 East 20th Street (between Broadway and Park Avenue South), New York, NY 10003. 212-477-0777. www. gramercytavern.com.*

Il Giglio   TriBeCa   Italian $ $ $

Sometimes going out to dinner is like going to the theater. At least the waiters at Il Giglio seem to think so, because they put on quite a performance. What they're serving is predictable but beloved old-style Northern Italian cuisine. Imagine a meal of prosciutto and melon, spaghetti carbonara, and veal scaloppini alla Romana with zabaglione for dessert. *81 Warren Street (between Greenwich Street and West Broadway), New York, NY 10007. 212-571-5555. www. ilgigliorestaurant.com.*

Il Mulino   Greenwich Village   Italian $ $ $

The dining room décor isn't much, but the food and the supremely professional service more than make up for that. The menu is old-style Italian with scampis, scaloppines, and saltimbocca. You will be forced to have dessert. *86 West Third Street (between Sullivan and Thompson Streets), New York, NY 10012. 212-673-3783. www.ilmulinonewyork.com.*

Jewel Bako   East Village   Japanese $ $ $

Some say that tiny Jewel Bako, housed in a former video store, has the best sushi south of 14th Street. It made *New York Magazine*'s list of best new restaurants of 2006. And *Time Out New York* loved the wild salmon in sea urchin sauce. *239 East Fifth Street (between Second and Third Avenues), New York, NY 10003. 212-979-1012.*

Nobu   TriBeCa   Japanese $ $ $

Is Nobu, around since 1994, still the king of all Japanese restaurants? The surrealistic dining room evokes the Japanese countryside. The menu includes yellowtail sashimi with jalapeño, sashimi tacos, and squid pasta with garlic sauce. *105 Hudson Street (at Franklin Street), New York, NY 10013. 212-219-0500. www.myriadrestaurantgroup.com.*

STAR SYSTEM

Keep in mind that one star from Michelin is roughly equal to three stars in *The New York Times*. It's not that one set of critics is superior to the other; rather, they simply use different systems. At the moment, only seven New York restaurants have won more than one Michelin star. (And fewer than three dozen have won even one.) The Zagat guides, which rely on regular customers rather than professional food critics, don't award stars at all. They use numerical ratings for food, décor, and service, then list the restaurants with the highest ratings by cuisine and neighborhood.

Old Homestead   Meat Packing District   American/Steak $\boxed{\$}\boxed{\$}\boxed{\$}$

Some of us could do without the big plastic cow out front, but when you've been around since 1868 (Andrew Johnson was president), as the Old Homestead has, you can get away with a lot. Anyway, the place looks good inside—traditional to the point of Victorian. The menu offers a little of everything, but it's all about steak. You might have the 10-oz. filet mignon for $36 or the sirloin au poivre for $42. Or, you could go completely nuts and have the 10-ounce Japanese Kobe steak for $195. (The Kobe burger is $41.) There's also an impressive wine list, heavy on the Californians. *56 Ninth Avenue (between 14th and 15th Streets), New York, NY 10011.* **212-242-9040.** *www. theoldhomesteadsteakhouse.com.*

Perry Street   Greenwich Village   American $\boxed{\$}\boxed{\$}\boxed{\$}$

Go for the view; stay for the food. Housed in a glamorous glass Richard Meier building facing the West Side Highway, the sleek, spare, and elegant Perry Street offers fabulous Hudson River sunsets. But look down at the menu, too. You might have butter-poached lobster Bearnaise with fingerling potatoes. The very first New York Michelin Guide gave the place a coveted star. *176 Perry Street (at West Street), New York, NY 10014.* **212-352-1900.** *www. jean-georges.com.*

Union Square Café   Union Square   American $ $ $

A favorite with New Yorkers since it opened in the mid–'80s, the Union Square Café is a low-key place with casual elegance and an eclectic menu. Among the memorable dishes are herb-roasted Amish chicken with Parmigiano bread pudding and an Indian-spiced vegetarian special that includes glazed eggplant, mushroom basmati, chickpeas, and spinach. *21 East 16th Street (between Fifth Avenue and Union Square West), New York, NY 10003. 212-243-4020. www.unionsquarecafe.com.*

Veritas   Flatiron District   American $ $ $

So there were these two wine collectors who realized one day that they had far many more bottles in their cellars than they'd ever be able to drink in their lifetimes. So, they acquired partners and opened a restaurant. The roast squab, braised veal, and spiced venison loin are recommended. *43 East 20th Street (between Broadway and Park Avenue South), New York, NY 10003. 212-353-3700.*

Wallsé   Greenwich Village   Austrian $ $ $

Okay, there are at least two notable Austrian restaurants in town. This one, named for the chef's hometown, has striking black-and-white dining rooms dominated by large pieces of twentieth-century art. With the menu, you can go traditional with wiener schnitzel and the like, or you can try something different such as cod strudel with wild mushrooms. *344 West 11th Street (at Washington Street), New York, NY 10014. 212-352-2300. www.wallse.com.*

WD-50   Lower East Side   American $ $ $

The chef at WD-50 is a risk taker: who else would mix foie gras and anchovies? Other unusual dishes include monkfish with red-pepper oatmeal, pork belly with black soybeans and turnips, and a parsnip tart with bok choy. It's all served in a diner atmosphere. *50 Clinton Street (between Rivington and Stanton Streets), New York, NY 10002. 212-477-2900. www.wd-50.com.*

Moderate

Aquagrill   SoHo   Seafood 💲💲

Aquagrill is so neighborhoody, so unintimidating, so (dare we say it?) friendly
that it sometimes surprises people that the place serves exceptional, award-
winning foods. Start with the pepper tuna carpaccio or the clam chowder—
then move on to your favorite seafood entrée (maybe the grilled jumbo white
shrimp with plantains, zucchini, and chutney in a coriander yogurt sauce).
210 Spring Street (at Sixth Avenue), New York, NY 10012. **212-274-0505.** *www.
aquagrill.com.*

Balthazar   SoHo   French 💲💲

If you'd really rather be in Paris, head for Balthazar—where the illusion of
being in some wonderful faded French bistro is strong. You've got the zinc
bar, the red banquettes, and the old-looking tile—not to mention steak frites,
escargot, and tarte tatin on the menu. *80 Spring Street (between Broadway and
Crosby Street), New York, NY 10012.* **212-965-1414.** *www.balthazarny.com.*

Chinatown Brasserie   NoHo   Chinese 💲💲

It's romantic and glamorous, but it's not in Chinatown. It has all the standards,
such as crispy orange beef, General Tso's chicken, and kung pao shrimp—but
dim sum is the way to go. *380 Lafayette Street (at Great Jones Street), New York,
NY 10003.* **212-533-7000.** *www.chinatownbrasserie.com.*

Dévi   Flatiron District   Indian 💲💲

Michelin gave it a star. The Zagat's readers rated it one of the best Indian
restaurants in the city. Dévi offers an exotic retreat from the real world with
jewel-like lighting, a curving marble staircase, inventive dishes (perhaps halibut cooked in banana leaves), and more familiar favorites (coconut shrimp curry and tandoori prawns). *8 East 18th Street (between Broadway and Fifth Avenue),
New York, NY 10013.* **212-691-1300.** *www.devinyc.com.*

Fleur de Sel   Flatiron District   French 💲💲

A touch of Bretagne, unexpected flavor combinations, and sometimes outstanding presentation make Fleur de Sel a special place. The imaginative
dishes include parsnip soup, steamed sea bream, and sweetbread ravioli with

crêpes. *5 East 20th Street (between Broadway and Fifth Avenue), New York, NY 10003. **212-460-9100.** www.fleurdeselnyc.com.*

⊘ Fraunces Tavern   Financial District   American 💲💲

It's interesting that in 1783, when George Washington retired from the U.S. Army to his home in Mount Vernon, he said farewell to his officers at a dinner here. Fraunces Tavern, owned by Samuel Fraunces but originally known as the Queen's Head, was founded in 1762. Apparently it was good enough for the father of our country, but the kitchen has changed hands a few times since then—and these days, the food is mostly forgettable. *54 Pearl Street (at Broad Street), New York, NY 10004. **212-968-1776.** www.frauncestavern.com.*

Knickerbocker Bar and Grill   Greenwich Village   American 💲💲

Part steakhouse, part bistro, and all New Yorker, the Knickerbocker has only been around since the 1970s but seems older. Maybe it's the 100-year-old marble bar, the live jazz on weekends, or all the memorabilia on the walls. Or maybe it's the retro menu, which includes caviar pie with toast points, pork loin Wellington, and veal goulash. The bartender also makes a mean Gibson. *33 University Place (between Eighth and Ninth Streets), New York, NY 10003. **212-228-8490.** www.knickerbockerbarandgrill.com.*

La Lunchonette   Chelsea   French 💲💲

The *New York Observer* called it "dark, funky, and romantic." I'd agree (with an emphasis on the funky). And the name is not a typographical error; the French owner didn't know how to spell luncheonette. He's much better at cooking, and this unpretentious bistro is a solid hit. Both the lunch and dinner menus include trout amandine, roast chicken, linguine, and grilled lamb sausages with sautéed apple. *130 Tenth Avenue (at 18th Street), New York, NY 10011. **212-675-0342.***

Le Gigot   Greenwich Village   French 💲💲

It's that little French place you've been looking for. In addition to its namesake, gigot d'agneau, Le Gigot serves typical bistro dishes, including mussels, pâté de campagne, bouillabaisse, and lots of salads. The $15 prix fixe brunch offers three kinds of eggs Benedict and the hard-to-find (in the United States) omelette paysanne. *18 Cornelia Street (between Bleecker and West Fourth Streets), New York, NY 10014. **212-627-3737.***

Little Owl Greenwich Village American $ $

Order the grilled pork chop. It's the star of the menu, although the "meatball sliders" (tiny sandwiches on garlic rolls), the crispy chicken, and the grilled strip steak topped with pancetta have earned great reviews, too. The other attraction here is monster-size windows, creating a lovely street-corner setting and a real sense of hospitality. *90 Bedford Street (at Grove Street), New York, NY 10014.* ***212-741-4695.*** *www.thelittleowlnyc.com.*

Mary's Fish Camp Greenwich Village Seafood $ $

The place is tiny, cramped, and very popular. It serves good old-fashioned seafood such as lobster, lobster rolls, pan-roasted monkfish, and fried cod sandwiches. Takeout, yes; reservations, no. *64 Charles Street (at West Fourth Street), New York, NY 10014.* ***646-486-2185.*** *www.marysfishcamp.com.*

Mercadito East Village Mexican $ $

Mercadito is a small, festive place that serves small tapas-style portions and does a great job of simultaneously creating atmosphere and dishing out good Mexican food. *179 Avenue B (between 11th and 12th Streets), New York, NY 10009.* ***212-529-6490.*** *www.mercaditony.com.*

Mercer Kitchen SoHo French/American $ $

For such a chic place, the Mercer Hotel's house restaurant makes some homey meals. Consider roast chicken with French beans, baby carrots, and mashed potatoes or the grilled lamb chops with butter beans. On the other hand, the individual pizzas come with combinations such as black truffle and fontina. *99 Prince Street (at Mercer Street), New York, NY 10012.* ***212-966-5454.*** *www. jean-georges.com.*

Mermaid Inn East Village American/Seafood $ $

A favorite of some of New York's best-known chefs, Mermaid Inn strives to look like an old fish shack. The menu and the pretty backyard garden throw off that plan, however. Offerings include grilled mahi-mahi, lobster sandwiches, and the very popular clam fritters. *96 Second Avenue (between Fifth and Sixth Streets), New York, NY 10003.* ***212-674-5870.*** *www.beanstalkrestaurants.com.*

Odeon   TriBeCa   French/American 💲💲

There's a photo of Andy Warhol standing out front on the Odeon's website. Its familiar red Deco-neon sign was on the cover of the novel *Bright Lights, Big City*. In other words, Odeon has been around for a while. But it remains hip in an established late-night way and still offers satisfying bistro classics such as steak frites, French onion soup, and a crôque monsieur—along with BLTs, brook trout, and ravioli. *145 West Broadway (between Duane and Thomas Streets), New York, NY 10013.* **212-233-0507.** *www.theodeonrestaurant.com.*

Ono   Meat Packing District   Japanese 💲💲

Hotel Gansevoort's multilevel house restaurant is big on mood-setting. Its outdoor Japanese garden even has a reflecting pool. Yet, critics find the place frenetic. Luckily, they like the sushi as well as the crispy pork and vegetable dumplings, the grilled skewers of chicken liver and shiitake mushrooms, and the citrus tart. *18 Ninth Avenue (at 13th Street), New York, NY 10014.* **212-660-6766.** *www.chinagrillmgt.com.*

Pastis   Meat Packing District   French 💲💲

Named for the national drink of France (or at least Provence), Pastis is a professionally casual, intensely fashionable bistro with the requisite zinc bar and summertime outdoor café. You might have a big meal, including roasted rack of lamb with mustard crust and flageolet beans, or maybe just an omelet or a crôque monsieur. *9 Ninth Avenue (at Little West 12th Street), New York, NY 10014.* **212-929-4844.** *www.pastisny.com.*

Pearl Oyster Bar   Greenwich Village   American/Seafood 💲💲

How many bests can one restaurant claim? The Pearl has had that honor bestowed on its lobster rolls, oyster po' boys, and bouillabaisse by publications including *Gourmet* magazine and *The New Yorker*. The owner, who was inspired by the Maine vacations of her childhood, likes to see this as an oasis of Yankee charm in the big city. *18 Cornelia Street (between Bleecker and West Fourth Streets), New York, NY 10014.* **212-691-8211.** *www.pearloysterbar.com.*

Pó   Greenwich Village   Italian $ $

Pó is small, romantic, and traditionally Italian. You'll find spaghetti carbonara and veal marsala on the menu, but you'll also find grilled Portobello
mushrooms with arugula and shaved Parmigiana Reggiano. Or, try the $50
six-course tasting menu. *31 Cornelia Street (between Bleecker and West Fourth
Streets), New York, NY 10014.* **212-645-2189.** *www.porestaurant.com.*

Pure Food and Wine   Gramercy Park   Vegan $ $

If you're already a vegan and/or a proponent of raw food, Pure Food and Wine
is probably already your favorite restaurant. If you're not, that doesn't mean
the food won't knock you out. And as magazines including *Forbes* and *Japanese
Vogue* have pointed out, it's quite normal. The menu includes Caesar salad,
zucchini and tomato lasagna, smoked Portobello mushrooms, and even potato
salad. *54 Irving Place (between 17th and 18th Streets), New York, NY 10003.* **212-
477-1010.** *www.purefoodandwine.com.*

Red Cat   Chelsea   American $ $

You don't see many restaurants decorated with both Moroccan hanging lamps
and barn siding. But that's a helpful hint about the Red Cat's mixed identity—
part neighborhood tavern, part chic gallerygoers' hangout. Recommended dishes
include the lamb chop Milanese, sautéed zucchini, and the orange panna cotta.
The downside: It's often mobbed. *227 10th Avenue (between 23rd and 24th Streets),
New York, NY 10011.* **212-242-1122.** *www.beanstalkrestaurants.com.*

Strip House   Greenwich Village   American/Steak $ $

It's a double-entendre, get it? You can order a New York strip steak, but there are
also pictures of old-time strippers on the wall. Yet this isn't one of those tough,
macho-style steakhouses. In fact, the restaurant's most-praised dish seems to be
the vegetables en papillote. *13 East 12th Street (between Fifth Avenue and University
Place), New York, NY 10003.* **212-328-0000.** *www.theglaziergroup.com.*

TriBeCa Grill   TriBeCa   American $ $

TriBeCa Grill had instant chic when it opened in 1990, partly because Robert
De Niro is a co-owner. But it probably would have succeeded anyway, with
its industrial-grand décor, fashionable but hearty menu, and award-winning
wine list (heavy on the Châteauneuf du Pape and California Cabernets). Try

the scallops with chanterelle and sweet potato risotto or the roasted venison loin. And the mahogany bar may look familiar to old-timers: it came from Maxwell's Plum, the original Upper East Side singles bar. *375 Greenwich Street (at Franklin Street), New York, NY 10013.* **212-941-3900.** *www.tribecagrill.com.*

Zen Palate   Financial District   Vegetarian $ $

You don't have to be vegetarian to like Zen Palate. Not when you can start a meal with basil peanut moo shu rolls, scallion pancakes, or hot and sour soup. The food has Chinese, Japanese, Indian, and Mexican influences. E. T. here means eggplant and tofu. The menu is predominantly vegan too, but a few dishes contain dairy ingredients. No alcohol is served, but you can bring your own bottle of wine for a corkage fee. *104 John Street (between Cliff and Pearl Streets), New York, NY 10038.* **212-962-4208.** *www.zenpalate.com.*

Affordable, With and Without Atmosphere

Corner Bistro   Greenwich Village   American $

When great chefs are in the mood for a really great hamburger, where do they go? Right here. This place is just what the name suggests, an inexpensive, often crowded neighborhood place that serves until the wee hours. Burgers start at $5.50. The menu also features chili, BLTs, grilled cheese sandwiches, and fries. *331 West Fourth Street (at Jane Street), New York, NY 10014.* **212-242-9502.**

Dim Sum Go Go   Chinatown   Chinese $

First of all, it doesn't have only dim sum and it doesn't serve food only "to go." This cheerful downtown diner specializes in Chinese food with a French accent, good enough to earn a star from *The New York Times.* Favorites include the shredded duck with ginger, spinach and bean curd soup and stuffed Swiss chard. *5 East Broadway (off Chatham Square), New York, NY 10038.* **212-732-0797.**

Empire Diner   Chelsea   American $

The Empire is a real stainless-steel railroad-car diner, circa 1946, straight out of an Edward Hopper painting, only shinier. And it's open 24 hours a day, so you can have any kind of meal you want. They have eggs, Belgian waffles, French toast, salads, burgers, chicken-fried steak, and a long-ago New York classic, the chocolate egg cream. *210 Tenth Avenue (at 22nd Street), New York, NY 10011.* **212-243-2736.** *www.empire-diner.com.*

Fuleen Seafood Chinatown   Chinese/Seafood $

Rumor has it that the chefs of some of the most expensive restaurants in town come to this very unstylish spot for great seafood. Fuleen certainly has dishes you won't find everywhere, such as crispy black jellyfish; braised shark's fin; and a frog, ginger, and scallion casserole. They also have 42 kinds of rice. *11 Division Street (between Market and Catherine Streets), New York, NY 10002.* **212-941-6888.**

Gobo Greenwich Village   Vegetarian $

Gobo serves international meatless cuisine in a pleasant dining room with clean lines meant to encourage mealtime serenity. In addition to a juice bar and organic wines, the restaurant offers a choice between small plates (such as seitan skewers with green-tea mustard sauce) and large plates (such as butternut squash risotto with toasted almonds). *401 Avenue of the Americas (between Eighth Street and Waverly Place), New York, NY 10014.* **212-255-3902.** *www. goborestaurant.com.*

Gray's Papaya Greenwich Village   American $

Maybe you've already checked out the Upper West side location of this glorified (and beloved) hot dog stand. Order a frank or two and a fruit drink, and you have what may be the cheapest lunch in town. *402 Sixth Avenue (at Eighth Street), New York, NY 10011.* **212-260-3532.**

Great Jones Café NoHo   American/Cajun $

Southern comfort food in a no-frills atmosphere at budget prices sounds like heaven to me. The menu changes constantly, but you might find blackened catfish, firehouse chili, St. John's gumbo, and garlic mashed potatoes on it. The place is renowned for its Bloody Marys. And the jalapeño cornbread is only 95 cents. *54 Great Jones Street (between Lafayette Street and Bowery), New York, NY 10012.* **212-674-9304.** *www.greatjonescom.*

Itzocan East Village   Mexican

Like its uptown sister, the East Village Itzocan is Mexican with a French accent. There are quesadillas and burritos at lunch, but at dinner the fusion is more obvious. The sweet corn appetizer is made with truffle oil. The roasted stuffed chicken breast features both goat cheese and red mole sauce. *438 East Ninth Street (between Avenue A and First Avenue), New York, NY 10009. 212-677-5856.*

Katz's Delicatessen   Lower East Side   American $\boxed{\$}$

You know that scene in the movie *When Harry Met Sally* where Meg Ryan gets all orgasmic at a restaurant and an older customer (played by Rob Reiner's mother) says, "I'll have what she's having"? That was filmed at Katz's Deli. If there's a real old-style New York Jewish deli extant, this one, founded in 1888, is it. You can get lox and bagels, pastrami, chopped liver, matzo ball soup, knishes, cheesecake, and an egg cream, although maybe not all at once. *Gourmet* magazine once declared Katz's hot dogs the best in town, too. *205 East Houston Street (at Ludlow Street), New York, NY 10002. 212-254-2246. www.katzdeli.com.*

Mandarin Court   Chinatown   Chinese $\boxed{\$}$

Here's a great place for dim sum. Mandarin Court has 40 different kinds. The almost endless menu also includes a dozen clay-pot casseroles, numerous varieties of buns, and a variety of rice and noodle dishes. The lunch specials include some old favorites, such as lemon chicken, orange beef, and sweet-and-sour pork. *61 Mott Street (between Bayard and Canal Streets), New York, NY 10013. 212-608-3838.*

OKAY, I GIVE UP ... WHAT'S DIM SUM?

In most parts of New York City, brunch means omelets, scrambled eggs, pancakes, or French toast. In Chinatown, it means dim sum, a parade of tiny, inexpensive dishes that arrive at your table by cart (if the restaurant is doing things the traditional way). There are egg rolls, fried wontons, potstickers, and lots and lots of dumplings. You just eat as many as you want and stop when you're full. What a concept!

Oriental Garden   Chinatown   Chinese

Excellent Cantonese seafood, outstanding dim sum, and low prices make Oriental Garden a real find. Try the salt-and-pepper prawns or the razor clams in black bean sauce. *14 Elizabeth Street (between Bayard and Canal Streets), New York, NY 10013.* **212-619-0085.**

Pete's Tavern   Gramercy Park   American

The story is that O. Henry wrote "The Gift of the Magi" here, sitting at his regular booth in the front. Pete's Tavern opened in 1864, making it the oldest continuously operating bar/restaurant in the city. (During Prohibition, it posed as a flower shop.) It's still going strong, with a casual American menu with Italian accents. There are burgers, veal parmigiana, filet of sole, steak sandwiches, and onion rings. *129 East 18th Street (at Irving Place), New York, NY 10003.* **212-473-7676.**

Ping's Seafood   Chinatown   Chinese

New Yorkers always say you can tell a really good Chinese restaurant by the number of Chinese customers you see there. And Ping's, where the specialty is seafood fresh from the tank, is very popular with Asian patrons. *The New York Times* restaurant critic gave the place two stars, praising the braised abalone and the winter melon soup. *22 Mott Street (between Bayard and Pell Streets), New York, NY 10013.* **212-602-9988.**

White Horse Tavern   Greenwich Village   American

It's a little strange that the White Horse is best known for someone famous having drunk himself to death there (the poet Dylan Thomas in 1953), but the mystique seems to keep drawing locals, students, and visiting out-of-towners. Besides drinks, there's basic pub food, a lively atmosphere and an outdoor café. *567 Hudson Street (at West 11th Street), New York, NY 10014.* **212-243-9260.**

Downtown Sights, A to Z

Because Downtown is the oldest part of the city, there's a real sense of history here, if you know where to look for it. For one thing, you'll find the three oldest churches in the city here, all within two miles of one another. Not to mention parks, museums, schools, and New York's first real skyscrapers.

Battery Park   Financial District

It's been called the front lawn of the Financial District, and it's a big one—25 acres of waterfront parkland. Its centerpiece, the Castle Clinton National Monument (now the ticketing center for the Staten Island, Statue of Liberty, and Ellis Island ferries), has had past lives as a theater and as an aquarium. The whole thing began as a fort, built for the War of 1812. Now it's a pretty garden, with 75,000 square feet of perennials and a great view of a certain statue standing in the harbor. *Battery Place (southern tip of West Street, Greenwich Street and Broadway, along State Street), New York, NY 10004.* **212-344-3491.** *www.thebattery.org.*

Brooklyn Bridge   Financial District

Thomas Wolfe loved it enough to exclaim "Good God, the only bridge of power, life and joy!" in print. Since it was completed in 1883, the Brooklyn Bridge has been a lot more than just a way to get to Brooklyn from Manhattan and vice versa. It's no longer the longest suspension bridge in the world (far from it), but those neo-Gothic granite towers and that web of wire cables, as delicate as harp strings, are as seductive as ever. The view at night is fabulous. Walking across the bridge on the wide pedestrian walkway is a memorable experience. *From Park Row, Manhattan, to Cadman Plaza, Brooklyn. www.nyc.gov.*

City Hall   Financial District

When it was built, between 1803 and 1812, City Hall sat at the very northern tip of the city. Now it's only at the northern end of the Financial District. It's still quite grand, though, with its French-influenced Federal styling, arched windows, and Corinthian columns. The interior is American Georgian with a sweeping staircase, a landmarked rotunda, and an impressive collection of nineteenth-century portraits. The Mayor of New York does have his office here, the City Council meets here, and City Hall Park is a favored site for political demonstrations. *260 Broadway (junction of Broadway, Park Row, and Chambers Street), New York, NY 10007. Free tours on weekdays.* **212-788-3000.** *Tour reservations* **311** *(within New York City) or* **212-NEW-YORK** *(from out of town). www.nyc.gov.*

IF YOU ABSOLUTELY MUST BE ATHLETIC

In another era, you might have gone down to these piers to meet your friends arriving on the Titanic. (Well, maybe the survivors who came in on the Carpathia.) Today this 30-acre stretch of waterfront is devoted to sports and entertainment in a complex known as Chelsea Piers. Here are some of the recreational possibilities:

Pier 59/Golf

Between Piers 59 and 60/300 New York (bowling)

Pier 60/Sports Center (health club)

Pier 61/Sky Rink (skating)

Between Piers 61 and 62/The Field House (includes batting cages, basketball, exercise classes, and a gym for toddlers)

Chelsea Piers, Hudson River waterfront from 17th Street to 23rd Street. www. chelseapiers.com.

Ellis Island   New York Harbor

Whether you know much about your ancestors or not, chances are about 50-50 that at least one of them passed through Ellis Island. Some 22 million immigrants, other passengers, and ships' crews entered the United States via Ellis Island between 1892 and 1924. And since 1990, you've been able to check up on them in the American Family Immigration History Center and visit the immigration museum here. There are photographs, prints, artifacts, video presentations, and interactive displays. *New York Harbor. Ferry from Battery Park 9 A.M.–5 P.M. daily (open later in summer). Adults $12, children 4–12 $5. $6 extra for audio tour.* **1-877-LADY-TIX.** *www.nyc.gov., www.ellisisland.org, www.statuecruises.com.*

Flatiron Building   Flatiron District (naturally)

It was really called the Fuller Building, after the construction company, but New Yorkers immediately noticed its resemblance to turn-of-the-century clothing irons and the nickname stuck. The 22-story Flatiron Building went up in 1902 and was the tallest skyscraper of its day. The Italian Renaissance façade is still impressive, and it's still a functioning office building. *175 Fifth Avenue (at Broadway, near 23rd Street), New York, NY 10010.*

General Theological Seminary   Chelsea

Clement Clarke Moore, whose family owned all of Chelsea (it was their country estate), donated the land to this Episcopal seminary, which was founded in 1817. Today its chapel, another dozen buildings, its grounds, and its gardens make up the most serene landscape in the neighborhood. *Ninth Avenue to Tenth Avenue and 20th Street to 21st Street, New York, NY 10011.* **212-243-5150.** *www.gts.edu.*

Ground Zero   See World Trade Center Site

National Museum of the American Indian   Financial District

The museum is also called the George Gustav Heye Center, because Heye (pronounced "high"), an investment banker born in 1874, made his private collection the basis of this one. There are, among other things, wood and stone carvings, masks, hides, clothing, feather bonnets, pottery, and basketry from North America, archaeological objects form the Caribbean, jade from the Olmec and Maya civilizations, and ceramics from Peru. *Alexander Hamilton U.S. Custom House, One Bowling Green (corner of Battery Place and State Street at the northeastern corner of Battery Park), New York, NY 10004. Fridays through Wednesdays 10 A.M.–5 P.M., Thursdays 10 A.M.–8 P.M. Free.* **212-514-3700.** *www.nmai.si.edu.*

New Museum   East Village

Like the Guggenheim, the New Museum of Contemporary Art is destined to be talked about more for its building than for its art. The museum was founded in 1977 but kept a low profile until it moved into its new building on the gritty Lower East Side 30 years later. Japanese architects suspended aluminum mesh over gray corrugated aluminum panels and sheathed the ground floor in glass. The effect is a little like a series of translucent boxes on top of one another, about to topple over. Inside you'll find high-ceilinged galleries filled with what management hopes is cutting-edge, even radical art. *235 Bowery (at Prince Street), New York, NY 10002. Wednesdays, Saturdays, and Sundays 12 P.M.–6 P.M., Thursdays–Fridays 12 P.M.–10 P.M. Closed Mondays and Tuesdays. Adults $12, students $6, young people 18 and under free.* **212-219-1222.** *www. newmuseum.org.*

New York Stock Exchange   Financial District

Here's where it all happens, the ups and downs of America's volatile stock market. You'll have to take the traders' word for it, though, because the Stock Exchange doesn't do tours anymore. You can appreciate the building, though, an example of Classical Revival, built in 1903, with tall Corinthian columns and marble sculpture in the pediment dedicated to the concept of integrity. Hmmm. *11 Wall Street (between New and Broad Streets), New York, NY 10005. Mondays–Fridays 9:30 A.M.–4 P.M., but not open to the public. 212-656-3000. www.nyse.com.*

GEORGE WASHINGTON'S BIG DAY

Just a few yards from the Stock Exchange you'll see a tall, handsome statue of George Washington. It stands exactly where Washington was inaugurated on April 30, 1789, as the first President of the United States. The building behind him, known as Federal Hall National Memorial, was built in 1842, replacing the original Federal Hall, which stood here in Washington's day, when New York was briefly the nation's capital city. Washington took the oath of office on the earlier building's balcony. *26 Wall Street, New York, NY 10005. 212-825-6888. www.nps.gov/feha.*

New York University   Greenwich Village

With some 40,000 students and 14 different schools and colleges (including the prestigious film school), NYU is the largest private university in the United States. It was founded in 1831 and has just grown. You'll find many of its buildings surrounding Washington Square Park. And all around the neighborhood. *Washington Square and points north, south, east, and west, New York, NY 10001. 212-998-8100. www.nyu.edu.*

St. Luke in the Fields   Greenwich Village

When it was dedicated in 1822, St. Luke's, the third oldest church building in the city, overlooked the Hudson River (these were pre-landfill days) and was surrounded by farms. Today it's in the middle of the Village, but it still has beautiful gardens that are open to the public. An Episcopal church, it started out as the country chapel of Trinity Church, and its first warden was Clement Clarke Moore (the aforementioned author of "A Visit From St. Nicholas"), who was obviously a very important and busy guy. The Federal-style church was severely damaged in a 1981 fire, but three exterior walls and the tower survived and the sanctuary was restored. *487 Hudson Street (between Grove and Christopher Streets), New York, NY 10014. North Garden, Mondays–Saturdays 7 A.M.–8 P.M. South Garden, daily 8 A.M.–8 P.M. Rector's Garden, Mondays–Thursdays 10 A.M.–5:30 p.m.* **212-924-0562.** *www.stlukeinthefields.org.*

St. Mark's in the Bowery   East Village

And here's the second oldest church building in New York. St. Mark's, a rather plain Georgian-style Episcopal church, was dedicated in 1799. The steeple was added in 1828 and the Italianate portico in 1854. The church has a longstanding relationship with the arts. In addition to religious services, St. Mark's houses the Ontological Hysteric Theater, the Poetry Project, and the Danspace Project. Both Martha Graham and Isadora Duncan danced here. *131 East 10th Street (at Second Avenue), New York, NY 10003.* **212-674-6377.** *www. stmarkschurch-in-the-bowery.com.*

Not for sale: the Brooklyn Bridge, spanning the East River since 1883.

St. Paul Chapel   Financial District

George Washington went to church here. Yes, we have finally come to the oldest church building in New York. In fact, St. Paul's is the city's oldest public building of any kind in continuous use. Washington headed here right after his inauguration in 1789 and attended services here as long as New York was the national capital. Completed in 1766, the church re-established its reputation after the terrorist attacks of September 11, 2001, when it served as a makeshift memorial spot as well as a place of rest and refuge for emergency workers. Although it stood in the shadow of the World Trade Center, the church survived without even a broken window. St. Paul's is a Georgian building with a classical portico, standing on land granted by Queen Anne of Britain. *209 Broadway (at Fulton Street), New York, NY 10007. Church Weekdays 10 A.M.–6 P.M., Saturdays 8 A.M.–3 P.M., Sundays 7 A.M.–3 P.M. Churchyard: Mondays–Saturdays 10 A.M.–4 P.M., Sundays 7 A.M.–3:30 P.M.* **212-233-4164.** *www.saintpaulschapel.org.*

A TOUGH GUY'S GRAVE

Peter Stuyvesant is buried beneath the chapel of St. Mark's in the Bowery, and he deserves that place of honor. Stuyvesant, who was a Dutch-born seventeenth-century director-general of New Amsterdam (before the English took over and it became New York), owned this land. It was his farm, or bowery (a variation on the Dutch word), and before his death in the 1670s he built a chapel on what is now the site of St. Mark's. Stuyvesant's name (pronounced, roughly, STY-vuh-zunt) is all over New York. Unfortunately as a politician, he was a tough guy and not very big on religious freedom, but that's another story.

South Street Seaport   Financial District

The South Street Maritime Museum is the big attraction at this historic waterfront site, which bustled with real maritime activity from 1815 to 1860 or so. There are outdoor concerts, places to eat (from Häagen Dazs to a real seafood restaurant), and places to buy things (from Victoria's Secret to Sharper Image). See "Great Shopping, in Its Way," later this chapter. *Corner of Fulton and South Streets, Pier 17, New York, NY 10038. 212-SEA-PORT. www. southstreetseaport.com.*

Statue of Liberty   New York Harbor

What the Eiffel Tower is to Paris, the Statue of Liberty is to New York. And we have the French to thank for it. This colossal copper statue was a gift from France in 1886, shipped here in 350 pieces and then reassembled on its own 12-acre island. If you plan ahead, you can get a free monument-access pass (it's a "first come, first served" deal), which lets you visit the museum gallery and the observation level in the pedestal. Nobody goes any higher these days. *Liberty Island, New York, NY 10004. Ferry from Battery Park 9 A.M.–5 P.M. daily (open later in summer). Adults $12, children 4–12 $5. $6 extra for audio tour. Tickets at Castle Clinton National Monument in Battery Park. 1-877-LADY-TIX. Visitor information 212-363-3200. www.statueofliberty.org, www.nps.gov, or www. statuecruises.com.*

IT'S A NICE STATUE, BUT …

If spending half a day (or longer) just to visit the Statue of Liberty on its island doesn't really fit into your tight schedule, there are other ways to get a good look at this icon of icons. The Circle Line tour people (see Chapter 11) do a two-hour boat trip that takes you quite close. The Staten Island Ferry (about 25 minutes each way) works too.

Staten Island Ferry   Financial District

It's only a five-mile trip that takes 25 minutes or so, but the Staten Island Ferry offers a memorable view of New York and New York Harbor. It was never meant as a tourist attraction. The ferry takes some 60,000 passengers every weekday, most of them commuters, and has been operating since 1897. It doesn't cost a nickel (the original price) any more. After the fare started creeping up, the powers that be just decided to make the trip free. *Whitehall Terminal, corner of Whitehall Street and Water Street, New York, NY 10006. See the following schedule.* **718-815-BOAT.** *www.siferry.com.*

TAKE A FREE RIDE

The Staten Island Ferry operates seven days a week, shuttling between Whitehall Terminal in Downtown Manhattan and St. George on Staten Island. Since 1997, the trip is absolutely free.

Weekdays: Departs Manhattan every 15–20 minutes, 6:30 A.M.–9:30 A.M. and 4 P.M.–8 P.M. At other times, every half-hour.

Saturdays: Departs Manhattan every half-hour, 7 A.M.–7:30 P.M. At other times, every hour.

Sundays: Departs Manhattan every hour on the half-hour.

Return trips from Staten Island generally mirror the Manhattan to Staten Island schedule.

To reach Whitehall Terminal by subway, take the No. 1 or 9 to South Ferry or the No. 4 or 5 to Bowling Green.

Trinity Church   Financial District

Trinity is the mother of all of New York's churches, founded in 1697 by charter of King William III of Britain. The first church building went up the following year but was destroyed in the great New York fire of 1776. The second building was torn down in 1839 because of severe snow damage. The present church, with its neo-Gothic spire, was dedicated in 1846. Alexander Hamilton, William Bradford, and Robert Fulton are buried in its churchyard. *Broadway and Wall Street, New York, NY 10006. Church: Weekdays 7 A.M.–6 P.M., Saturdays 8 A.M.–4 P.M., Sundays 7 A.M.–4 P.M. Churchyard: Weekdays 7 A.M.– 4 P.M., Saturdays and holidays 8 A.M.–3 P.M., Sundays 7 A.M.–3 P.M. Free tours daily at 2 P.M.* **212-602-0800.** *www.trinitywallstreet.org.*

Washington Square Park   Greenwich Village

The park looks harmless now (at least during the day), but this peaceful 9.7-acre spot was once the site of public executions. Before that, as early as 1797, it was a Potter's Field. Today Washington Square is a haven for strollers, students, musicians, chess players, children, dog owners, and the random tourist. Its best-known asset is, of course, Washington Arch, built in 1892 to honor George Washington. The park is surrounded by well-preserved Greek Revival and Federal townhouses, many of them owned by New York University. A renovation is under way, promising a restoration of the central fountain, new plantings, and more unpaved green space. *Waverly Place to West Fourth Street and MacDougal Street to University Place, New York, NY 10003. www.nycgovparks. org.*

Woolworth Building   Financial District

In 1913, when it was completed, the 57-story Woolworth Building was the tallest building in the world. They called it the Cathedral of Commerce, and this Gothic-style building does have a religious feel with a sumptuous cruciform lobby with vaulted ceilings, lots of marble, bronze, and even gargoyles. But be warned: Security guards have been known to turn visitors away with the words "No sightseeing." *233 Broadway (between Park Place and Barclay Street), New York, NY 10279.* **212-397-8200.**

World Trade Center Site   Financial District

No matter how much respect we show to the site and to the more than 2,700 people who died in the terrorist attacks here on September 11, 2001, there is still something distasteful about the spot where the World Trade Center towers once stood having turned into a tourist attraction. On the other hand, I went downtown to see the damage as soon as civilians were allowed below Canal Street—when that awful burned smell still hung in the air—so I understand the impulse to visit. This is now a construction site (for the 1,776-foot-tall building to be called the Freedom Tower), so for the time being, visitors may want just to pass by and to pay their respects at nearby St. Paul Chapel instead. *Vesey Street to Liberty Street and Church Street to West Side Highway, New York, NY 10007.*

Great Shopping, in Its Way

No shopping district like the grand sweep of Midtown Fifth Avenue exists in Lower Manhattan. But it does have pockets of shopping opportunity, some larger than others.

Bleecker Street in Greenwich Village

I've been around long enough to remember when the **Magnolia Bakery,** at the corner of Bleecker and 11th Street, was a pet store specializing in colorful, noisy birds. I don't miss the birds so much, but it is a shame that so many neighborhood shops have been replaced by designer boutiques.

Our misfortune is your good luck, though, if you're looking for a compact, brand-name shopping area to explore while you check out the Village's other charms. The best route is to start at the corner of Bleecker and Bank Streets and walk southeast.

On the first block, things still look like old times, with **Leo Design,** an antiques shop, at 413 Bleecker, and **Treasures & Trifles,** at 409.

But in between those shops is the first of two **James Perse** stores, known for California style (and chic T-shirts).

It's good to see **Biography Bookshop,** with its well-chosen collection, still at the corner of West 11th Street on the right. Glamorous **Marc Jacobs** is across the street. (That designer's two other stores, a **Marc Jacobs** and a **Little Marc Jacobs,** with clothing, books, and fuzzy bears for young shoppers, are at two different corners of Bank Street and West Fourth Street, one block off Bleecker.)

Next comes the **Magnolia Bakery,** which may not look high-style to you, but this place has single handedly made cupcakes the coolest dessert in town. Across the street, at 394 Bleecker, is **Lulu Guinness,** outpost of the British designer. It's followed by **Double RL Denim,** at 390, and **Robert Marc**'s designer eyewear, at 386.

By the time you visit 383 Bleecker Street (corner of Perry Street), **L'Uomo** will probably be gone, replaced by yet another **Ralph Lauren** store. Before the shift it was just Ralph's two Bleecker Street stores, next door at 381 Bleecker and across the street.

Ralph's neighbors on the south side of the street include **Olive & Bette's,** another **Marc Jacobs** shop and **Cynthia Rowley,** with that American designer's sophisticated fashions, at 376 Bleecker.

Before we hit Charles Street, we pass **Tommy Hilfiger, Coach, Ruehl, Juicy Couture,** and **Les Pierre Antiques** (formerly Pierre Deux).

Crossing Charles, we find **Intermix** (London, fashions and accessories); another **James Perse** shop; **Arleen Bowman,** known for classic, grown-up fashion; and **Verve,** which has great bags, watches, and other accessories.

The next block, after West 10th Street, gives us the colorful women's fashions of **Miguelina,** at 347 Bleecker, across from an old standby, **Village Apothecary.** Crossing Christopher Street, we find **Smoke Shop,** at 324. The bongs, hookahs, and rolling papers in the window suggest that we have found an old-fashioned Village head shop, and our designer-shop excursion has come to an end … for now.

Century 21 in the Financial District

It's the closest thing to real discount outlet shopping in Manhattan, with prices billed as 40 to 70 percent off suggested retail. **Century 21** (which is very close to the World Trade Center site and was closed for five months because of damage from the terrorist attacks) sells men's fashions, women's fashions, children's fashions, handbags, shoes, accessories, and items for the home. I haven't had great luck here, but my friends have. *22 Cortlandt Street (west of Broadway, between Dey Street and Liberty Street), New York, NY 10007. Mondays, Tuesdays, Wednesdays, and Saturdays 7:45 A.M.–8 P.M., Thursdays 7:45 A.M.–10 P.M., Fridays 7:45 A.M.–8:30 P.M., Sundays 11 A.M.–7 P.M.* **212-227-9092.** *www.c21stores.com.*

Chelsea Market in Chelsea

In the 1890s, this complex was the National Biscuit Company (later Nabisco), where all the goodies were baked. But they moved out in 1958, and decades later **Chelsea Market** was born. The market is known for its restaurants and bakeries and the Food Network studios, but there are also shops worth checking out.

Bowery Kitchen Supply has cookware, knives, utensils, gadgets, tools, and even kitchen furniture. **Chelsea Market Baskets** sells gift baskets for various occasions (or just the ingredients). **Imports From Marrakesh** has Moroccan tiles, lamps, rugs, and other items for home décor.

Chelsea Wine Vault, which stocks wines from around the world, sponsors wine classes and in-store tastings. And the upscale **Chelsea Wholesale Flower Market** does sell retail as well, carrying flowers and green plants and doing floral arrangements.

Ninth Avenue to Tenth Avenue, 15th to 16th Streets, New York, NY 10011. Market doors open Mondays–Fridays 7 A.M.–9 P.M., Saturdays–Sundays 10 A.M.–8 P.M. Various shops have different hours. (Three-hour tours of Chelsea Market and Meat Packing District, including on-the-go tastings, $40. **212-209-3370.** *www.foodsofny. com. or www.chelseamarket.com.*

SoHo

It probably wasn't anybody's plan when artists started moving into the cast-iron buildings here, but once SoHo became cool, the retailers followed. Today the neighborhood is one of the most fashionable shopping areas in the city.

If you're in the market for fashion, there are dozens of choices, including **Dolce & Gabbana,** at 434 West Broadway, specializing in the designers' bridge line; **Prada,** at 575 Broadway; **Barbara Bui,** at 115 Wooster Street; **A.P.C.,** at 131 Mercer Street; **Ted Baker London,** at 107 Grand Street; **Chanel,** at 139 Spring Street; **Marc Jacobs,** at 163 Mercer Street; and **Ralph Lauren,** at 379 West Broadway.

Other intriguing fashion stores: **Wink,** at 155 Spring Street; **Shecky's Shop,** at 489 Broome Street; **Jack Spade,** at 56 Greene Street; **Costume National,** at 108 Wooster Street; and a branch of **Anthropologie,** at 375 West Broadway.

For shoes, the possibilities include **Irregular Choice,** at 276 Lafayette Street; **Vitto,** at 424 West Broadway; and **Te Casan,** at 382 West Broadway. For leather goods and handbags, there are **Coach,** at 143 Prince Street; **Kate Spade,** at 454 Broome Street; **Louis Vuitton,** at 116 Greene Street; and, for luggage, **Il Bisonte,** at 120 Sullivan Street.

Several places carry interesting jewelry, among them **Fragments,** at 116 Prince Street; **So Good Jewelry,** at 496 Broadway; **Robert Lee Morris,** 400 West Broadway; and **Girlprops,** at 153 Prince Street.

If you're traveling with children or bringing gifts back for some, you can shop for toys at **Alphaville,** at 226 West Houston Street; **Kid Robot,** at 126 Prince Street; and **Pylones,** at 69 Spring Street, which also carries home décor items.

Clio, at 92 Thompson Street, also sells home décor, as well as kitchen and bath items. **Sur la Table,** at 75 Spring Street, also has kitchen and bath things. Or if you want to go all the way and buy furniture while you're here, sources include **BDDW,** at 5 Crosby Street; **Room & Board,** at 105 Wooster Street; **Moss,** at 146 Greene Street; and a branch of **Crate & Barrel,** at 611 Broadway.

There's an **Apple Store** at 103 Prince Street. A unique store called **Kiosk,** at 95 Spring Street, sells unusual items (dish towels, soap, notebooks, pens, toys, pillows, you name it) from many countries. However, they only sell one country at a time. And of course there's **Bloomingdale's SoHo,** at 504 Broadway, an honest-to-goodness department store.

South Street Seaport in the Financial District

The stores here include many you could find in almost any city, such as **Victoria's Secret, J. Crew, Ann Taylor, Gap, Gap Kids,** and **Godiva Chocolates.** If you're looking for something with an actual New York connection, you might try the **Metropolitan Museum Store** and the **New York Yankees Clubhouse Shop.** Other stores include **Sharper Image, Coach, United Colors of Benetton, Foot Locker, Bath & Body Works,** and **Sunglass Hut.**

*Fulton Street and South Street, Pier 17, New York, NY 10038. Mall open
Mondays–Saturdays 10 A.M.–7 P.M., Sundays 11 A.M.–6 P.M.* **212-SEA-PORT.**
www.southstreetseaport.com.

Fabulous Cocktail Hours

If it still isn't clear to you that Downtown is a study in contrasts, where Bohe-
mia and Wall Street pass in the night, take a look at these very different places
to have a drink or two. As in other parts of town, go early, If you can, to avoid
the crowds.

The Angel's Share   East Village

Right away, you feel like an insider, because you know that you have to go up
to the second floor and walk through a Japanese restaurant to get to the front
door of the Angel's Share. What you'll find inside is the civilized perfection of
beautifully made cocktails and, if you're lucky enough to get a window table, a
charming East Village view. *8 Stuyvesant Street (just off Ninth Street and Third
Avenue), New York, NY 10003.* **212-777-5415.**

Death & Company   East Village

Wouldn't you love a Pink Lady, a Black Market Manhattan, or a Slanted
Grouse? The people at Death & Company take cocktails very seriously. Or
you could just have a glass of wine or a scotch and soda. And if you're hungry
too, there are all sorts of snacks (sashimi, crab cakes, oysters, etc.), some real
food (fish & chips, filet mignon), and desserts. *433 East Sixth Street (at First
Avenue), New York, NY 10009.* **212-388-0882.** *www.deathandcompany.com.*

The Ear Inn   SoHo

The Federal-style house has been around since at least 1817, when James
Brown (not the godfather of soul, but an African American tobacconist) lived
there and had his shop on the ground floor. Over the years it served as a drugstore, a boot maker's shop, and a grocery store before becoming a bar. In 1977
the current owner, who was publishing a music journal called *Ear,* painted
over part of the B on the sign outside, turning the word Bar into Ear. It's a
wonderfully ramshackle old place with live music (jazz and blues) on Sundays
and many other nights. *326 Spring Street (between West and Washington Streets),
New York, NY 10013.* **212-226-9060.** *www.earinn.com.*

Mercbar SoHo

A co-owner of MercBar, next to the Mercer Hotel, describes the place's décor as a cross between an Adirondacks camp and an old boathouse. Others just call it rustic, rugged, or, as *The Village Voice* said, "relentlessly comfy." So relax in this incongruous mountain-lodge setting in the city and have a glass of Veuve Clicquot, a shot of 12-year-old scotch, a sour apple martini, or a California pinot noir. Make up your own scenario. *151 Mercer Street (between Houston and Prince Streets), New York, NY 10012.* **212-966-2727.** *www.mercbar.com.*

Plunge Meat Packing District

Up on the roof of the Hotel Gansevoort is a world of beautiful people, refreshing drinks, a garden, a big pool (that's for hotel guests only), and 360-degree views of the Hudson River and Lower Manhattan. You can even look down, literally and figuratively, at the people at the Soho House pool. To keep things beautiful, there's a dress code: no shorts, no flip-flops, no football jerseys or T-shirts with funny (or unfunny) slogans. *18 Ninth Avenue (at 13th Street), 15th Floor, New York, NY 10014.* **1-877-426-7386.**

Rise Bar and Terrace Financial District

It's on the 14th floor of the gorgeous Ritz-Carlton Battery Park, overlooking the Statue of Liberty and New York Harbor. Really, does anything else need to be said? *2 West Street (at First Place), New York, NY 10004.* **212-344-0800.**

Entertainment and Nightlife

If it's true that New York is the city that never sleeps, Downtown is where many of its citizens are staying awake. The top pop-music and jazz venues are here, along with a lot more theater than you might think.

Arlene's Grocery Lower East Side

You never know who might turn up on the bill at Arlene's Grocery, which took its name from the sign outside (the building used to be a bodega). Past acts include Señor Tadpole, Zerobridge, Jesse Kilguss, Julie Belle, Tall Black Girls, and the Swinging Fingers. The real institution here is rock 'n' roll karaoke night, Mondays at 10 p.m. There is a $7 cover charge. *95 Stanton Street (between Orchard and Ludlow Streets), New York, NY 10002.* **212-995-1652.** *www.arlenesgrocery.net.*

Blue Note   Greenwich Village

Jazz is alive and well in the Village, especially at the Blue Note, which has been around since 1981. You can catch both established names and up-and-coming musicians at this club. There's a full dinner menu too and jazz brunches on Sundays. *131 West Third Street (between Sixth Avenue and Macdougal Street), New York, NY 10012. Shows at 8 P.M. and 10:30 P.M. on weeknights, 8 P.M., 10:30 P.M. and 12:30 A.M. on weekends.* *212-475-8592. www.bluenote.net.*

Bowery Ballroom   Lower East Side

New York Magazine declared it the best music club in the city. Certainly the Bowery Ballroom has a lot going for it: a 1929 Art Deco–accented building (it was finished just before the big stock market crash), a 500-person-capacity concert hall, and a great bar. You'll find up-and-coming indie rockers onstage. Past headliners have included Super Furry Animals, Black Mountain, Tokyo Police Club, and Big Head Todd and the Monsters. *6 Delancey Street (between Chrystie Street and Bowery), New York, NY 10002.* *212-533-2111. www.boweryballroom.com.*

The Fillmore at Irving Plaza   Union Square

It used to be just plain Irving Plaza. But the branding game struck again, in 2007, attaching the name of the Fillmore, the magic clubs of the '60s, with which it has no real connection. Irving Plaza has its own rich history, thank you, with some major players on its stage in the past (such as, oh, Bob Dylan). Also Patti Smith, the Dave Matthews Band, Barenaked Ladies, Wilco, Willie Nelson, Keith Urban, the Goo-Goo Dolls, the New York Dolls, and the Pussycat Dolls. The place may have been around since 1992, but it still rocks. *17 Irving Place (at 15th Street), New York, NY 10003.* *212-777-6800. www.irvingplaza.com.*

Joe's Pub   East Village

The stage is small, the club is intimate, and management practices what it calls "genre-blind booking." That means you may find anything from a jazz band to a comedian at Joe's Pub, next door to the Public Theater. In the past, you might have caught musical stars from David Byrne to Dolly Parton and funny people from Sarah Silverman to Mort Sahl. *425 Lafayette Street (between Astor*

Place and East Fourth Street), New York, NY 10003. Two-drink or $12 food minimum in addition to ticket price. **212-967-7555** *(show tickets only) or* **212-539-8778** *(show and dinner reservations). www.joespub.com.*

Joyce Theater   Chelsea

More than 270 dance companies have performed at the Joyce since it was transformed, from a defunct movie theater, into a class-act dance venue in 1982. Come here and you might find flamenco, a ballet company from Rotterdam, the Khmer Arts Ensemble doing Cambodian dance, the Stephen Petronio Company, Philippe Decouflé, a showcase of works by Twyla Tharp, the Ballet de Monterrey (Mexico), or Savion Glover tapping away. *175 Eighth Avenue (at 19th Street), New York, NY 10011.* **212-242-0800.** *www.joyce.org.*

The Knitting Factory   TriBeCa

Founded in 1987 on Houston Street, the Knitting Factory has become a well-known venue for new music. Sonic Youth played here in the olden days. More recent bookings: Soul Purpose, Chris Brokaw, the Loved Ones, Donna Jean, and the Tricksters. *74 Leonard Street (between Church Street and Broadway), New York, NY 10013.* **212-219-3132.** *www.knittingfactory.com.*

Mercury Lounge   East Village

Here's one of the city's best small venues for live music, with a capacity for an audience of about 250. Acts that have performed in recent times have included Dax Riggs, Dirty on Purpose, Nashkato, Be Your Own Pet, Firekrotch, and the Dead Trees. You get the idea. *217 East Houston Street (between Ludlow Street and Essex Street/Avenue A), New York, NY 10002.* **212-260-4700.** *www. mercuryloungenyc.com.*

Off-Broadway Theaters   All Over

Considering how expensive Broadway theater is these days (over $100 a ticket for musicals and almost that much for plays) and how derivative it is (as I write this, there are at least nine shows playing that are based on hit movies), it's surprising that so many visitors who want to make a theater evening part of their New York visit never even think about off-Broadway. Much less off-off-Broadway.

Movie and TV stars do off-Broadway (Ethan Hawke, Calista Flockhart, Bebe Neuwirth). Famous playwrights and directors have worked off-Broadway (Neil Simon, Woody Allen, Neil LaBute, Mike Leigh). Ticket prices are lower. The theaters are more intimate. You can avoid the crowds.

Off-Broadway runs tend to be shorter than on Broadway runs, where a hit show can run for years. Check the theater listings in *The New York Times, New York Magazine, The New Yorker,* and *Time Out New York* to find out what's on during your stay. Then be sure to take note of the reviews, because there are both masterpieces and stinkers at all levels of theater.

The Public Theater, in the East Village, is probably the best-known downtown venue, with a longtime reputation for excellence. But there are many, many others. (See the Appendix for a list with addresses, website information, and box office telephone numbers.)

S. O. B.'S   SoHo

The initials stand for Sounds of Brazil, but the music is much more international. You'll find African; Brazilian; and French Caribbean, and Asian influences. You'll find salsa, reggae, hip-hop, and R&B. Past headliners have included Erykah Badu, Gil Scott Heron, Issac Delgado, and John Legend. The food is Brazilian and Latin too. *200 Varick Street (at West Houston Street), New York, NY 10014. 212-243-4940. www.sobs.com.*

Village Vanguard   Greenwich Village

The Vanguard has been around since 1935, but it started out as a venue for poetry and sketch comedy. Today it's considered the grand old man of the jazz world, but I took some music-loving out-of-town visitors there not that long ago and we were treated pretty much like cattle. *178 Seventh Avenue South (below West 11th Street, at the junction of Waverly Place and Perry Street), New York, NY 10014. Most shows are $30 Sundays–Thursdays and $35 Fridays–Saturdays, including a $10 drink minimum. Credit cards accepted for reservations but not at the club itself. 212-255-4037. www.villagevanguard.com.*

Plan My Trip: One-Day Downtown Itinerary

There are an inordinate number of fashionable Downtown neighborhoods, but not too many to see in one day. This itinerary gives you a taste of Chelsea, the Village, SoHo, TriBeCa, and the Financial District.

8 A.M.–9 A.M. Breakfast:	Start your day in Chelsea with a big breakfast at the **Empire Diner.** Some of your fellow breakfasters will have just gotten up. Others may have been out all night.
9 A.M.–10 A.M.:	Take a look around the seminary blocks, West 20th and 21st Streets, where the lovely nineteenth-century campus of **General Theological Seminary** stands. Then set off walking south on Ninth Avenue to the Village (you'll pass through the Meat Packing District) or grab the subway to 14th Street.
10 A.M.–12 P.M.:	It's time to hit Bleecker Street for a little shopping. This is one of the Village's prettiest streets, and it's also become a mecca for upscale shoppers.
12 P.M.–2 P.M. Lunch:	Have a relaxing lunch at **Gotham Bar & Grill.** (There's a prix fixe lunch menu.) Catch a glimpse of Washington Square Park afterward, then head downtown to the Financial District.
2 P.M.–3 P.M.:	Pass by the construction at the **World Trade Center** site and visit nearby **St. Paul Chapel,** which played an important role on and after September 11, 2001. It also happens to be the oldest church building in the city.
3 P.M.–4:30 P.M.:	Take the **Staten Island Ferry** for a gorgeous view of the Downtown skyline and a close-up look at the **Statue of Liberty.**
4:30 P.M.–5:30 P.M.:	Now enjoy a longer-distance but very satisfying view of the statue as you have a drink at the **Rise Bar & Terrace** at the Ritz-Carlton Battery Park.

5:30 P.M.–6:30 P.M.:	Do a little more Financial District sightseeing, checking out the **New York Stock Exchange,** the **Woolworth Building,** the **Brooklyn Bridge,** and **City Hall.** If you're still not tired, keep going north and you'll hit **Chinatown.**
6:30 P.M.–8 P.M.:	Time for rest and recuperation back at your hotel.
8 P.M.–9:30 P.M. Dinner:	Have dinner at **Aquagrill** in SoHo. (Or, if you feel like splurging and have reserved ahead, go to **Chanterelle** in TriBeCa instead.)
9:30 P.M.–Midnight:	Enjoy the street life in SoHo or TriBeCa, then zip back to the Village and catch the 10:30 show at the **Blue Note.**

What the Statue of Liberty sees: The Lower Manhattan skyline, from New York Harbor.

Side Trip: Brooklyn

Newspaper and magazine articles are always announcing that moving to some newly discovered outer-borough neighborhood is just as good as living in Manhattan. But nobody really believed that until the last few years, as parts of Brooklyn became almost impossibly cool. At first it was just Williamsburg, where so many artists (priced out of SoHo and TriBeCa) had settled. These days, great places seem to be all over the borough. (The way things are going, maybe the Dodgers will come back.)

Sights

Brooklyn Heights Promenade   Brooklyn Heights

If there were a contest for best view of Manhattan, this 1,826-foot (about ⅓ of a mile) esplanade would stand an excellent chance of winning. Looking across the East River to the skyline, just south of the Brooklyn Bridge, this area is a mecca for walkers, runners, inline skaters, and lovers. It's built above the Brooklyn Queens Expressway (better known as the BQE) and was dedicated in 1950. *Montague Street to Middagh Street, Brooklyn, NY 11201. Subway: No. 2 or 3 to Clark Street.* **718-965-8900.** *www.nycgovpark.org.*

Brooklyn Museum   Prospect Heights

The Brooklyn Museum has one of the world's greatest collections of Egyptian art, going back to roughly 3,500 B.C.E., the Predynastic Period. The permanent collections also include European, American, African, and Asian art, as well as a section on American decorative arts that includes 26 period rooms (from 1675 Dutch to 1928 Park Avenue). *200 Eastern Parkway (at Washington Avenue), Brooklyn, NY 11238. Wednesdays–Fridays 10 A.M.–5 P.M., Saturdays–Sundays 11 A.M.–6 P.M. Closed Mondays and Tuesdays. Adults $8, students $4, children under 12 free.* **718-638-5000.** *www.brooklynmuseum.org.*

Coney Island   West of Brighton Beach

A hundred years or so ago, Coney Island would probably have been near the top of your things-to-see list in New York. Starting out as a beach resort in the nineteenth century, it became a day-trip destination as transportation improved over the decades. But for the last half-century or so, it's been mostly an exercise in nostalgia. In winter, all you can visit is the beach and the boardwalk. In summer (Memorial Day to Labor Day), you can go on amusement-park rides, see attractions such as the New York Aquarium and the Sideshow Museum and eat a Nathan's hot dog (the hot dog, they say, was invented at Coney Island in 1867). Between Easter and Memorial Day and in September after Labor Day, things are open on weekends only. It's about a 45-minute trip from Midtown. *1000 Surf Avenue, Brooklyn, NY 11224. Subway: D, Q, N or F to Stillwell Avenue.*

New York Transit Museum   Brooklyn Heights

If you find the subway system even vaguely interesting, take a look at this unusual museum, housed in a 1930s subway station. There are artifacts (such as vintage turnstiles), interactive exhibits and, for the children, educational workshops. And if you never make it out to Brooklyn at all, you can drop by the museum's annex at Grand Central Terminal. *Corner of Boerum Place and Schermerhorn Street, Brooklyn Heights, NY 11201. Tuesdays–Fridays 10 A.M.– 4 P.M., Saturdays 12 P.M.–5 P.M. Closed Mondays. Adults $5, children 3–17 $3. Subway: No. 2, 3, 4, or 5 to Borough Hall. Bus: B25, B26, B37, B38, and others. 718-694-1600. www.mta.info.*

Restaurants

Al Di La   Park Slope   Italian 💲💲

You may have to stand in line (the place is very popular and they don't take reservations), but fans and food critics alike say the wait is worth it. Venetian dishes are the specialty. The braised rabbit with olives and polenta and the hanger steak come highly recommended. *248 Fifth Avenue (at Carroll Street), Brooklyn, NY 11215. 718-783-4565. www.aldilatrattoria.com.*

Peter Luger   Williamsburg   American/Steak 💲💲

It gets the highest rating of any steakhouse in New York City in the Zagat's guide. People have been making the trip to Peter Luger since 1877, and the consensus among those who should know is that it has the best porterhouse in town. But you might also try the lunch specials: Thursday is corned beef and cabbage day. *178 Broadway (at Driggs Avenue), Brooklyn, NY 11211. 718-387-7400. www.peterluger.com.*

Pó   Carroll Gardens   Italian 💲💲

Just like its mother restaurant in Manhattan, this Pó offers an outstanding menu of rustic Italian dishes. The six-course tasting menu is $50. *276 Smith Street (between Sackett and Degraw Streets), Brooklyn, NY 11231. 718-875-1980. www.porestaurant.com.*

Quercy   Carroll Gardens   French $\boxed{\$}$ $\boxed{\$}$

Think of it as La Lunchonette's confident country sister. Same owner, and much the same elegant-bistro-style menu. Have a little French comfort food, maybe coq au vin, boeuf bourguignon, or steak au poivre. *242 Court Street (between Baltic and Kane Streets), Brooklyn, NY 11201.* **718-243-2151.**

River Café   Dumbo   American $\boxed{\$}$ $\boxed{\$}$ $\boxed{\$}$

Aside from the stunning river and Manhattan skyline view, the venerable River Café has an award-winning wine list and a classic menu. Choices include rack of lamb, sirloin, duck breast, lobster, salmon, and a veggie plate. There's also a $45 three-course brunch. *1 Water Street (between Furman and Old Fulton Street), Brooklyn, NY 11201.* **718-522-5200.** *www.rivercafe.com.*

Saul   Boerum Hill   American $\boxed{\$}$ $\boxed{\$}$

The Michelin food critics (who gave Saul a coveted star) loved the pan-roasted veal, the scallops, and the baked Alaska. The *Times* liked the seafood chowder. *140 Smith Street (between Bergen and Dean Streets), Brooklyn, NY 11201.* **718-935-9844.** *www.saulrestaurant.com.*

WHO NEEDS CHERRY GARCIA?

Let's say you've just had brunch at the River Café. Or you've enjoyed a concert at Bargemusic. The logical thing to do is pop into the Brooklyn Ice Cream Factory, a deceptively modest spot in an old fireboat house right between the two. You can sit and relax with your dessert or take it with you and stroll across the Brooklyn Bridge. The owner is an ice cream purist, who prefers the classic flavors (you remember vanilla, chocolate, and strawberry, right?), but he does semi-exotic ones too, such as peaches and cream, vanilla chocolate chunks, and butter pecan. *Water Street and Old Fulton Street, Brooklyn, NY 11201.* **718-246-3963.**

Cocktails

Brooklyn Social Club   Carroll Gardens

The name makes the point: this place used to be an honest-to-goodness Italian men's social club. Bada bing. Now the old-timers stare down from framed sepia prints and the hip young people order the drinks. Both *New York Magazine* and *The Village Voice* have sung its praises. *335 Smith Street (between Carroll and President Streets), Brooklyn, NY 11231.* **718-858-7758.**

Entertainment

Bargemusic   Dumbo

Back in 1977, somebody inexplicably said, "We want to give chamber music concerts. Let's do it on an old abandoned coffee barge floating in the East River." And the enchantment of Bargemusic was born. Normally there's a quartet (maybe flute, violin, cello, and piano) or quintet doing Beethoven, Mozart, Schubert, Mendelssohn, or one of their classical brethren, while the audience gazes at the river and the Manhattan skyline beyond. Note: If you're exclusively a classical fan, don't go on a Thursday. That's jazz night. *Fulton Ferry Landing, Brooklyn, NY 11201. Subway: No. 2 or 3 to Clark Street or A to High Street or F to York Street. Wednesdays–Saturdays 8 P.M., Sundays 4 P.M. Adults $35, students $20.* **718-624-2083.** *www.bargemusic.org.*

Brooklyn Academy of Music   Fort Greene

I guess you could call BAM off-off-off-off-Broadway. You can see some amazing theater (Patrick Stewart once starred in a sold-out *Macbeth* here), not to mention dance, musical performances, and film (at the BAM Rose Cinemas). The main theater, known as the opera house, seats more than 2,100. You can have drinks or pre-theater dinner at BAMcafé. *30 Lafayette Avenue (at Ashland Place), Brooklyn, NY 11217. Subway: No. 2, 3, 4, or 5 to Atlantic Avenue. D, M, N, or R to Pacific Street. BAMbus: Leaves from 120 Park Avenue (at 42nd Street) one hour before performance time. $5.* **718-636-4100.** *www.bam.org.*

Luna Lounge   Williamsburg

Like a lot of Manhattanites (Luna Lounge began on Ludlow Street in the '90s), this club moved to Brooklyn and got a lot more space for the money.

In the past you might have seen acts varying from the Strokes, Kid Rock, and Interpol to Jon Stewart and Wanda Sykes. More recent acts have included Bugs in the Dark and One Small Step for Landmines. *361 Metropolitan Avenue (at Havemeyer Street), Brooklyn, NY 11211. Subway: L to Bedford or J to Marcy Avenue.* **718-384-7112.** *www.lunalounge.com.*

Side Trip: Staten Island

As long as you've taken the ferry to Staten Island, you might as well stay awhile and look around. Staten Island is the smallest of New York City's five boroughs. It's the least populous, although almost half a million people live there. Some of its sights are within walking distance of the ferry terminal; others can be reached by taxi or bus.

Sights

Snug Harbor Cultural Center

These grand Greek Revival buildings were once the center of a home for re-tired sailors. Today they house art exhibitions, performing-arts events, and educational programs. You'll also find the John A. Noble Maritime Collection museum, the Staten Island Children's Museum and the Staten Island Botani-cal Garden (see below) here. *1000 Richmond Terrace (two miles west of ferry ter-minal), Staten Island, NY 10301. Daily 9 A.M.–5 P.M. Free.* **718-448-2500.** *www. snug-harbor.org.*

Staten Island Botanical Garden

There are perennial, shade, herb, butterfly, and a variety of other gardens here, but the star attraction is the Chinese Scholar's Garden. Just the names of the elements are calming: Gurgling Rock Bridge, Tea House of Hearing Pines, Assured Tranquility Pavilion, and Moon Gate of Uncommon Beauty. *1000 Richmond Terrace (on the grounds of Snug Harbor Cultural Center), Staten Island, NY 10301. Grounds open dawn to dusk every day. Free. Chinese Scholar's Garden: Tuesdays–Sundays 10 A.M.–5 P.M. (12 P.M.–4 P.M. in winter). Adults $5, students and children under 12 $4.* **718-273-8200.** *www.sibg.org.*

Staten Island Museum

The focus here used to be the history and culture of Staten Island itself, but the collection has expanded to include art from Europe, Africa, Asia, other parts of the United States and ancient civilizations. *75 Stuyvesant Place (at Wall Street, two blocks from ferry terminal), Staten Island, NY 10301. Mondays–Fridays and Sundays, 12 P.M.–5 P.M. Saturdays, 10 A.M.–5 P.M. Adults $2, students $1, children under 12 free.* **718-727-1135.** *www.statenislandmuseum.org.*

Staten Island Zoo

The reptile wing is the main attraction here, but there are also meerkats, mandrills, ring-tailed lemurs, North American river otters, and other representatives of the animal kingdom. *614 Broadway, Staten Island, NY 10310. Daily 10 A.M.–4:45 P.M. Adults $7, children 3–14 $4, children under 3 free.* **718-442-3100.** *www.statenislandzoo.com.*

Restaurants

¢ Denino's Pizzeria   Italian $

Denino's has been around since the 1930s, and regulars say they've perfected pizza-making. Prices are low too. The only problems are noise and long waits. *524 Port Richmond Avenue (between Hooker Place and Walker Street), Staten Island, NY 10302.* **718-442-9401.**

Marina Café   Seafood $ $

It's all about the setting here (the Great Kills Harbor views), but the food isn't bad either. *154 Mansion Avenue (at Hillside Terrace), Staten Island, NY 10308.* **718-967-3077.** *www.marinacafegrand.com.*

Now you know all about Downtown. And you've covered all five of the boroughs that make up New York City. All that's left is to go out and enjoy it.

Part **5**

Plan My Trip— All Around Town

There's nothing more fun than choosing all the things you want to do and mapping an itinerary for every day of your vacation—unless you don't have time. In that case, consider some ready-made itineraries that cover all parts of the city, whether you have a day, four days, or even longer to make New York your own.

Chapter 11

Twelve More Fabulous Itineraries

In This Chapter

- 🍎 Itineraries, depending on who you are
- 🍎 Itineraries, depending on how much time you have
- 🍎 Pointers on creating your own itinerary

Whenever anyone asks, "What should I see while I'm in New York?" the answer has to be, "It depends." If you think most twentieth- and twenty-first-century art looks like something your nephew once did with crayons on the kitchen wall, you probably won't want to spend much time at the Guggenheim. If you consider New York's heyday to have been right after the war (WWII? WWI? Civil?), you may want to seek out landmarks from past eras to feed your love of tradition and nostalgia. If you have only one day in the city, you probably don't want to spend half of it on the Circle Line tour and the other half on the Statue of Liberty outing. Here are some possibilities based on your passions and your schedule.

Depending on Who You Are

Everyone who comes to New York has his or her own picture of the city. If musical theater represents the meaning of life to you, then you should probably spend a lot of time on or near Broadway. If you're 85 and have visited the city every year since you were in first grade, you can probably afford to enjoy the city at a slower pace and skip the obvious sightseeing. And of course, if you're a Renaissance person with several of the interests or characteristics targeted in these itineraries, feel free to mix and match.

Itinerary #1: Theater Lovers

Day 1: Get into the Broadway mood this morning. Check out the **Museum of the City of New York,** which has a fascinating collection of theater memorabilia going back to the eighteenth century. Have a yummy Italian lunch in the neighborhood at **Sfoglia.** Check out what's being shown at the **Costume Institute** at the **Metropolitan Museum of Art.** Have pre-theater dinner at **Orso,** on Restaurant Row. Go to see the **Broadway show** that's No. 1 on your things-to-do list.

Day 2: Take a tour (or give yourself one) of **Grand Central Terminal** this morning. If you're in the mood, you can shop there. Have lunch right there at **Metrazur** or **Michael Jordan's Steakhouse,** with grand views of the main concourse. Get on the subway and head for the **Bronx Zoo.** Have pre-theater dinner at **Angus McIndoe,** where lots of stage actors and directors hang out. Go to see whatever won the Tony Award for **best play** this year.

Day 3: Make this a shopping morning at the **Shops at Columbus Circle** in the **Time Warner Center.** There's also a great view of **Central Park** from this urban mall. Try a little Mexican food for lunch at the Lincoln Center location of **Rosa Mexicano.** Spend the afternoon at the **Library of Performing Arts at Lincoln Center.** There are lots of videotapes of great musicals and plays you might have missed. Have dinner at **Café Luxembourg.** Go to see whatever is playing at either the **Vivian Beaumont** or the **Mitzi Newhouse Theater,** just because it's fun to go to the theater at **Lincoln Center.**

Day 4:   Do a combination of shopping, window shopping, and sightseeing this morning on the Midtown stretch of **Fifth Avenue.** Wander right into **Central Park** for a lakeside lunch at the **Boathouse.** Take the short version of the **Circle Line** cruise this afternoon, tipping your hat to the **Statue of Liberty.** Have an early, very casual seafood dinner at **Pearl Oyster Bar** in the Village. Try out what **off Broadway** has to offer tonight, maybe the latest production at the **Public Theater** or something offbeat by the **Atlantic Theater Company** or at **Playwrights Horizons.**

Day 5:   Spend the morning in the **Village,** maybe with a walk down Bleecker Street and a stop in **Washington Square Park.** Zip uptown for lunch at an old theater-industry hangout, the **Edison Café** (also known as the **Polish Tea Room**) in the **Edison Hotel.** Go to a **Broadway matinée.** Make it whatever won the most recent Tony for best musical. Take a night off from theater. Spend the whole evening doing a long, splashy, expensive dinner at **Jean Georges.**

Day 6:   Take yourself on a walking tour of the **Financial District,** ending with a visit to **St. Paul's** next to the **World Trade Center site.** Moving slightly uptown, have a fashionable Southwestern lunch at **Mesa Grill.** Steel yourself for waiting in line and go to the observation deck at the **Empire State Building.** Hope for a clear day. Go to see a Broadway musical revival. Sometimes they're actually as good as (or better than) the originals. Do after-theater dinner tonight at **Sardi's,** where you'll be surrounded by all those stage-star caricatures on the walls (and possibly some night-owl stage stars themselves).

Day 7:   Spend some time in Chelsea this morning, with a visit to the **Chelsea Market** and an art gallery or two. Have lunch (French) nearby at **La Lunchonette.** Visit the **New Museum** on the **Lower East Side,** and see how the **Bowery** has changed. Go Pan-Asian tonight with dinner at the festive Times Square **Ruby Foo's.** See a Broadway comedy tonight, and exit laughing.

Itinerary #2: Art Lovers

Day 1:   Throw yourself into the New York art world by starting at the top, with a morning at the **Metropolitan Museum of Art.** Take a break for lunch at **Le Refuge,** a charming little French place a few blocks away. After lunch, grab the Madison Avenue bus and head uptown (way uptown) to the **Cloisters.** (Your museum button from this morning is good for admission here, too.) Spend the afternoon appreciating Medieval art and the lovely Hudson River view. For a change of pace and a look at a new neighborhood, go downtown to **TriBeCa** and have dinner at **Odeon,** which has been popular since the first arty types started moving in Downtown.

Day 2:   The **Museum of Modern Art** in Midtown is your first stop today. Be sure to see the sculpture garden as well as the indoor collections. Have a sophisticated lunch inside the museum at **the Modern.** (If you can't get reservations, try one of the in-house cafés upstairs.) As long as you're in the neighborhood, walk a few blocks south to **Rockefeller Center** and go to **Top of the Rock** for a spectacular 65th-floor view of the city. You can appreciate the mural and Art Deco styling of 30 Rockefeller Plaza while you're there. If you feel like seafood, have dinner at the **Sea Grill,** right in Rockefeller Plaza. Or have Italian at **Insieme** a couple of blocks west.

Day 3:   The Upper West Side has museums, too. Start your day at the **New-York Historical Society.** The collection includes beautiful Hudson River School landscapes. Go a little out of your way, almost 10 blocks south, for lunch at **Café des Artistes.** Besides the food, there are gorgeous murals to enjoy. Head uptown again and devote a couple of hours to the **American Museum of Natural History.** There's the **John James Audubon gallery,** and even the most serious art connoisseur can appreciate the dinosaur exhibits. Stay in the neighborhood for dinner at **Ouest.**

Day 4:   This will be another Upper East Side day, beginning with a morning with the masterpieces at the intimate **Frick Collection.** At lunchtime, stroll into **Central Park** and enjoy a tranquil lunch at the **Boathouse,** overlooking the lake. Spend a little time exploring the park before you walk back to Fifth Avenue. In the afternoon, spend some time with the modern art at the **Guggenheim Museum,** and take a good look at the building's unique Frank Lloyd Wright architecture. Go south to **Chinatown** and have dinner at **Oriental Garden.**

Day 5:   It's time to be brave and visit another borough besides Manhattan. Hop on the subway and go directly to the **Brooklyn Museum,** which has a remarkable Egyptian art collection. As long as you're in Brooklyn, have French comfort food for lunch at **Quercy.** There's still time for a couple of hours with the American art at the **Whitney Museum.** And when you're ready to sit down and discuss your thoughts on the collection, you're only a block away from **Bemelmans Bar,** which has its own playful murals to admire during cocktail hour. While you're still in an American mood, make this steak night. Have dinner at the **Old Homestead,** which has been around since the 19th century, in the now-fashionable **Meat Packing District.**

Day 6:   After breakfast, visit the **Neue Galerie,** a palace of German and Austrian art in an old Vanderbilt mansion. Have a casual lunch at **Sarabeth's** on Madison Avenue. Then take a break from museum-hopping and go shopping this afternoon in **SoHo,** where you can admire all those great cast-iron buildings. Keep heading downtown to the **Financial District** and treat yourself to a drink at the **Rise Bar** in the **Ritz Carlton Battery Park.** You can admire the **Statue of Liberty** in the harbor while you relax. Give yourself a night off and have dinner in your hotel room. You need time to admire your gift-shop purchases, after all.

Day 7:   Start in the upper reaches of the Upper East Side with a visit to the **Museum of the City of New York.** Don't miss the old prints and photographs here. Before heading downtown, have a little Mexican food for lunch at **Itzocan,** just a few blocks from the museum. **Chelsea** is the center of the Manhattan art-gallery world these days. Shows change frequently, so take a look at the listings in *New York Magazine, The New Yorker,* or *The New York Times* and choose a couple of places to visit this afternoon. End the day with dinner at the **Red Cat.** If you feel like a walk afterward, stroll by **London Terrace** and the nearby seminary.

Itinerary #3: Movie Lovers

Day 1:   Set out on a half-day **tour of movie and television locations** in New York (tour operators in the Appendix). You'll visit locations from films of all eras, such as *Ghostbusters, Spider-Man, Manhattan,* and *The Devil Wears Prada.* Stroll up to the **Time Warner Center,** where many scenes in *Enchanted* were filmed, and grab a quick late lunch at **Bouchon Bakery.** Spend the rest of the afternoon in **Central Park,** where scenes from too many movies to count have been shot. (*Hair, The Out-of-Towners,* and *Manhattan* come to mind.) Be sure to drop by **Bethesda Fountain.** Keep going toward the East Side and have Italian food there tonight at **Felidia.**

Day 2: Start out on **Fifth Avenue** at the ultimate toy store, **FAO Schwarz,** where children stand in line to dance on the giant piano keys the way Tom Hanks did in *Big*. A number of other films, including *Baby Boom* and *Eyes Wide Shut,* have included scenes set here. Across the street, stop to admire the grandness of the **Plaza** (formerly a hotel, now a combination of hotel and apartments), where many great movie scenes have been filmed, including the poignant final one ("See ya, Hubbell") in *The Way We Were*. Shop or window shop, walking south on Fifth, and stop at **Tiffany,** where Audrey Hepburn as Holly Golightly communed with the jewelry display windows in *Breakfast at Tiffany's*. Grab a hot dog or a kabob at a vendor's cart and wander down to **Rockefeller Center.** Admire the ice skaters or the umbrella-dotted restaurant (depending on what time of year it is) and the setting you've seen in a thousand films. Pay your respects to **Radio City Music Hall** on Sixth Avenue, the greatest tribute to the days when movie theaters were palaces (now Radio City just presents stage shows). Catch an **afternoon flick** in the neighborhood (maybe at the Ziegfeld, the Paris, or one of the Times Square multiplexes). Have an all-American dinner in a lovely setting at the **Bryant Park Grill.**

Day 3: Explore the **Upper West Side** today, starting at **55 Central Park West,** Sigourney Weaver's apartment building in the original *Ghostbusters*. Walk six blocks north to the **Dakota,** one of New York's grandest apartment buildings, and the eerie setting for *Rosemary's Baby*. (It is also, of course, where John Lennon lived and died.) Enjoy a leisurely lunch at nearby **Café des Artistes.** Diane Keaton, Goldie Hawn, and Bette Midler gathered there in *The First Wives Club*. Go over to Broadway and stroll through **Lincoln Center,** the setting for numerous movie scenes, including Cher's beauty-makeover "after" scene in *Moonstruck*. Then, head northwest to **Riverside Park.** You'll want to end up at the gorgeous gardens around **91st Street** where Tom Hanks and Meg Ryan did their big romantic finale in *You've Got Mail*. Pass by **817 West End Avenue,** the building where Michael Douglas and Anne Archer lived in *Fatal Attraction*. End your sightseeing with a nod to a landmarked Art Deco movie theater, the **Metro** (*Broadway, between 99th and 100th Streets*), now closed and dwarfed by glass-tower apartment buildings. The theater appeared in *Hannah and Her Sisters*. Tonight, go down to the **Madison Square** area for barbecue at **Blue Smoke.** There's jazz downstairs if you feel like a musical evening.

Day 4: Take yourself on a walking tour of the **Lower East Side** (*Hester Street, Crossing Delancey,* and so on). Just be sure you end up at **Katz's Delicatessen** for lunch. That's where Meg Ryan played her "faking it" scene with Billy Crystal in *When Harry Met Sally*. Spend the afternoon in the Village, being sure to stop by **Washington Square Park,** which has appeared in many movies. But Robert Redford and Jane Fonda's scenes in *Barefoot in the Park* are best known. Catch whatever is playing at **Film Forum,** known for great retrospectives, themed festivals of classic films, and indie-film premieres. Afterward, grab a late dinner in **Chinatown,** maybe at **Ping's Seafood.** (Sadly, *Chinatown* was not filmed here but in Los Angeles.)

Day 5:   Every movie lover has to go to the observation deck at the **Empire State Building,** following in the footsteps of the stars of *An Affair to Remember* (and the other versions of *Love Affair*) and *Sleepless in Seattle.* Plus, you'll enjoy the view. Bring a fan magazine or a movie-star biography to read while you wait in line. How about a giant slab of red meat for lunch? **Michael Jordan's Steakhouse** is inside **Grand Central Terminal,** not far away. Going there is a good excuse to take a look at that building's beautiful architecture. Spend the afternoon at the **Museum of Modern Art.** After you've enjoyed the nonmotion pictures, you may be able to catch a screening. Relax over a casual dinner at **Mexicana Mama** in the **Village.** You deserve a margarita.

Day 6:   Pay a visit to the **Library of Performing Arts** around back at **Lincoln Center.** The emphasis is mostly on music and theater (including a lot of stage plays and musicals that were turned into movies). Take a break for an early lunch at **Picholine** (near Lincoln Center). In fact, take a break from movie-related sightseeing altogether and go on a **sightseeing cruise** around the island on the **Circle Line.** Tonight, check out whatever series, festival, or other kind of screening they're doing at the **Leonard Nimoy Thalia Theater at Symphony Space.** Have a late dinner at **Picnic,** a few blocks north. Or go back to the hotel and order room service.

Day 7:   If the **Museum of the Moving Image in Queens** is still closed for renovations, do the next best thing: drop into the **Paley Center for Media** on 52nd Street. (But if the museum has reopened, head immediately for Queens. The Paley Center is great, but it's TV-oriented.) Have lunch at **'21,'** right next door. Michelle Pfeiffer spent a harried cocktail hour here in *One Fine Day.* Back in the 1950s, Burt Lancaster's evil character held court here in *The Sweet Smell of Success.* Go to a matinee at **Anthology Film Archives** or the **IFC Center,** both downtown venues with inventive programming. Splurge on a farewell dinner at **Asiate** in the **Mandarin Oriental Hotel.** This paragon of Asian-French fusion hasn't been in any classic movies yet, but you'll feel as if you're in one.

Itinerary #4: Senior Travelers

Day 1:   Take it easy this morning, just exploring your hotel's neighborhood and doing a little window-shopping. Start your vacation officially with a sophisticated Midtown lunch at **Aquavit.** Spend the afternoon on the **Circle Line cruise,** just sitting back and watching the sights of Manhattan go by. Enjoy a big steak dinner at **Bull & Bear** in the **Waldorf-Astoria.**

Day 2: In late morning, head for **Saks Fifth Avenue.** Check out a couple of floors, then go upstairs and have a civilized lunch at **Café S. F. A.** After lunch, spend an hour or so at the **Museum of Modern Art,** which is only a few blocks away. Take a break back at the hotel. Then, when everyone else is heading out for theater performances and concerts and dinners, go directly to the **Empire State Building.** The lines are much shorter then, and the nighttime view is fantastic. Order a light dinner from room service.

Day 3: After a late breakfast, taxi to the **Intrepid** aircraft-carrier museum and immerse yourself in the World War II history or later exhibits like the **Concorde.** Have a sort of French-country-house lunch at **La Mangeoire,** on the East Side. Treat yourself to an afternoon massage at a hotel spa, maybe at the **Mandarin Oriental,** the **Peninsula,** or the **Gansevoort.** Enjoy an old-fashioned musical floor show (with celebrity headliner) over dinner at **Feinsten's at the Regency.**

Day 4: Have a big breakfast at the hotel. Make a day of it on the cruise to the **Statue of Liberty** and **Ellis Island,** maybe to look up your ancestors, maybe just for the sense of history. Skip lunch and have tea (with all the trimmings, of course) at the **Palm Court** at the **Plaza** instead. After a rest and relaxation break at the hotel, go down to **Il Mulino** for Italian food done with great style (and high prices).

Day 5: Sleep late, then do a little late-morning shopping in **SoHo.** Stay in the neighborhood and have lunch at **Balthazar.** Enjoy a low-key afternoon, just strolling in **Central Park** or sitting on a bench and watching the infinite variety of New York go by. It's time to enjoy an evening at the theater (maybe a Broadway-musical revival), after pre-theater dinner at **Marseille.**

Day 6: Spend the morning resting up after your big night. Enjoy a big, fancy lunch at **Aureole** on the Upper East Side. (Prix fixe, if you're budgeting.) Sign up for a guided shopping, food, historical, or movie-sites tour. Let someone else do all the work. Have a casual barbecue dinner at **Virgil's** in **Times Square.**

Day 7: On your last morning, spend at least an hour at the **Metropolitan Museum of Art.** Grab a burger or something else light and casual at **P. J. Clarke's.** You're not far from **Bloomingdale's.** Drop in. Have an early but festive Chinese dinner at **Shun Lee West.** For your last evening, treat yourself to a concert, the ballet, or the opera (your choice, of course) at **Lincoln Center.** Afterward, sip a farewell nightcap at the **Empire Hotel** across the street.

Itinerary #5: Nostalgia Buffs

Day 1:   Check into the **Inn on 23rd** in Chelsea. (Naturally you've reserved the 1940s Room.) Have brunch or lunch at the **Empire Diner,** circa 1946. Go to **Rockefeller Center** to enjoy the Art Deco buildings and the view from **Top of the Rock,** which first opened in 1933. Pop into **Saks Fifth Avenue,** across the way, and **St. Patrick's Cathedral.** Go down to the **Village** for dinner at the **Knickerbocker Bar & Grill.** Have the shrimp cocktail, the shell steak, and the chocolate soufflé, and listen to mellow jazz.

Day 2:   Spend the morning at the elegant early twentieth-century **Morgan Library & Museum.** Have lunch in the **Morgan Dining Room,** the financier Pierpont Morgan's original family dining room, where the menu is inspired by early twentieth-century cuisine. Go downtown and catch the **Staten Island Ferry.** You'll get a good look at the **Statue of Liberty,** unchanged over the years, and the Lower Manhattan skyline, which has (but from a distance, it doesn't matter so much). When you come back, spruce up a bit and take yourself out for drinks at the **Algonquin Hotel,** where the witty writers and editors of the '20s and '30s held court at the **Round Table.** Have dinner nearby at **Café Un Deux Trois,** which feels like a French bistro that's been here forever.

Day 3:   Spend the day at **Coney Island,** pretending that it's still this Brooklyn beach resort's heyday. You can still ride the Cyclone (assuming you're visiting in summer) and have an old-fashioned **Nathan's** hot dog. Spend the evening at the dinner show at the sophisticated **Café Carlyle.** Whoever is playing there, it's very likely that you'll hear a little Gershwin or Cole Porter.

Day 4:   Check out of your hotel and into the **Blue Moon Hotel,** with its great period furnishings, on the Lower East Side. Ask for the George Raft Room or the Benny Goodman Room. Pay a visit to the **Frick Collection,** with its collection of great paintings in an old Fifth Avenue mansion. Have lunch at the new-old **Oak Room** at the new-old **Plaza.** Afterward, cross the street and go shopping at **Bergdorf Goodman,** one of the few grand old Fifth Avenue stores still around. Follow that with a stroll in the city's greatest nineteenth-century treasure, **Central Park.** Tonight take yourself to a serious Broadway play (you're more likely to find traditional theatergoers there than at a musical based on a movie). Or take in a Broadway-musical revival, and you can pretend that you're back in 1954 or whenever the show originally opened. End the evening with after-theater dinner at **Sardi's,** where the theater crowd has hung out for generations.

Day 5: This morning, check out the **Lower East Side Tenement Museum,** near your hotel, for a reminder that the good old days weren't good for everybody. Stay in the neighborhood for lunch at **Katz's Delicatessen.** It may be a little taken with its own celebrity these days, but the old-fashioned Jewish deli in its character is still there. In the afternoon, give yourself a tour of the Beaux-Arts beauty of **Grand Central Terminal.** If you feel like shopping while you're there, there are lots of stores to visit. As cocktail hour approaches, seek out the private Grand Central entrance to the **Campbell Apartment,** a 1920s office/residence transformed into a period cocktail lounge. Have a glass of Prohibition Punch. Stay in the same era with an early dinner at **'21,'** which started out as a speakeasy.

Day 6: Change hotels again, this time moving on to the **Madison Square** area and **Hotel Giraffe,** where all the rooms are done in '20s–'30s moderne. Spend the rest of the morning at the **Museum of the City of New York,** where all manner of artifacts, fashions, and decorative arts bring back a bygone era. Treat yourself to lunch at **Aureole,** in a beautiful East Side townhouse. Pay an afternoon visit to the **Mount Vernon Hotel and Museum** in the East 60s and imagine what it was like to be a guest there when this part of Manhattan was the countryside. Have dinner at **One if by Land, Two if by Sea.** The setting is an eighteenth-century Village carriage house, and there's piano music at the bar.

Day 7: Spend your last day Downtown, the oldest part of the city, starting with a walk through the **Financial District.** Be sure to see the statue of **George Washington** at the site of his inauguration, **Trinity Church** on lower Broadway and **St. Paul Chapel** a few blocks north. Go uptown a bit and take a stroll around **Gramercy Park,** surrounded by nineteenth-century houses, before having lunch at **Pete's Tavern,** where O. Henry used to hang out. Visit **Washington Square Park.** Then head west and do some shopping and architecture-admiring in the Village. Admire the Manhattan skyline while you have dinner at the **River Café** in **Brooklyn.** Come home over the **Brooklyn Bridge,** lit up in all its glory.

Itinerary #6: A Romantic Getaway

Day 1: Order room service breakfast for two, and enjoy it at your leisure in your bathrobes. Spend the morning strolling through the southeastern end of **Central Park.** The duck pond and Bethesda Fountain are worth stopping to admire. Have lunch at the **Boathouse,** overlooking the lake in the park. Exit the park on Fifth Avenue and head straight for the intimate **Frick Museum** for an afternoon of art appreciation à deux. Have dinner in the Village at **One if by Land, Two if by Sea,** one of the most romantic restaurants in the city. Get there early if you can to enjoy the piano player by the bar.

Day 2: Grab coffee and bagels for breakfast, then spend the morning window-shopping in the neighborhood of your choice. Hold hands and admire the sexy murals (naked sprites, frolicking) over a memorable lunch at **Café des Artistes.** While you're in the neighborhood (the Upper West Side), check out **Lincoln Center** and the shops around it. Make it an early dinner at **Marseille** in the Theater District, then go to a cheery Broadway musical. (Or a play, if you can find one that isn't about a dysfunctional couple or family.)

Day 3: Spend the morning at the **Metropolitan Museum of Art** (make sure to pay a visit to the roof to see the great view of the park). You can't see everything in the museum, so choose just one or two exhibits or periods that you both like. Almost nobody doesn't like the Impressionists, and there's something mysteriously romantic about the ancient Temple of Dendur. Have a cozy French lunch at **Le Refuge,** just a few blocks away. Take the Madison Avenue bus to the Metropolitan's uptown Medieval branch, the **Cloisters.** It's the next best thing to being in Europe. Travel back to the Upper East Side for a spectacular French dinner at **Daniel.**

Day 4: Spend the day in the Village, including a walk through **Washington Square Park** and some shopping time on Bleecker Street. Have lunch at **Gotham Bar & Grill.** At dinnertime, cross the **Brooklyn Bridge** and go to the **River Café** with its unrivaled view of the downtown Manhattan skyline.

Day 5: Follow in the footsteps of screen lovers (from Charles Boyer and Irene Dunne to Tom Hanks and Meg Ryan) and ascend to the observation deck of the **Empire State Building** for the famous view. (You may want to pick up breakfast or a sandwich at a takeout place beforehand. You can enjoy it while standing in line.) Have some wine and cheese at nearby **Artisanal.** Then head back to the hotel, pick up the phone, order Chinese food or pizza and enjoy dinner in bed in front of a movie on TV. It's a very New York thing to do.

Day 6: Start the day shopping or window-shopping along **Fifth Avenue** (Tiffany's! Cartier! Bulgari! Mickey Mouse!). Stop at **Rockefeller Plaza** and watch the ice skaters (or, if it's summer, just admire the scenery). Pick up some lunch goodies at **Dean & DeLuca** (there's a wine store next door) and take a picnic to the park. In the evening, catch the dinner show at the **Café Carlyle,** where someone fabulous is almost always playing.

Day 7: Spend your last morning doing nothing. Just pick up an overpriced cappuccino or latté and watch the world go by, maybe at a café or maybe on a park bench. Have a long, French-accented lunch at **La Grenouille.** Pick up those gifts for friends and family back home at the **Museum of Modern Art** gift shop (or another museum gift shop, if there's one nearer). Have an early but impressive New American dinner at **Telepan** in the West 60s.

Depending on How Much Time You Have

No matter how long you're staying in New York, there's never enough time to see everything that you want to see. But with a little careful planning, you can make the most of the available hours here, even if you have only 24.

Itinerary #7: One Day Only

Start your busy day with a hearty breakfast at **Sarabeth's** on the Upper East Side. Spend the morning walking 10 blocks on **Fifth Avenue,** starting at **Rockefeller Center** (if you have time, take a quick peek at the great city view from **Top of the Rock**) and winding up at 59th Street and **Central Park.** Travel to the West Side for a Mediterranean lunch at **Picholine.** Afterward, walk a couple of blocks to see **Lincoln Center.** Devote your afternoon to your favorite art genre at the **Metropolitan Museum** on the Upper East Side. Now subway or taxi to the southern end of Manhattan for drinks with a view. Have a cocktail at the **Rise Bar** at the **Ritz Carlton Battery Park.** Hello, **Statue of Liberty** out there in the harbor! Wind up your day with dinner at **TriBeCa Grill.** Walk around this fashionable neighborhood a little and make a vow to stay a little longer on your next trip.

Itinerary #8: Two-Day Weekend

Day 1:   Hit the deck running with a morning visit to the **Metropolitan Museum of Art.** It's not far to the **Boathouse** in **Central Park,** where you can have a scenic lakeside lunch, then take a stroll in the park. Explore the heart of Midtown **Fifth Avenue,** working from 59th to 49th Streets, from **FAO Schwarz** to **Rockefeller Center** this afternoon. Pop up to the **Rainbow Room Bar** for a drink with a fabulous view. Wrap up the day with a casual pre-theater dinner at **Joe Allen's,** in the theater district, and a Broadway show around **Times Square.**

Day 2:   Spend the morning exploring the **Financial District,** including **Wall Street, Trinity Church,** and **St. Paul Chapel.** Head for the **Village** to enjoy a luxurious European brunch (or just coffee and a basket of Viennese pastries) at **Wallsé.** Take the short version of the **Circle Line cruise,** for the fresh air and the **Statue of Liberty.** Have a drink at the rooftop bar of the **Hotel Gansevoort** in the hip **Meat Packing District.** Splurge on a farewell dinner at **Le Bernardin.**

Itinerary #9: Three-Day Weekend

Day 1:   Start your vacation in Midtown with a morning visit to the **Museum of Modern Art** and its sculpture garden. Have lunch at **the Modern,** the museum's glamorous restaurant, or in one of its upstairs cafés. This afternoon, take the 75-minute **Circle Line cruise** down the Hudson River to see the **Statue of Liberty** and other sights. (If you're feeling ambitious, take the three-hour version.) Go out for an affordable luxury tonight. Have the prix fixe dinner at the caviar palace **Petrossian.**

Day 2:   Do the Midtown **Fifth Avenue** walk this morning, starting at **Rockefeller Center** and ending up at 59th Street and **Central Park,** shopping and sightseeing along the way. Relax over a lakeside lunch at the **Boathouse** in Central Park, giving you an excuse to stroll the park's southern end. Head to the West Side of the park for a shopping excursion at the **Time Warner Center.** Have pre-theater dinner at **Café Un Deux Trois** in the Theater District. Then go and enjoy a Broadway show.

Day 3: Check out the **Metropolitan Museum** on the Upper East Side this morning for an hour or two. Then go downtown and explore the **Financial District,** including **St. Paul Chapel** next to the **World Trade Center site.** Have lunch in **SoHo** at **Mercer Kitchen.** Take a quick look around the neighborhood, then point yourself north toward 34th Street. This afternoon, be prepared to stand in line for the view from the **Empire State Building'**s observatory. The wait is worth it. Eventually. Have drinks at the **Plaza Athenée'**s sexy **Bar Seine,** then an elegant dinner at the hotel's chic restaurant, **Arabelle.**

Itinerary #10: Three-Day Winter Holiday Weekend

Day 1: Get up early and go immediately to **Rockefeller Center** to see the towering Christmas tree, before the crowds arrive. Go across the street to see **Saks Fifth Avenue'**s holiday windows. (Be prepared to stand in line to see department-store windows at times.) Hang around long enough to watch the store's outdoor light-and-music show. Have lunch at the **Sea Grill** in Rockefeller Plaza, with a view of the ice-skaters on the rink beneath the tree. In the afternoon, walk north on **Fifth Avenue** to see the store and street decorations, including the giant snowflake above 57th Street. Join the crowds waiting to get inside **FAO Schwarz,** the ultimate toy store. Have dinner at the Times Square location of **Ruby Foo's,** where it feels like Christmas year-round. Walk over to Sixth Avenue and see the **Radio City Holiday Spectacular**—a show that truly has something for everyone.

Day 2: Start the morning with a visit to **Macy's** (and, if you're traveling with children, to Santa Claus). It can be a long wait, but there are all sorts of colorful distractions en route to Santa. Afterward, stop and take a look at the Macy's holiday windows. It's only four blocks or so north to **Lord & Taylor'**s animated holiday windows, which have a reputation for being the most traditional of their kind. Stroll north a few blocks and have lunch at the **Bryant Park Grill.** In the afternoon, check out the holiday windows (usually wacky ones) at **Barneys** on the **Upper East Side.** Then, in a more reverent mood, go to the **Metropolitan Museum's Medieval Sculpture Hall** to see its Christmas tree with eighteenth-century ornaments and a Neapolitan baroque crèche at its foot. Have dinner at the **Four Seasons,** if you're feeling extravagant, or its next-door sister property, **the Brasserie,** if you're feeling more like Scrooge. After dinner, either taxi or walk up **Park Avenue** to appreciate its almost 50 blocks of lighted trees in the avenue's median.

Day 3: Go shopping in the **Fifth Avenue stores** for gifts, cards, ornaments, and other holiday decorations. Time things so you'll be at Saks at lunchtime, then go upstairs and have a festive holiday lunch at **Café S. F. A.** Drop in for a visit to the **Museum of Natural History** in its holiday finery, complete with origami Christmas tree. Have pre-theater dinner at **Café des Artistes.** Walk a few blocks to **Lincoln Center,** take note of its Christmas tree in the plaza, then go inside the New York State Theater and settle in for the beloved holiday ballet **"The Nutcracker."** Happy holidays!

Itinerary #11: Four-Day Weekend

Day 1: Start your vacation with a morning visit to **Grand Central Terminal.** Admire the Beaux-Arts architecture, check out the shops, and have lunch at the famous **Oyster Bar.** Now get thee to the Hudson River and acquaint yourself with all of Manhattan on the **Circle Line** cruise, which includes a close-up view of the **Statue of Liberty.** Travel down to the **Village** for an elegant Italian dinner at **Babbo.**

Day 2: Do the traditional **Fifth Avenue** day, beginning this morning with a couple of hours at the **Metropolitan Museum of Art.** For lunch, just grab a hot dog and an ice cream from a street vendor in or right outside **Central Park.** Your Fifth Avenue shopping/sightseeing walk begins at the park's end (59th Street) and ends 10 blocks later at **Rockefeller Center.** Visit the **Flatiron District** at dinnertime and have great American cuisine at **Gramercy Tavern.**

Day 3: Right after breakfast, get in line to see the **Empire State Building**'s observation deck and its killer view. Have a real "Noo Yawk" sandwich at the **Carnegie Deli.** After lunch, walk a few blocks west and wander through the shops in the **Time Warner Center** on **Columbus Circle.** Enjoy a hearty pre-theater barbecue dinner at **Virgil's** in **Times Square.** Then rush to the theater and see a **Broadway show.**

Day 4: Spend the morning exploring the **Financial District,** from **Battery Park** up to **St. Paul Chapel,** next to the **World Trade Center site.** On your way uptown, stop in the Village at Perry Street, with its great Hudson River views, for lunch. Drop in at the **Museum of Modern Art** to see the permanent collections or whatever the current must-see exhibition is. On your last night, have American "greenmarket cuisine" at **Telepan** and stroll by **Lincoln Center** afterward.

Itinerary #12: Seven Fun-Filled Days

Day 1:	Hop on a double-decker tour bus in **Times Square** and spend a half-day getting acquainted with the city. Have lunch in a beautiful park setting at the **Bryant Park Grill**. Walk another couple of blocks east and explore **Grand Central Terminal** and its shops. Stay and have a drink at the **Campbell Apartment,** right inside the terminal. Do dinner in **Chinatown** tonight, at **Oriental Garden.**
Day 2:	Start the day by visiting **Top of the Rock** and enjoying the 70th-floor view. Then take a look around the rest of **Rockefeller Center** and **St. Patrick's Cathedral,** across the street. Pop into **Saks Fifth Avenue** and go upstairs for a lovely lunch at **Café S. F. A.** Walk north on **Fifth Avenue,** shopping or window-shopping, until you hit 59th Street and **Central Park.** If you're thirsty or tired, stop for a drink at the **Oak Bar** or tea at the **Palm Court,** both at the **Plaza.** Go the **Village** tonight for an elegant American cuisine at **Annisa.** Take a stroll around the neighborhood afterward.
Day 3:	Spend part of the morning at the **Metropolitan Museum of Art.** Then walk a few blocks up or down Fifth Avenue to see the nineteenth- and early twentieth-century mansions. Have lunch at the **Boathouse** in Central Park, overlooking the lake. Then stroll south or southwest through the park, ending up at the **Time Warner Center** on **Columbus Circle,** with just enough time for shopping. Have Mexican food tonight at **Zarela** in the East 50s.
Day 4:	Appreciate some American art this morning at the **Whitney Museum.** Then appreciate some French food with lunch at **Payard Bistro** just a couple of blocks away. It's also a patisserie. After lunch, hop on the subway and go directly to the **Bronx Zoo,** even if you aren't traveling with kids. Give yourself a night off and either have room service or call up and have a pizza delivered.
Day 5:	Go and see the dinosaurs at the **Museum of Natural History** on the **Upper West Side.** While you're on the Upper West Side, go a little farther north and have Southern comfort food for lunch at **Rack & Soul.** This afternoon, bring a good book and stand in line at the **TKTS booth** in Times Square for discount Broadway tickets. Have a pre-theater Italian dinner at **Orso** on Restaurant Row. Go to a Broadway show, half price.
Day 6:	Give yourself a morning off. (If you feel guilty about doing nothing, take a scenic neighborhood walk.) Go down to the **Village** and have a burger at the **Corner Bistro.** Take a walk through the **Financial District,** then get on the ferry to see the **Statue of Liberty** and visit the immigration museum on

Ellis Island. Back on dry land, treat yourself to a drink at the **Rise Bar,** with its harbor view, at the Ritz Carlton Battery Park. Visit **SoHo** for dinner at the chic but somehow homey **Mercer Kitchen.** Stroll around the neighborhood afterward.

Day 7:   Make a morning of it at the sleek, contemporary **Museum of Modern Art.** Have lunch at the museum's glamorous restaurant, **the Modern.** Then switch genres and visit the **Frick Collection** on the Upper East Side, grand old paintings in gilt frames in a former private home. Say goodbye to New York with an ultra-glamorous dinner at **Asiate** at the **Mandarin-Oriental Hotel,** complete with **Central Park** view.

Create Your Own Itinerary

And there you have it. East Side, West Side, all around the town. Now you know about New York's many neighborhoods, its culture, its hotels great and small, and its restaurants extravagant and modest, grand and casual. You know how to get a taxi, take the subway, or ask for directions, how to walk and talk like a native, where to shop for fabulous stuff, and even how to save a few pennies here and there.

The Complete Idiot's Guides have one goal: to make things as easy as possible for you. That's why this one includes a big selection of detailed itineraries. So if you want to, you can just toss the book into your luggage, carry it with you as you explore the city, and follow the directions day by day or even hour by hour. (And don't forget the block-by-block walks in various parts of the city.)

But if you're an independent soul, it's understandable that you might want to put a little of your own thought and unique tastes into the mix. Just do a quick analysis of what you love and what you have the time and energy for. Then, pick your favorite things—and the next thing you know, you have a custom-made itinerary. *Your* New York City.

Whether you're seeing the glories of New York City for the first time or the hundredth, trust me: this wonderful town is going to show you a good time.

New York City A to Z: Facts at Your Fingertips

Here, for ready reference, is a list of selected companies, venues, services, and agencies that could be helpful to you before and during your New York City stay.

AAA

Don Glo Auto Service of Manhattan, 409 West 218th Street (at Ninth Avenue), New York, NY 10034. 212-567-1767. www.aaa.com.

Elite Auto Repair, 524 Bryant Avenue (between Randall and Oak Point Avenues), Bronx, NY 10474. 718-842-9500. www.aaa.com.

54th Street Auto Center, 415 West 54th Street (between Ninth and Tenth Avenues), New York, NY 10019. Collision repair: 212-265-3120. www.aaa.com.

Accessibility and Disability Resources

Mayor's Office for People With Disabilities, 212-788-2830. www.nyc.gov/mopd.

Metropolitan Transit Authority (public transportation), 718-596-8585. www.mta.info. (Under NYC Transit: Accessibility.)

Theater Access Project of the Theater Development Fund, 212-719-4537. www.tdf.org.

Airlines

Aeromexico, 1-800-237-6639. www.aeromexico.com.

Air Canada, 1-888-247-2262. www.aircanada.com.

Air France, 1-800-237-2747. www.airfrance.com.

AirTran Airways, 1-800-247-8726. www.airtran.com.

Alaska Airlines, 1-800-252-7522, www.alaskaair.com.

American Airlines, 1-800-433-7300. www.aa.com.

British Airways, 1-800-247-9297. www.britishairways.com.

Continental Airlines, 1-800-523-3273. www.continental.com.

Delta Airlines, 1-800-221-1212. www.delta.com.

Frontier Airlines, 1-800-432-1359. www.frontierairlines.com.

Japan Airlines, 1-800-525-3663. www.jal.com.

JetBlue Airways, 1-800-538-2583. www.jetblue.com.

Lufthansa, 1-800-645-3880. www.lufthansa.com.

Northwest Airlines, 1-800-225-2525. www.nwa.com.

Philippine Airlines, 1-800-435-9725. www.philippineairlines.com.

Qantas Airways, 1-800-227-4566. www.qantas.com.

South African Airways, 1-800-722-9675. www.flysaa.com.

Southwest, 1-800-435-9792. www.southwest.com.

United Airlines, 1-800-864-8331. www.ual.com.

US Airways, 1-800-428-4322. www.usairways.com.

Virgin Atlantic, 1-800-862-8621. www.virgin-atlantic.com.

Airports

John F. Kennedy International Airport (JFK), www.panynj.gov.
General and AirTrain information: 1-800-AIR-RIDE.
Airport information: 718-244-4444.
Lost and found: 718-244-4225.
Police and emergency services: 718-244-4333.
Medical services (Building 198): 718-656-5344.

LaGuardia Airport (LGA), www.panynj.gov.
General information: 1-800-AIR-RIDE.
Lost and found: 718-533-3988.
Police emergencies: 718-533-3900.
Medical services: 718-476-5575.
Dental services: 718-507-7800.
Recorded information: 718-533-3400.

Long Island Islip MacArthur Airport (ISP), www.macarthurairport.com.
General information: 631-467-3210.
Lost and found: 631-467-2577 for items lost at security checkpoints or
631-467-3315 for items lost in public areas of the airport.

Newark Liberty International Airport (EWR), www.panynj.gov.
General and AirTrain information: 1-800-AIR-RIDE or 1-800-EWR-INFO.
Police emergencies, medical emergencies, and lost and found: 973-961-6230.
Medical emergency building (No. 339): 973-643-8383.
Airport information: 973-961-6000.

Better Business Bureau

Better Business Bureau, 275 Park Avenue South (between 21st and 22nd
Streets), New York, NY 10010. 212-533-7500. www.bbb.org.

Better Business Bureau, 70 West 36th Street (between Fifth and Sixth
Avenues), New York, NY 10018. 212-754-1320. www.nadreview.org.

To check out a business or charity: www.newyork.bbb.org.

Bicycle Rentals

Bike and Roll, Hudson River Park, Pier 84, New York, NY 10036. 1-866-736-8224. www.bikeandroll.com.

Bike the Big Apple, 1306 Second Avenue (between 68th and 69th Streets), New York, NY 10021. 201-837-1133. www.bikethebigapple.com.

Central Park Bicycle Tours/Rentals, 203 West 58th Street (at Seventh Avenue), New York, NY 10019. 212-541-8759. www.centralparkbiketour.com.

Broadway Theaters

Al Hirschfeld Theater, 302 West 45th Street (between Eighth and Ninth Avenues), New York, NY 10036. Telecharge: 212-239-6200.

Ambassador Theater, 219 West 49th Street (between Broadway and Eighth Avenue), New York, NY 10019. Telecharge: 212-239-6200.

American Airlines Theater, 227 West 42nd Street (between Seventh and Eighth Avenues), New York, NY 10036. Box Office: 212-719-1300. www.roundabouttheatre.org.

August Wilson Theater, 245 West 52nd Street (between Eighth Avenue and Broadway), New York, NY 10019. Telecharge: 212-239-6200.

Belasco Theater, 111 West 44th Street (between Sixth Avenue and Broadway), New York, NY 10036. Telecharge: 212-239-6200.

Bernard B. Jacobs Theater, 252 West 45th Street (between Eighth Avenue and Broadway), New York, NY 10036. Telecharge: 212-239-6200.

Biltmore Theater, 261 West 47th Street (between Seventh and Eighth Avenues), New York, NY 10036. Telecharge: 212-239-6200.

Booth Theater, 222 West 45th Street (between Broadway and Eighth Avenue), New York, NY 10036. Telecharge: 212-239-6200.

Broadhurst Theater, 235 West 44th Street (between Broadway and Eighth Avenue), New York, NY 10036. Telecharge: 212-239-6200.

Broadway Theater, 1681 Broadway (between 52nd and 53rd Streets), New York, NY 10019. Telecharge: 212-239-6200.

Brooks Atkinson Theater, 256 West 47th Street (between Broadway and Eighth Avenue), New York, NY 10036. Ticketmaster: 212-307-4100. www. brooksatkinsontheater.com

Circle in the Square Theater, 1633 Broadway (at 50th Street), New York, NY 10019. Telecharge: 212-239-6200.

Cort Theater, 138 West 48th Street (between Sixth and Seventh Avenues), New York, NY 10036. Telecharge: 212-239-6200.

Ethel Barrymore Theater, 243 West 47th Street (between Eighth Avenue and Broadway), New York, NY 10036. Telecharge: 212-239-6200.

Eugene O'Neill Theater, 230 West 49th Street (between Eighth Avenue and Broadway), New York, NY 10019. Telecharge: 212-239-6200.

Gershwin Theater, 222 West 51st Street (between Eighth Avenue and Broadway), New York, NY 10019. Ticketmaster: 212-307-4100.

Helen Hayes Theater, 240 West 44th Street (between Seventh and Eighth Avenues), New York, NY 10036. Telecharge: 212-239-6200.

Hilton Theater, 213 West 42nd Street (between Seventh and Eighth Avenues), New York, NY 10036. Ticketmaster: 212-307-4100.

Imperial Theater, 249 West 45th Street (between Eighth Avenue and Broadway), New York, NY 10036. Telecharge: 212-239-6200.

Longacre Theater, 220 West 48th Street (between Eighth Avenue and Broadway), New York, NY 10036. Telecharge: 212-239-6200.

Lunt-Fontanne Theater, 205 West 46th Street (between Eighth Avenue and Broadway), New York, NY 10036. Ticketmaster: 212-307-4747. www. luntfontannetheatre.com.

Lyceum Theater, 149 West 45th Street (between Sixth Avenue and Broadway), New York, NY 10036. Telecharge: 212-239-6200.

Majestic Theater, 245 West 44th Street (between Eighth Avenue and Broadway), New York, NY 10036. Telecharge: 212-239-6200.

Marquis Theater, Marriott Marquis Hotel, 1535 Broadway (between 45th and 46th Streets), New York, NY 10036. Ticketmaster: 212-307-4100. marquistheatre.com.

Minskoff Theater, 200 West 45th Street (between Seventh and Eighth Avenues), New York, NY 10036. Ticketmaster: 212-307-4100.

Music Box Theater, 239 West 45th Street (between Eighth Avenue and Broadway), New York, NY 10036. Telecharge: 212-239-6200.

Nederlander Theater, 208 West 41st Street (between Seventh and Eighth Avenues), New York, NY 10036. Ticketmaster: 212-307-4100. www. nederlander.org.

Neil Simon Theater, 250 West 52nd Street (between Eighth Avenue and Broadway), New York, NY 10019. Ticketmaster: 212-307-4100. www. neilsimontheatre.com.

New Amsterdam Theater, 214 West 42nd Street (between Seventh and Eighth Avenues), New York, NY 10036. Ticketmaster: 212-307-4747. www. disneyonbroadway.com.

Palace Theater, 1564 Broadway (between 46th and 47th Street), New York, NY 10036. Ticketmaster: 212-307-4747. www.palacetheatreonbroadway.com.

Schoenfeld Theater, 236 West 45th Street (between Eighth Avenue and Broadway), New York, NY 10036. Telecharge: 212-239-6200.

Richard Rodgers Theater, 226 West 46th Street (between Eighth Avenue and Broadway), New York, NY 10036. Ticketmaster: 212-307-4100.

Shubert Theater, 225 West 44th Street, New York, NY 10036. Telecharge: 212-239-6200.

St. James Theater, 246 West 44th Street (between Seventh and Eighth Avenues), New York, NY 10036. Box Office: 212-239-5800.

Studio 54, 254 West 54th Street (between Eighth Avenue and Broadway), New York, NY 10019. Telecharge: 212-239-6200.

Vivian Beaumont Theater, Lincoln Center, 160 West 65th Street (between Amsterdam Avenue and Broadway), New York, NY 10023. Telecharge: 212-239-6200. www.lincolncenter.org.

Walter Kerr Theater, 219 West 48th Street (between Eighth Avenue and Broadway), New York, NY 10036. Telecharge: 212-239-6200.

Winter Garden Theater, 1634 Broadway (between 50th and 51st Streets), New York, NY 10019. Telecharge: 212-563-5544.

Car Rental Companies

Alamo, 1-800-462-5266. www.alamo.com.

Avis, 1-800-331-1212. www.avis.com.

Budget, 1-800-527-0700. www.budget.com.

Dollar, 1-800-800-4000. www.dollar.com.

Enterprise, 1-800-261-7331. www.enterprise.com.

Hertz, 1-800-654-3131. www.hertz.com.

National, 1-800-227-7368. www.nationalcar.com.

Chamber of Commerce

Manhattan Chamber of Commerce, 1375 Broadway (at 37th Street), New York, NY 10018. 212-479-7772. www.manhattancc.org.

Convention Bureaus

NYC & Company, 810 Seventh Avenue (between 52nd and 53rd Streets), New York, NY 10019. 212-484-1200. www.nycvisit.com.

Cruise Lines and Ferries

Circle Line, Pier 83 (at West 42nd Street), New York, NY 10036. 212-563-3200. www.circlineline42.com.

Circle Line Downtown, Pier 16, South Street Seaport, New York, NY 10038 or Brooklyn Navy Yard, Pier C, Brooklyn, NY 11205. 1-866-925-4631. www.circlelinedowntown.com.

Classic Harbor Line, Chelsea Piers, Suite 5912, New York, NY 10011. General information: 646-336-5270. Public sails and cruises: 212-209-3370. Private charters: 212-627-1825. www.sail-nyc.com.

New York Water Taxi, South Street Seaport, New York, NY 10038. 212-742-1969, ext. 0. www.nywatertaxi.com.

Prestige Yacht Charters, New York Skyport Marina (23rd Street and F.D.R. Drive), the Marina at Chelsea Piers, the Queens World's Fair Marina, and other points of departure. 212-717-0300. www.prestigeyachtcharters.com.

Spirit Cruises, Pier 62, Chelsea Piers, New York, NY 10011. 1-866-483-3866. www.spiritcruises.com.

Skyline Cruises, World's Fair Marina, Flushing Meadows, Queens, NY 11368 and other points of departure. 718-446-1100. www.skylinecruises.com.

Staten Island Ferry, Whitehall Terminal Manhattan, Whitehall Street at Water Street, New York, NY 10006. 718-815-BOAT. www.siferry.com.

Gay and Lesbian Resources

Lesbian, Gay, Bisexual, & Transgender Community Center, 208 West 13th Street (between Seventh and Greenwich Avenues), New York, NY 10011. 212-620-7310. www.gaycenter.org.

GMHC (Gay Men's Health Crisis), 119 West 24th Street, New York, NY 10011. 212-367-1000. www.gmhc.org.

Hospitals

Beth Israel Medical Center, First Avenue and 16th Street, New York, NY 10003. 212-420-2000.

Cabrini Medical Center, 227 East 19th Street (between Second and Third Avenues), New York, NY 10003. 212-995-7173.

Harlem Hospital Center, 506 Lenox Avenue (at 135th Street), New York, NY 10037. 212-939-1000.

Lenox Hill Hospital, 100 East 77th Street (between Lexington and Park Avenues), New York, NY 10021. 212-434-2000. www.lenoxhillhospital.org.

Manhattan Eye, Ear, & Throat Hospital, 210 East 64th Street (between Second and Third Avenues), New York, NY 10021. 212-838-9200.

Memorial Sloan-Kettering Cancer Center, 1275 York Avenue (at 68th Street), New York, NY 10065. 212-639-2000.

Mount Sinai Hospital, 1190 Fifth Avenue (at 100th Street), New York, NY 10029. 212-241-6500. www.mountsinai.org.

New York Downtown Hospital, 170 William Street (at Ann Street), New York, NY 10038. 212-312-5000.

New York Eye & Ear Infirmary, 310 East 14th Street (between First and Second Avenues), New York, NY 10003. 1-800-449-4673.

New York-Presbyterian Hospital/Columbia University, 622 West 168th Street (west of Broadway), New York, NY 10032. 212-932-4000. Emergency: 212-305-2255.

New York-Presbyterian/Weill Cornell, 525 East 68th Street (at York Avenue), New York, NY 10065. 212-746-5454. Emergency: 212-746-5050.

NYU Medical Center, 550 First Avenue (at 31st Street), New York, NY 10016. 212-263-7300 or 1-888-769-8633.

Roosevelt Hospital, 1000 10th Avenue (at 58th Street), New York, NY 10010. 212-523-4000.

Sloane-Kettering. See Memorial Sloane-Kettering Medical Center.

St. Luke's Hospital, 1111 Amsterdam Avenue (at 114th Street), New York, NY 10025. 212-523-4000.

St. Vincent's Catholic Medical Center of New York, Seventh Avenue and 11th Street, New York, NY 10014. 212-604-7000.

St. Vincent's Midtown Hospital, 415 West 51st Street (at Ninth Avenue), New York, NY 10019. 212-586-1500.

Limousine and Towncar Services

Allstate, 1-800-453-4099 or 212-333-3333.

Bermuda Limousine International, 212-647-9400 or 1-800-223-1383.

Carmel, 1-800-922-7635 or 212-666-6666.

Chris & Gina Limousines, online reservations: www.chrislimousines.com.

Dial 7 (formerly Tel Aviv), 1-800-777-8888 or 212-777-7777.

Movie Theaters

East Side:

AMC Loews Kips Bay 15, 570 Second Avenue (between 31st and 32nd Streets), New York, NY 10016. 212-447-0638.

AMC Loews Orpheum 7, 1538 Third Avenue (between 86th and 87th Streets), New York, NY 10028. 212-876-2111.

AMC Loews 72nd Street East, 1230 Third Avenue (at 72nd Street), New York, NY 10021. 212-472-0153.

City Cinemas East 86th Street Cinema, 210 East 86th Street (at Third Avenue), New York, NY 10028. 212-734-4427.

Clearview First and 62nd, 400 East 62nd Street (at First Avenue), New York, NY 10021. 212-777-3456.

UA East 85th, 1629 First Avenue (at 85th Street), New York, NY 10028. 212-249-5488.

UA 64th Street and Second Avenue, 1210 Second Avenue (at 64th Street), New York, NY 10021. 212-832-1671.

West Side:

AMC Empire 25, 234 West 42nd Street (between Seventh and Eighth Avenues), New York, NY 10036. 212-398-3939.

AMC Loews 84th Street 6, 2310 Broadway (at 84th Street), New York, NY 10024. 212-877-3892.

AMC Loews Lincoln Square 13 With IMAX, 1998 Broadway (at 68th Street), New York, NY 10023. 212-336-5020.

AMC Loews 34th Street 14, 312 West 34th Street (at Eighth Avenue), New York, NY 10001. 212-244-8850.

AMC Magic Johnson Harlem 9, 2309 Frederick Douglass Boulevard (at 124th Street), New York, NY 10027. 212-665-6923.

Leonard Nimoy Thalia, Symphony Space, 2537 Broadway (at 95th Street), New York, NY 10025. 212-864-5400. www.symphonyspace.org.

Lincoln Plaza, 1886 Broadway (at 62nd Street), New York, NY 10023. 212-757-2280.

Paris Theater, 4 West 58th Street (off Fifth Avenue), New York, NY 10019. 212-688-3800. www.theparistheatre.com.

Regal E-Walk Stadium 13, 247 West 42nd Street (between Seventh and Eighth Avenues), New York, NY 10036. 212-840-7761.

Ziegfeld Theater, 141 West 54th Street (between Sixth and Seventh Avenues), New York, NY 10019. 212-307-1862. www.clearviewcinemas.com.

Downtown:

AMC Loews 19th Street East 6, 890 Broadway (at 19th Street), New York, NY 10003. 212-260-8173.

AMC Loews Village 7, 66 Third Avenue (at 11th Street), New York, NY 10003. 212-982-2116.

Angelika Film Center, 18 West Houston Street (at Mercer Street), New York, NY 10012. 212-995-2000. www.angelikafilmcenter.com.

Anthology Film Archives, 32 Second Avenue (at Second Street), New York, NY 10003. 212-505-5181.

Clearview Chelsea, 260 West 23rd Street (between Seventh and Eighth Avenues), New York, NY 10011. 212-505-2463.

Film Forum, 209 West Houston Street (west of Sixth Avenue), New York, NY 10014. 212-727-8110. www.filmforum.org.

IFC Center, 323 Avenue of the Americas (at West Third Street), New York, NY 10014. 212-924-7771. www.ifccenter.com.

Landmark's Sunshine Cinema, 143 East Houston Street (between Eldridge and Forsyth Street), New York, NY 10002. 212-330-8182. www. landmarktheatres.com.

Regal Battery Park Stadium 11, 102 North End Avenue (at Vesey Street), New York, NY 10282. 212-945-4370.

Regal Union Square Stadium 14, 850 Broadway (at 14th Street), New York, NY 10003. 212-253-6266.

Village East Cinemas, 181-189 Second Avenue (between 11th and 12th Streets), New York, NY 10003. 212-529-6799. www.angelikafilmcenter.com.

Off-Broadway Theaters

American Place Theater, 111 West 46th Street (between Sixth and Seventh Avenues), New York, NY 10036. Telecharge: 212-239-6200. www. americanplacetheatre.com.

Astor Place Theater, 434 Lafayette Street (between Astor Place and West Fourth Streets), New York, NY 10003. Ticketmaster: 212-307-4100.

Atlantic Theater Company. See Linda Gross Theater.

Cherry Lane Theater, 38 Commerce Street (between Seventh Avenue and Hudson Street), New York, NY 10014. Telecharge: 212-239-6200.

Daryl Roth Theater, 101 East 15th Street (at Union Square East/Park Avenue South), New York, NY 10003. Telecharge: 212-239-6200.

Dixon Place, 258 Bowery (between Stanton and East Houston Streets), New York, NY 10012. 212-219-0736. www.dixonplace.org.

Douglas Fairbanks Theater. 432 West 42nd Street (between Ninth and Tenth Avenues), New York, NY 10036. Telecharge: 212-239-6200.

Ensemble Studio Theater, 549 West 52nd Street (between 10th and 11th Avenues), New York, NY 10019. 212-247-4982. www.ensemblestudiotheatre. org.

59E59 THEATERS, 59 East 59th Street (between Park and Madison Avenues), New York, NY 10022. Ticket Central: 212-279-4200. www.59e59.org.

Flea Theater, 41 White Street (between Church Street and Broadway), New York, NY 10013. 212-266-2407. www.theflea.org.

45 Bleecker Street (between Mott Street and the conjunction of Mulberry and Lafayette Streets), New York, NY 10012. 212-353-9983. www.45bleecker.com.

Here Arts Center, 145 Avenue of the Americas (at Dominick Street, just below Spring Street), New York, NY 10013. Box office: 212-352-2101. www.here.org.

Irish Repertory Theater, 132 West 22nd Street (between Sixth and Seventh Avenues), New York, NY 10011. 212-727-2737. www.irishrepertorytheatre. com.

Joseph Papp Public Theater, 425 Lafayette Street (between Astor Place and Fourth Street), New York, NY 10003. Telecharge: 212-239-6200.

The Kitchen, 512 West 19th Street (between 10th and 11th Avenues), New York, NY 10011. 212-255-5793. www.thekitchen.org.

Linda Gross Theater, Atlantic Theater Company, 336 West 20th Street (between Eighth and Ninth Avenues), New York, NY 10011. Telecharge: 212-239-6200. www.atlantictheater.org.

Lucille Lortel Theater, 122 Christopher Street (off Hudson Street), New York, NY 10014. Telecharge: 212-239-6200.

Manhattan Theater Club. NY City Center (Stage I and II), 131 West 55th Street (between Sixth and Seventh Avenues), New York, NY 10019. (MTC also does productions at the Biltmore Theater.) Citytix: 212-581-1212. www.nycitycenter.org.

Minetta Lane Theater, 18 Minetta Lane (at Sixth Avenue, south of West Third Street), New York, NY 10012. Ticketmaster: 212-307-4100.

Mitzi E. Newhouse Theater, Lincoln Center, 150 West 65th Street (between Broadway and Amsterdam Avenues), New York, NY 10023. Telecharge: 212-239-6200. www.lincolncenter.org.

New Victory Theater, 209 West 42nd Street (between Eighth Avenue and Broadway), New York, NY 10036. Box Office: 646-223-3020.

Pearl Theater, 80 St. Marks Place (between First and Second Avenue), New York, NY 10003. Box Office: 212-598-9802. www.pearltheatre.org.

Playwrights Horizons. 416 West 42nd Street (between Ninth and Tenth Avenues), New York, NY 10036. Ticket Central: 212-279-4200. www.playwrightshorizons.org.

P. S. 122, 150 First Avenue (at Ninth Street), New York, NY 10009. Theatermania: 212-352-3101. www.ps122.org.

Public Theater. See Joseph Papp Public Theater.

Samuel Beckett Theater. 410 West 42nd Street (between Ninth and Tenth Avenues), New York, NY 10036. 212-584-2826.

Signature Theatre Company, 555 West 42nd Street (between 10th and 11th Avenues), New York, NY 10036. Box Office: 212-244-7529. www.signaturetheatre.org.

Vineyard Theater, 108 East 15th Street (between Fourth Avenue and Irving Place), New York, NY 10003. 212-353-0303. www.vineyardtheatre.org.

Westside Theater, 407 West 43rd Street (between Ninth and Tenth Avenues), New York, NY 10037. Telecharge: 212-239-6200.

Police

NYPD Switchboard: 646-610-5000

Emergency: 911

Nonemergency: 311

Sex Crimes Report Line: 212-267-RAPE

Terrorism Hot Line: 1-888-NYC-SAFE

Post Offices

General Post Office, James A. Farley Building, 421 Eighth Avenue (31st to 33rd Streets), New York, NY 10001. 212-330-2900. Open 24 hours a day, 7 days a week. www.usps.com.

Address of the New York post office branch nearest you: 1-800-275-8777. www.usps.com.

Tour Operators

Beyond Times Square, 231 West 29th Street (at Seventh Avenue), New York, NY 10001. 212-564-1001. www.beyondtimessquare.com.

Big Onion Walking Tours, 476 13th Street (between Eighth Avenue and Prospect Park West), Brooklyn, NY 11215. 212-439-1090. www.bigonion.com.

City Sights NY, 47-25 27th Street, Long Island City, NY 11101. Most tours leave from the Times Square area. 212-819-2700 or 1-877-486-8769. www.citysightsny.com.

Destination Secrets of NYC, 11 Penn Plaza (at 32nd Street), New York, NY 10001. 212-946-4885. www.destinationnycinc.com.

Enthusiastic Gourmet, 245 East 63rd Street (between Second and Third Avenues), New York, NY 10021. 646-209-4724. www.enthusiasticgourmet.com.

Family in New York, 244 Fifth Avenue (at 28th Street), New York, NY 10001. 212-726-1008. www.familyinnewyork.com.

Grayline New York Sightseeing, 777 Eighth Avenue (at 47th Street), New York, NY 10036. 212-445-0848 or 1-800-669-0051. www.grayline.com.

Harlem Heritage Tours, Harlem Heritage Tourism and Cultural Center, 104 Malcolm X Boulevard (between 115th and 116th Streets), New York, NY 10026. 212-280-7888. www.harlemheritage.com.

Harlem, Your Way! Tours, 129 West 130th Street (at Lenox Avenue), New York, NY 10027. 212-690-1687. www.harlemyourwaytours.com.

Joyce Gold History Tours of New York, 141 West 17th Street (between Sixth and Seventh Avenues), New York, NY 10011. 212-242-5762. www.nyctours. com.

New York Water Taxi, South Street Seaport, New York, NY 10038. 212-742-1969, Extension 0. www.nywatertaxi.com.

OnBoard New York Tours, 110 West 40th Street (between Sixth and Seventh Avenues), New York, NY 10018. 212-277-8018. www.newyorkpartyshuttle. com.

On Location Tours, 347 Fifth Avenue (at 34th Street), New York, NY 10016. 212-683-1961. www.screentours.com.

Rockefeller Center Tours, 30 Rockefeller Plaza (between 48th and 49th Streets), New York, NY 10112. 212-664-3700. www.nbcuniversalstore.com.

Safari Shopping, 244 Fifth Avenue (at 28th Street), New York, NY 10001. 212-920-4438. www.safarishopping.com.

Scene on TV. Information: 212-683-2027. Tickets (Zerve): 212-209-3370. www.sceneontv.com.

1792 Wall Street Walks, 382 Central Park West (at 98th Street), New York, NY 10025. 212-666-0175. www.1792wallstreetwalks.com.

1654 Society, 8 West 70th Street (off Central Park West), New York, NY 10023. 212-873-0300. www.1654society.org.

Tribute WTC Visitor Center, 120 Liberty Street (between Greenwich and Church Streets), New York, NY 10006. 212-422-3520. www.tributewtc.org.

Walkin' Broadway, 226 West 47th Street (between Broadway and Eighth Avenue), New York, NY 10036. 212-997-5004. www.walkingbroadway.com.

Visitor Information

NYC & Company, 810 Seventh Avenue (between 52nd and 53rd Streets), New York, NY 10019. 212-484-1200. www.nycvisit.com.

Times Square Alliance, 1560 Broadway (between 46th and 47th Streets), New York, NY 10036. 212-768-1560. www.timessquarenyc.org.

Brooklyn Tourism & Visitors Center, Borough Hall, 209 Joralemon Street (at Court Street), Brooklyn, NY 11201. 718-802-3846. www.visitbrooklyn.org.

Index